THE BAVLI'S INTELLECTUAL CHARACTER
The Generative Problematic:
In Bavli Baba Qamma Chapter One
And Bavli Shabbat Chapter One

SOUTH FLORIDA STUDIES IN THE HISTORY OF JUDAISM

Edited by
Jacob Neusner
William Scott Green, James Strange
Darrell J. Fasching, Sara Mandell

Number 62
The Bavli's Intellectual Character
The Generative Problematic:
In Bavli Baba Qamma Chapter One
And Bavli Shabbat Chapter One

by
Jacob Neusner

THE BAVLI'S INTELLECTUAL CHARACTER
The Generative Problematic:
In Bavli Baba Qamma Chapter One
And Bavli Shabbat Chapter One

by
Jacob Neusner

Scholars Press
Atlanta, Georgia

THE BAVLI'S INTELLECTUAL CHARACTER
The Generative Problematic:
in Bavli Baba Qamma Chapter One
and Bavli Shabbat Chapter One

©1992
University of South Florida

Publication of this book was made possible by a grant from the Tisch Family
Foundation, New York City. The University of South Florida acknowledges
with thanks this important support for its scholarly projects.

Library of Congress Cataloging in Publication Data
Neusner, Jacob, 1932-
    The Bavli's intellectual character : the generative problematic :
in Bavli Baba qamma chapter one and Bavli Shabbat chapter one / by
Jacob Neusner.
        p. cm. — (South Florida studies in the history of Judaism ;
no. 62)
    Includes index.
    ISBN 1-55540-773-0
    1. Talmud. Bava kamma I—Criticism, interpretation, etc.
2. Talmud. Shabbat I—Criticism, interpretation, etc. 3. Talmud—
Criticism, interpretation, etc.   I. Title.   II. Series: South
Florida studies in the history of Judaism ; 62.
BM506.B23N45   1992
296.1'25—dc20   92-33003
                                                    CIP

Printed in the United States of America
on acid-free paper

Table of Contents

Preface

By the "intellectual character" of a document, I mean the program of thought and inquiry that brings about the writing of that document. In these pages I argue a twin proposition: first, that the Bavli constitutes an intellectual document, not merely an informative one; second, that the intellectual program of the document, replicated in countless details but everywhere uniform, can be identified and defined. It is an informative document – important parts of the Bavli do set forth information and explanation. But it is also a highly intellectual piece of writing – important parts of the Bavli also identify problems and solve them; more to the point, they use information as a medium for the investigation of propositions that vastly transcend concrete data. The Bavli is both concrete – everywhere, all the time, always very concrete – but it is also abstract; it is practical but also speculative; it is detailed but, in many ways (though not everywhere) also cogent. The description of the Bavli's intellectual character requires me to spell out this claim for abstraction and intellectual vigor and transcendence: Why is the Bavli a statement, not merely a compilation of information?

Much of the Bavli consists of explanations of words and phrases of the Mishnah; identification of scriptural bases for the Mishnah's rules; discovery of the authority behind an unattributed law; and similar problems of an essentially factual nature. But the Bavli is a richly argumentative document. It not only presents facts, it solves problems. But how do the framers of the Bavli's large-scale composites know a problem from a fact, and what tells them that a problem requires attention? By that I mean, what constitutes the problematic of the document, its philosophical hermeneutic? The thesis of this book is that the Mishnah exegetes of the Bavli proposed to take the two-dimensional chess of the Mishnah and to transform it into a three-dimensional game: changing the game from chess on a flat board to cubic chess defines the generative problematic of the Bavli. The rest of this monograph spells out that simple sentence through a two of substantial examples.

In this little experiment I continue my inquiry into the commonalities of the Bavli, meaning, how in many diverse topics, the framers of the document undertake a single labor of thought and analysis. What I propose to do is set forth a thesis on how the Bavli does its work, what, throughout, characterizes its program of inquiry. For having left no doubt at all that the Bavli forms a cogent literary document, one that exhibits integrity over the surface of its thirty-seven tractates, I owe myself the answer to the following question: If the medium coheres, does the message prove coherent, too? In a variety of monographs I have addressed that question, and in this one, I offer a proposition and illustrations. Only a sustained inquiry into the whole of the Bavli to determine where and to what extent, in the document overall, the basic traits of mind and the fundamental conceptions I lay out here characterize the whole will determine whether my proposition proves sound.

It is now a well-demonstrated fact that the Bavli in formal terms adheres to a few entirely visible rhetorical patterns, which time and again, without limitation by reason of subject matter, make possible a limited inquiry into some few problems and propositions. In adhering to a restricted repertoire of rhetoric, the writing speaks for an authorship, serving as a formally coherent statement, not merely a collection of received opinions. The framers of the document not only choose and reframe what they have inherited but place the stamp of their own rhetorical and logical program upon the writing they produced. On formal, therefore factual and easily replicable, literary-analytical grounds it is beyond reasonable doubt that the Bavli speaks in particular for those who put it together, and not for indeterminate generations before that time except as mediated through those penultimate and ultimate framers of the whole.

Since that is now the fact, I move on from issues of rhetoric and logic to ask about the implications of their uniformity for the character of the topical and propositional program of the document. What I want to know is this: Beyond the diverse subjects that are treated, does the document throughout put forth a cogent propositional program at all, and if so, how are we to identify it? Since the Bavli speaks for some one group of authors (an "authorship") and is a document of remarkable integrity, repeatedly insisting upon the harmony of the parts within a whole and unitary structure of belief and behavior, I want to know what that authorship repeatedly says. So the question is, within the restricted rhetorical vocabulary of the document, can we identify the one thing that is repeated – always in some one simple rhetorical pattern – in regard to many things? If the limits of my language are the limits of my world, may I also say that the limits of my rhetoric restrict the thoughts that I may think about that world? Dismantling ("deconstructing") its components and identifying them, perhaps even describing the kinds of compilations that the authors of those components could have had in mind in writing their compositions – these activities of literary criticism yield no insight into the religious system that guided the document's framers. It is time to reconstruct, to see things whole, having carefully examined the parts.

What is at stake for my principal inquiry, which is into the formation of Judaism in late antiquity? To explain, I have to point out that the Talmud of Babylonia recapitulates in grand and acute detail a religious system. The generative problematic of that writing – once we have identified it – then directs our attention not to the aesthetics of writing as literature, but to the religion of writing as a document of faith in the formation of the social order. So we have now to turn to the message of the method of the Bavli: what the Bavli's one voice always wishes to convey, the proposition that animates the work throughout. In connection with my first finger exercise, I used the language, "a metaproposition." I stated what I conceived to be the particular character of one such metaproposition. But, those results told me, diverse metapropositions, if demonstrated to be present, all together will not give me the answer that I seek; the character of the one I believe I was able to show fully realized in a long and stunningly cogent discourse of the Bavli did not serve my larger inquiry. It lacked the requisite abstraction. So here I try again.

Accordingly, this monograph carries forward my description of the Talmud of Babylonia, specifically moving outward from *The Bavli's One Statement. The Metapropositional Program of Babylonian Talmud Tractate Zebahim Chapters One and Five* (Atlanta, 1991: Scholars Press for South Florida Studies in the History of Judaism). There I point to what I conceive to be a profound shift in the modes of thought inaugurated by the framers of the Mishnah. I review those findings in Chapter Two, and that leads me directly to the literary-analytical work of Chapters Three and Four. In Chapter Five I explain what is at stake in this work and how the rather witless definition of precisely the same problem by a rather mediocre mind provoked me to think about the problems that I solve in these pages.

Since I here present my fourteenth monograph on exactly the same problem of description, it is necessary to set this one in its larger context. In the appendix I summarize the first thirteen monographs. Each study is meant to identify a piece of the puzzle that the Bavli once seemed to me to present; now that I have a good grasp of all the types of writing comprising the Bavli and how these are to be classified in an entirely objective manner, I turn with confidence to the next stage in the description of the document. Once more to signal what I conceive to be at stake, I may point toward what will follow. That research in turn will make possible the synthetic and the comparative stages of research that, of course, are necessary. The works I plan in succession to this sequence of analytical monographs are projected as follows:

The Torah in the Talmud. A Taxonomy of the Uses of Scripture in the Talmud of Babylonia in Comparison with the Talmud of the Land of Israel.

The Bavli and the Yerushalmi. A Systematic Comparison. I. The Problem and a Preliminary Probe: Bavli and Yerushalmi to Mishnah-Tractate Niddah.

The Bavli and the Yerushalmi. A Systematic Comparison. II. Bavli and Yerushalmi to Selected Mishnah-Tractates in Moed.

The Bavli and the Yerushalmi. A Systematic Comparison. III. Bavli and Yerushalmi to Selected Mishnah-Tractates in Nashim.

The Bavli and the Yerushalmi. A Systematic Comparison. IV. Bavli and Yerushalmi to Selected Mishnah-Tractates in Neziqin. Conclusion: Does the Bavli Establish an Autonomous Discourse?

The Definition of Judaism. From the Yerushalmi's Religion to the Bavli's Theology. The Autonomous Discourse of the Bavli and Its Associated Midrash Compilations. The Traits and Program of the Normative, Dual Torah in Conclusion.

The Bavli and the Denkart. A Comparison of the Systemic Statements of Judaism and Zoroastrianism.

From Old Order to New: Judaism, Zoroastrianism, and Islam at the End of Antiquity.

The critical position of the Bavli translation and the analytical studies that it has made possible emerge in a clear way from that program, and the character of the translation best explained by the logic that generates it. What lies beyond God only knows – but isn't telling.

I express my genuine pleasure at the opportunity offered to me by the University of South Florida for learning, through both teaching and scholarly inquiry. I express thanks to my university for its generous support of my scholarly work.

JACOB NEUSNER

Distinguished Research Professor of Religious Studies
UNIVERSITY OF SOUTH FLORIDA
Tampa, St. Petersburg, Sarasota, Lakeland, Fort Myers

735 Fourteenth Avenue Northeast
St. Petersburg, Florida 33701-1413 USA

June 30, 1990

1

The Generative Problematic:
What Is It and What Is at Stake in It?
The Case of the Mishnah and Sifra

The Mishnah concentrates on the correct classification of things. The Bavli takes up the issue of the relationships between and among what has been classified, adding to a simple classification system of the Mishnah other, fitting classificatory grids (hence, "mixed grids"). The Mishnah's mode of thought therefore is static, the Bavli's, dynamic; the Mishnah addresses a world at rest, the Bavli calls that same world into motion. The meaning of these simple descriptive statements will emerge in these pages, for in this monograph I try to show that, in a variety of entirely unrelated topics, when the framers of the Bavli move beyond the labor of Mishnah exegesis and amplification, they address a single question over and over again. This they do at a great many points, though two will suffice to state my proposal.

The question that occupies the authors of analytical compositions and composites concerns the interplay of classifications of things that form the same thing, which is to say, in taxonomic terms, of the species of a genus. A given genus is made up of various species. Each of these species, by definition, exhibits distinctive traits. When these species are brought into relationship with other species of the same genus, how the various species interrelate, by reason of the distinctive taxonomic traits characteristic of each, allows us to compare like to like and identify points of unlikeness; or to compare unlike to unlike and discover points of commonality. In so doing, we probe deeper into the concrete laws that govern each of the species of a common genus. So this labor of dialectical comparison and contrast aims at moving ever more profoundly into the depths of the law. We see how laws form law, but

1

also, how law generates laws: the unity of the law in its diversity, the power of diversity, too, to emerge out of unity.

Now these are exceedingly abstract formulations, and to make them stick, I have to show how diverse, concrete compositions and especially composites in acute detail illustrate them. If I can show that for a number of important passages in the Bavli, what is in play at the surface realizes what sits in the deep structure of thought, I can establish the prima facie plausibility of these readings of what makes the Bavli work.

So what I propose is that at the most profound and abstract layer of discourse, what gives the Bavli its dynamic and power of dialectic is this question of how to sort out the diverse ways in which different things form the same thing. That is not what occupies the framers of the Mishnah and shapes the character of their inquiry into any given topic, but it is a question that depends upon their work and forms the logically consequent inquiry. So while what generates inquiry and shapes analysis of things in the Mishnah is the taxonomic question, what does the same for the heirs of the Mishnah in the Bavli is the result of that taxonomy. A single process unfolds, but in clearly differentiated steps – just as the very presentation of the Bavli as a commentary and secondary amplification of the Mishnah is meant to indicate even in visual form. A simple analogy, drawn from music, will show what is at stake. The Mishnah may be compared to Ravel's *Bolero,* saying the same thing over and over again, pretty much in the same way, varying only the subject matter (in this, the analogy fails, being unfair to the brilliance of the Mishnah authorship, for Ravel says the same thing in the same way and never changes the musical counterpart to his subject matter). The Bavli then may be compared to a Beethoven or a Bruckner symphony, in which the same simple idea is reworked in countless variations, so that the whole exhibits both a rich complexity and also an essential simplicity.

I. Defining a Generative Problematic

The meaning of "generative problematic" then is very simple. When I address any topic whatever, is there something I want to know about that topic that is pretty much the same as what I want to know about any and every topic? In the Mishnah and in the Bavli, the answer to that question is affirmative. If I bring to bear a problem that provokes inquiry and focuses my attention on one thing, rather than some other, then that is what generates my work: makes me curious, requires me to answer a question (particularly of an analytical, not merely descriptive) character. By "problem" we may mean a variety of things, but by "problematic" only one: what persistently provokes curiosity and demands inquiry. The "generative problematic" then is that abstract problem that over and over again, in a variety of concrete settings, tells me what I want to know about this, that, and the other thing: which, for there to be a generative problematic, must always be the same thing.

In a variety of prior studies of not only the Mishnah but also various Midrash compilations, I have shown that some documents in the canon of Judaism (as it had taken shape by the end of late antiquity) repeatedly ask a single question or make a single point or focus on a single issue. Other documents do not do so. The former emerge as cogent, powerful illustration and advocacy of a single sustained proposition. The latter appear to be miscellaneous, informative but not argumentative. In the former, facts are active, in the latter, inert; in the former, topics are made to serve a larger purpose, in the latter, they serve themselves. Those writings that ask a single question over and over again may be characterized as documents formed in response to a single, recurrent issue, hence, shaped around a generative problematic. Those that do not often appear to be scrapbooks, mere collections. Among the former kind of documents in the Judaic canon, two strike me as the best evidence of how a single recurrent issue, transcending the data of discussion at any given point but present throughout the document as a whole, generates the problem to which the document overall is devoted. The first is the Mishnah, the second, Sifra. In that context, I have worked through a mounting number of monographs to show the same of the Bavli. Among the latter documents, the outstanding example is Mekhilta Attributed to R. Ishmael, though one can argue that some, though by no means all, Midrash compilations compile rather than shape data into propositions. But within all documents are compositions and composites that simply inform; for instance, the Bavli's massive miscellanies came out of authorships who did their work to illustrate themes, rather than to make points.

As to the Mishnah and Sifra: in a variety of works, I have shown that without regard to the limits of any given topic, the framers of the Mishnah time and again use the same method to produce results that are everywhere congruent with one another. The method is that of classification, and the results show how chaotic data may be shown to yield clear propositions through correct classification, that is, by appeal to the inherent traits of things. In respect to Sifra, I have shown that a single issue runs through the bulk of the document, which is the issue of the correct classification of things. Specifically, the traits of things by themselves do not yield reliable results. Only the Torah dictates how things truly are to be classified.

So that the exact sense in which I use the words "generative problematic" in relationship to a rabbinic document may be clear, let me now review my discussion of the taxonomic character of the Mishnah and the critique thereof by Sifra. Then the way in which a highly abstract inquiry may govern analysis of an unlimited number of concrete problems will be clear. Then, and only then, the question that I bring to the Bavli will be accessible, so my answer will be comprehensible.

II. The Generative Problematic of the Mishnah and that of Sifra: How the Former Set the Issue for the Latter

As we shall now see, the framers of the Mishnah ask the same thing of many things, which is, what is this, yielding, how is this like, or unlike, that, so that we may know what rule governs things of this classification, but not things of that classification. All things depend upon the taxa we select for the purpose of classification. The framers of the Mishnah classify things by their inherent traits, without reference to Scripture. Specifically, by systematically demolishing the logic that sustains an autonomous Mishnah and by equally thoroughly demonstrating the dependency, for the identification of the correct classification of things, not upon the traits of things viewed in the abstract, but upon the classification of things by Scripture in particular, the framers of Sifra recast the two parts of the Torah – the Written Torah and the Mishnah, which they read as a component of the Torah revealed by God to Moses at Sinai – into a single coherent statement through unitary and cogent discourse. At stake, therefore, for Sifra's authorship is the dependency of the Mishnah upon Scripture, at least for the encompassing case of the book of Leviticus.[1] So in choosing, as to form, the base text of Scripture, the authorship of Sifra made its entire statement *in nuce.* Then by composing a document that for very long stretches cannot have been put together without the Mishnah and at the same time subjecting the generative logical principles of the Mishnah to devastating critique, that same authorship took up its mediating position. The destruction of the Mishnah as an autonomous and free-standing statement, based upon its own logic, is followed by the reconstruction of (large tracts of the Mishnah) as a statement wholly within, and in accord with, the logic and program of the Written Torah in Leviticus. I therefore represent as a triumph of intellect the work of the authorship of Sifra, as we now know it in its recurrent and fixed forms of rhetoric and logic and equally

---

[1]That Sifra's authorship could have demonstrated the same propositions of topical program and order, logic of cogent discourse, and logic of probative demonstration of propositions for other parts of the Mishnah that relate to other legal codes in the Mosaic composite is beyond all doubt shown in the two Sifrés. But the program of our document certainly is not particular to the book of Leviticus, and the polemic and propositions encompass the entirety of the Dual Torah, wherever finally written down.

permanent protocol of relationships with other documents, particularly Scripture and Mishnah (with Tosefta). What we have in Sifra is simply one of the great, original, and successful works of the critical mind in the Judaism of the Dual Torah as it emerged from late antiquity.

The former, and dominant, approach to uniting the two Torahs, Oral and Written, into a single cogent statement, involved reading the Written Torah into the Oral. In form, this was done through inserting into the Oral Torah a long sequence of of prooftexts. That is the solution taken by the authorities who received the Mishnah, the initial and authoritative writing down of the Oral Torah, and subjected it to four hundred years of amplification and paraphrase and internal augmentation. They carried out that solution through the Tosefta, ca. A.D. 300, then the Talmud of the Land of Israel, ca. A.D. 400, and then, in the most successful, thoroughgoing manner, through the Talmud of Babylonia, ca. A.D. 600. The other solution required reading the Oral Torah into the written one, by inserting into the Written Torah citations and allusions to the oral one, and, as a matter of fact, also by demonstrating, on both philosophical and theological grounds, the utter subordination and dependency of the Oral Torah, the Mishnah, to the Written Torah – while at the same time defending and vindicating that same Oral Torah.

III. The Problem of the Mishnah and How That Problem Defined the Problematic That Generated Sifra as a Coherent and Cogent Inquiry

When, in ca. A.D. 200, the Mishnah reached closure and was received and adopted as law by the state-sanctioned Jewish governments in both the Roman empire, in the Land of Israel, and Iran, in Babylonia, respectively, the function and character of the document precipitated a considerable crisis. Politically and theologically presented as the foundation for the everyday administration of the affairs of Jewry, the Mishnah ignored the politics of the sponsoring regimes. Essentially ahistorical, the code hardly identified as authoritative any known political institution, let alone the patriarchate in the Land of Israel, the exilarchate in Babylonia. True, that political institutional flaw (from the viewpoint of the sponsoring authorities) scarcely could have proved critical.

But silence of the authorship of the Mishnah on the theological call for their document presented not a chronic but an acute problem. Since Jews generally accepted the authority of Moses at Sinai, failure to claim for the document a clear and explicit relationship to the Torah of Moses defined that acute issue. Why should people accept as authoritative the rulings of this piece of writing? Omitting reference to a a theological, as much as to a political myth, the authorship of the Mishnah also failed to signal the relationship between their document and Scripture. Since, for all Judaisms, Hebrew Scriptures in general, and the Pentateuch, in particular, represented God's will for Israel, silence on that matter provoked considerable response. Let me now spell out in some detail the political, theological, and literary difficulties presented by the Mishnah to any theory that the Mishnah formed part of God's revelation to Moses at Sinai. To make its way in Israelite life, the Mishnah as a constitution and code demanded for itself a theory of beginnings at (or in relation to) Sinai, with Moses, from God. The character of the Mishnah itself hardly won confidence that, on the face of it, the document formed part of, or derived from Sinai. It was originally published through oral formulation and oral transmission, that is, in the medium of memorization. But it had been in the medium of writing that, in the view of all of Israel until about A.D. 200, God had been understood to reveal the divine word and will. The Torah was a written book. People who claimed to receive further messages from God usually wrote them down. They had three choices in securing acceptance of their account. All three involved linking the new to the old.

Insofar as a piece of Jewish writing did not find a place in relationship to Scripture, its author laid no claim to present a holy book. The contrast between Jubilees and the Testaments of the Patriarchs, with their constant and close harping on biblical matters, and the several books of Maccabees, shows the differences. The former claim to present God's revealed truth, the latter, history. So a book was holy because in style, in authorship, or in (alleged) origin it continued Scripture, finding a place therefore (at least in the author's mind) within the canon, or because it provided an exposition on Scripture's meaning. But the Mishnah made no such claim. It entirely ignored the style of biblical Hebrew, speaking in a quite different kind of Hebrew altogether. It is silent on its authorship through sixty-two of the sixty-three tractates (the claims of Abot are post facto). In any event, nowhere does the Mishnah contain the claim that God had inspired the authors of the document. These are not given biblical names and certainly are not alleged to have been biblical saints. Most of the book's named authorities flourished within the same century as its anonymous arrangers and redactors, not in remote antiquity. Above all, the Mishnah contains scarcely a handful of exegeses of Scripture. These, where they occur, play a trivial and tangential role. So here is the problem of the Mishnah: different from Scripture in language and style, indifferent to the claim of authorship by a biblical hero or divine inspiration, stunningly aloof from allusion to verses of Scripture for nearly the whole of its discourse – yet authoritative for Israel.

IV. The Two Solutions to the Problem of the Mishnah

One response was represented by the claim that the authorities of the Mishnah stood in a chain of tradition that extended back to Sinai; stated explicitly in the Mishnah's first apologetic, tractate Avot, that circulated from approximately a generation beyond the promulgation of the Mishnah itself, that view required amplification and concrete demonstration. This approach treated the word *torah* as a common noun, as the word that spoke of a status or classification of sayings. A saying was *torah*, that is, enjoyed the status of torah or fell into the classification of *torah*, if it stood in the line of tradition from Sinai.

A second and distinct response took the same view of *torah* as a common noun. This response was to treat the Mishnah as subordinate to, and dependant upon, Scripture. Then *torah* was what fell into the classification of the revelation of *Torah* by God to Moses at Sinai. The way of providing what was needed within that theory was to link statements of the Mishnah to statements ("prooftexts") of Scripture. The Tosefta, ca. 300, a compilation of citations of, and comments upon, the Mishnah, together with some autonomous materials that may have reached closure in the period in which the work of redaction of the Mishnah was going on, as well as the Talmud of the Land of Israel, ca. 400, fairly systematically did just that.

The former solution treated Torah with a small *t*, that is to say, as a generic classification, and identified the Mishnah with the Torah revealed to Moses at Sinai by claiming a place for the Mishnah's authorities in the process of tradition and transmission that brought torah – no longer, the Torah, the specific writing comprising the Five Books of Moses – to contemporary Israel, the Jewish people. It was a theological solution, expressed through ideas, attitudes, implicit claims, but not through sustained rewriting of either Scripture or the Mishnah. The latter solution, by contrast, concerned the specific and concrete statements of the Mishnah and required a literary, not merely a theological, statement, one precise and specific to passages of the Mishnah, one after the other. What was demanded by the claim that the Mishnah depended upon, but therefore enjoyed the standing of, Scripture, was a line-by-line commentary upon the Mishnah in light of Scripture. But this, too, I stress, treated *torah* as a common noun.

The third way, which is Sifra's, would set aside the two solutions, the theological and the literary, and explore the much more profound issues of the fundamental and generative structure of right thought, yielding, as a matter of fact, both Scripture and the Mishnah. This approach insisted that *torah* always was a proper noun. There was, and is, only The Torah. But this – The Torah – demanded expansion and vast amplification.

When we know the principles of logical structure and especially those of hierarchical classification that animate The Torah, we can undertake part of the task of expansion and amplification, that is, join in the processes of thought that, in the mind of God, yielded The Torah. For when we know how God thought in giving The Torah to Moses at Sinai and so accounting for the classifications and their ordering in the very creation of the world, we can ourselves enter into The Torah and participate in its processes.

V. Sifra's Solution to the Problem of the Mishnah: Framing an Original Problematic in Place of the Mishnah's Generative Problematic

Sifra's authorship attempted to set forth the Dual Torah as a single, cogent statement, doing so by reading the Mishnah into Scripture not merely for proposition but for expression of proposition. On the surface that decision represented a literary, not merely a theological, judgment. But within the deep structure of thought, it was far more than a mere matter of how to select and organize propositions. Presenting the two Torahs in a single statement constituted an experiment in logic, that logic, in particular, that made cogent thought possible, and that transformed facts into propositions, and propositions into judgments of the more, or the less, consequential. It will take many pages of the shank of this book to demonstrate the profound layers of thought upon which the authorship of Sifra erected its remarkable writing. At this point, it suffices to warn that Sifra's authorship did something no one else in Judaic antiquity even imagined attempting to do, and that is, to state the Dual Torah in a single, coherent, cogent piece of writing, a piece of writing in which new thought came to expression in a very particular medium indeed.

While the Mishnah's other apologists wrote the Written Torah into the Mishnah, Sifra's authorship wrote the Oral Torah into Scripture. That is to say, the other of the two approaches to the problem of the Mishnah, the one of Sifra, to begin with claimed to demonstrate that the Mishnah found its correct place within the Written Torah itself. Instead of citing verses of Scripture in the context of the Mishnah, the authorship of Sifra cited passages of the Mishnah in the context of Scripture, Leviticus in particular. Let me concentrate on the other solution, the one that characterized authorities from Avot and the Tosefta through the Bavli, which we may call "the appeal to the Torah for a solution to the problem of the Mishnah."

Sifra's authorship's position is that the Mishnah is authoritative not because it is *torah* in the generic sense, but because it simply amplifies or depends upon the Torah, in the particular sense of the Five Books of

Moses. The earliest exegetical strata of the two Talmuds and the legal exegetical writings produced in the two hundred years after the closure of the Mishnah took the position that the Mishnah is wholly dependent upon Scripture and authoritative, in the status (*but not the classification!*) of the Torah, because of that dependency. Whatever is of worth in the Mishnah can be shown to derive directly from Scripture. So the Mishnah was represented as deemed distinct from, and subordinate to, Scripture. This position is expressed in an obvious way. Once the Talmuds cite a Mishnah pericope, they commonly ask, "What is the source of these words?" And the answer invariably is, "As it is said in Scripture." This constitutes not only a powerful defense for the revealed truth of the Mishnah. It presents, also, a stunning judgment upon the standing (and, as a matter of fact, the classification) of the Mishnah. For when the exegetes find themselves constrained to add prooftexts, they admit the need to acknowledge that the Mishnah is not (part of) The Torah but only a secondary expression or amplification of The Torah.

That judgment upon the Mishnah forms part of the polemic of Sifra's authorship – but only part of it. Sifra's authorship conducts a sustained polemic against the failure of the Mishnah to cite Scripture very much or systematically to link its ideas to Scripture through the medium of formal demonstration by exegesis. Sifra's rhetorical exegesis follows a standard redactional form. Scripture will be cited. Then a statement will be made about its meaning, or a statement of law correlative to that Scripture will be given. That statement sometimes cites the Mishnah, often verbatim. Finally, the author of Sifra invariably states, "Now is that not (merely) logical?" And the point of that statement will be, Can this position not be gained through the working of mere logic, based upon facts supplied (to be sure) by Scripture?

The polemical power of Sifra lies in its repetitive demonstration that the stated position, citation of a Mishnah pericope, is not only not the product of logic, but is, and only can be, the product of exegesis of Scripture. That is only part of the matter, as I shall explain, but that component of the larger judgment of Sifra's authorship does make the point that the Mishnah is subordinated to Scripture and validated only through Scripture. In that regard, the authorship of Sifra stands at one with the position of the authorships of the other successor writings, even though Sifra's writers carried to a much more profound level of thought the critique of the Mishnah. They did so by rethinking the logical foundations of the entire Torah.

VI. The Generative Problematic of the Mishnah: The Importance of Classification in the System of the Mishnah

The system of philosophy expressed through concrete and detailed law presented by the Mishnah consists of a coherent logic and topic, a cogent worldview and comprehensive way of living. It is a worldview which speaks of transcendent things, a way of life in response to the supernatural meaning of what is done, a heightened and deepened perception of the sanctification of Israel in deed and in deliberation. That paramount concern accounts for the centrality of classification, the appeal of the logic of hierarchical classification in the demonstration of comparisons and contrasts, in the formation of the thought of the document. For sanctification in the Mishnah's system means establishing the stability, order, regularity, predictability, and reliability of Israel in the world of nature and supernature in particular at moments and in contexts of danger. And it is through assigning to all things their rightful name, setting of all things in their proper position, that we discover the laws of stability, order, regularity, and predictability. Danger means instability, disorder, irregularity, uncertainty, and betrayal. Each topic of the system as a whole takes up a critical and indispensable moment or context of social being. Through what is said in regard to each of the Mishnah's principal topics, what the system as a whole wishes to declare is fully expressed. Yet if the parts severally and jointly give the message of the whole, the whole cannot exist without all of the parts, so well joined and carefully crafted are they all.

What this means for the requirements of logical demonstration is quite obvious. To show something to be true, one has to demonstrate that, in logic, it conforms to the regularity and order that form the guarantee of truth. Analysis is meant to discover order: the rule that covers diverse, by nature disorderly, things, the shared trait, the general and prevailing principle of regularity. And to discover the prevailing rule, one has to know how to classify things that seem to be each *sui generis*, how to find the rule that governs diverse things. And that explains the centrality in the system of the Mishnah of the classification of things. At issue between the framers of the Mishnah and the authorship of Sifra is the correct sources of classification. The framers of the Mishnah effect their taxonomy through the traits of things. The authorship of Sifra insists that the source of classification is Scripture. We shall now see two expressions of the considerable debate. In this chapter we shall show how Sifra's authorship time and again demonstrates that classification cannot be carried out without Scripture's data, and, it must follow, hierarchical arguments based on extrascriptural taxa always fail.

In the Mishnah we seek connection between fact and fact, sentence and sentence, by comparing and contrasting two things that are like and not alike. At the logical level the Mishnah falls into the category of familiar philosophical thought. Once we seek regularities, we propose rules. What is like another thing falls under its rule, and what is not like the other falls under the opposite rule. Accordingly, as to the species of the genus, so far as they are alike, they share the same rule. So far as they are not alike, each follows a rule contrary to that governing the other. So the work of analysis is what produces connection, and therefore the drawing of conclusions derives from comparison and contrast: the *and*, the *equal*. The proposition then that forms the conclusion concerns the essential likeness of the two offices, except where they are different, but the subterranean premise is that we can explain both likeness and difference by appeal to a principle of fundamental order and unity. To make these observations concrete, we turn to the case at hand. The important contrast comes at the outset. The high priest and king fall into a single genus, but speciation, based on traits particular to the king, then distinguishes the one from the other. All of this exercise is conducted essentially independently of Scripture; the classifications derive from the system, are viewed as autonomous constructs; traits of things define classifications and dictate what is like and what is unlike.

VII. Sifra's Critique of Designating Classifications without Scriptural Definition: A Preliminary View

Let us now examine one sustained example of how Sifra's authorship rejects the principles of the logic of hierarchical classification *as these are worked out by the framers of the Mishnah*. I emphasize that the critique applies to the way in which a shared logic is worked out by the other authorship. For it is not the principle that like things follow the same rule, unlike things, the opposite rule, that is at stake. Nor is the principle of hierarchical classification embodied in the argument a fortiori at issue. What Sifra's authorship disputes is that we can classify things on our own by appeal to the traits or indicative characteristics, that is, utterly without reference to Scripture. The argument is simple. On our own, we cannot classify species into genera. Everything is different from everything else in some way. But Scripture tells us what things are like what other things for what purposes, hence Scripture imposes on things the definitive classifications, and not traits we discern in the things themselves. When we see the nature of the critique, we shall have a clear picture of what is at stake when we examine, in some detail, precisely how the Mishnah's logic does its work. That is why at the outset I present a complete composition in which Sifra's authorship tests the modes of classification characteristic of the Mishnah, resting as they do on the traits of things viewed out of the context of Scripture's categories of things.

5. Parashat Vayyiqra Dibura Denedabah Parashah 3

VI.1   A.   "[If his offering is] a burnt-offering [from the herd, he shall offer a male without blemish; he shall offer it at the door of the tent of meeting, that he may be accepted before the Lord; he shall lay his hand upon the head of the burnt-offering, and it shall be accepted for him to make atonement for him]" (Lev. 1:2):

       B.   Why does Scripture refer to a burnt-offering in particular?

       C.   For one might have taken the view that all of the specified grounds for the invalidation of an offering should apply only to the burnt-offering that is brought as a freewill-offering.

       D.   But how should we know that the same grounds for invalidation apply also to a burnt-offering that is brought in fulfillment of an obligation [for instance, the burnt-offering that is brought for a leper who is going through a rite of purification, or the bird brought by a woman who has given birth as part of her purification rite, Lev. 14, 12, respectively]?

       E.   It is a matter of logic.

       F.   Bringing a burnt-offering as a freewill-offering and bringing a burnt-offering in fulfillment of an obligation [are parallel to one another and fall into the same classification].

       G.   Just as a burnt-offering that is brought as a freewill-offering is subject to all of the specified grounds for invalidation, so to a burnt-offering brought in fulfillment of an obligation, all the same grounds for invalidation should apply.

       H.   No, [that reasoning is not compelling. For the two species of the genus, burnt-offering, are not wholly identical and can be distinguished, on which basis we may also maintain that the grounds for invalidation that pertain to the one do not necessarily apply to the other. Specifically:] If you have taken that position with respect to the burnt-offering brought as a freewill-offering, for which there is no equivalent, will you take the same position with regard to the burnt-offering brought in fulfillment of an obligation, for which there is an equivalent? [For if one is obligated to bring a burnt-offering by reason of obligation and cannot afford a beast, one may bring birds, as at Lev. 14:22, but if one is bringing a freewill-offering, a less expensive form of the offering may not serve.]

       I.   Accordingly, since there is the possibility in the case of the burnt-offering brought in fulfillment of an obligation, in which case there is an acceptable equivalent [to the more expensive beast, through the less expensive birds], all of the specified grounds for invalidation [which apply to the in any case more expensive burnt-offering brought as a freewill-offering] should not apply at all.

       J.   That is why in the present passage, Scripture refers simply to "burnt-offering," [and without further specification, the meaning is then simple:] All the same are the burnt-offering brought in fulfillment of an obligation and a burnt-offering brought as a freewill-offering in that all of the same grounds for invalidation of the beast that pertain to the one pertain also to the other.

VI.2 A. And how do we know that the same rules of invalidation of a blemished beast apply also in the case of a beast that is designated in substitution of a beast sanctified for an offering [in line with Lev. 27:10, so that, if one states that a given, unconsecrated beast is to take the place of a beast that has already been consecrated, the already consecrated beast remains in its holy status, and the beast to which reference is made also becomes consecrated]?

B. The matter of bringing a burnt-offering and the matter of bringing a substituted beast fall into the same classification [since both are offerings that in the present instance will be consumed upon the altar, and, consequently, they fall under the same rule as to invalidating blemishes].

C. Just as the entire protocol of blemishes apply to the one, so in the case of the beast that is designated as a substitute, the same invalidating blemishes pertain.

D. No, if you have invoked that rule in the case of the burnt-offering, in which case no status of sanctification applies should the beast that is designated as a burnt-offering be blemished in some permanent way, will you make the same statement in the case of a beast that is designated as a substitute? For in the case of a substituted beast, the status of sanctification applies even though the beast bears a permanent blemish! [So the two do not fall into the same classification after all, since to begin with one cannot sanctify a permanently blemished beast, which beast can never enter the status of sanctification, but through an act of substitution, a permanently blemished beast can be placed into the status of sanctification.]

E. Since the status of sanctification applies [to a substituted beast] even though the beast bears a permanent blemish, all of the specified grounds for invalidation as a matter of logic should not apply to it.

F. That is why in the present passage, Scripture refers simply to "burnt-offering," [and without further specification, the meaning is then simple:] All the same are the burnt-offering brought in fulfillment of an obligation and a burnt-offering brought as a substitute for an animal designated as holy, in that all of the same grounds for invalidation of the beast that pertain to the one pertain also to the other.

VI.3 A. And how do we know [that the protocol of blemishes that apply to the burnt-offering brought as a freewill-offering apply also to] animals that are subject to the rule of a sacrifice as a peace-offering?

B. It is a matter of logic. The matter of bringing a burnt-offering and the matter of bringing animals that are subject to the rule of a sacrifice as a peace-offering fall into the same classification [since both are offerings and, consequently under the same rule as to invalidating blemishes].

C. Just as the entire protocol of blemishes apply to the one, so in the case of animals that are subject to the rule of a sacrifice as a peace-offering, the same invalidating blemishes pertain.
D. And it is furthermore a matter of an argument a fortiori, as follows:
E. If to a burnt-offering which is valid when in the form of a bird [which is inexpensive], the protocol of invalidating blemishes apply, to peace-offerings, which are not valid when brought in the form of a bird, surely the same protocol of invalidating blemishes should also apply!
F. No, if you have applied that rule to a burnt-offering, in which case females are not valid for the offering as male beasts are, will you say the same of peace-offerings? For female beasts as much as male beasts may be brought for sacrifice in the status of the peace-offering. [The two species may be distinguished from one another.]
G. Since it is the case that female beasts as much as male beasts may be brought for sacrifice in the status of the peace-offering, the protocol of invalidating blemishes should not apply to a beast designated for use as peace-offerings.
H. That is why in the present passage, Scripture refers simply to "burnt-offering," [and without further specification, the meaning is then simple:] All the same are the burnt-offering brought in fulfillment of an obligation and an animal designated under the rule of peace-offerings, in that all of the same grounds for invalidation of the beast that pertain to the one pertain also to the other.

The systematic exercise proves for beasts that serve in three classifications of offerings, burnt-offerings, substitutes, and peace-offerings, that the same rules of invalidation apply throughout. The comparison of the two kinds of burnt-offerings, voluntary and obligatory, shows that they are sufficiently different from one another so that as a matter of logic, what pertains to the one need not apply to the other. Then come the differences between an animal that is consecrated and one that is designated as a substitute for one that is consecrated. Finally we distinguish between the applicable rules of the sacrifice; a burnt-offering yields no meat for the person in behalf of whom the offering is made, while one sacrificed under the rule of peace-offerings does. What is satisfying, therefore, is that we run the changes on three fundamentally different differences and show that in each case, the differences between like things are greater than the similarities I cannot imagine a more perfect exercise in the applied and practical logic of comparison and contrast.

The authorship of Sifra concurs in the fundamental principle that sanctification consists in calling things by their rightful name, or, in philosophical language, discovering the classification of things and determining the rule that governs diverse things. Where that authorship differs from the view of the Mishnah's concerns is – I emphasize – *the origins of taxa*: how do we know what diverse things form a single classification of things. Taxa originate in Scripture. Accordingly, at stake in the critique of the Mishnah is not the principles of logic necessary for understanding the construction and inner structure of creation. All parties among sages concurred that the inner structure set forth by a logic of classification alone could sustain the system of ordering all things in proper place and under the proper rule. The like belongs with the like and conforms to the rule governing the like, the unlike goes over to the opposite and conforms to the opposite rule. When we make lists of the like, we also know the rule governing all the items on those lists, respectively. We know that and one other thing, namely, the opposite rule, governing all items sufficiently like to belong on those lists, but sufficiently unlike to be placed on other lists. That rigorously philosophical logic of analysis, comparison and contrast, served because it was the only logic that could serve a system that proposed to make the statement concerning order and right array. Let us first show how the logic of proving propositions worked, then review Sifra's authorship's systematic critique of the way in which the Mishnah's framers applied that logic, specifically, proposed to identify classifications.

VIII. Sifra's Critique of the Mishnah:
The Revealed Taxonomic Attack on Free-Standing Taxonomic Logic

As is now clear, the source of classifications proves to define the decisive point at issue between the authorship of Sifra and the framers of the Mishnah. No one denies the principle of hierarchical classification. That is an established fact, a self-evident trait of mind. The argument of Sifra's authorship is that, by themselves, things do not possess traits that permit us finally to classify species into a common genus. There always are traits distinctive to a classification. Accordingly, it is the argument of Sifra's authorship that without the revelation of the Torah, we are not able to effect any classification at all, are left, that is to say, only with species, no genus, only with cases, no rules. We shall now review a series of specific statements of that general position. Then, in the following chapter, we shall see the way in which, in the view of Sifra's authorship, we correctly carry out our scientific inquiry, through *Listenwissenschaft*, into the rules that govern.

IX. The Fundamental Critique:
The Limitations of (the Mishnah's) Monothetic Classification

The thrust of Sifra's authorship's attack on the Mishnah's taxonomic logic is readily discerned. Time and again, we can easily demonstrate, things have so many and such diverse and contradictory indicative traits that, comparing one thing to something else, we can always distinguish one species from another. Even though we find something in common, we also can discern some other trait characteristic of one thing but not the other. Consequently, we also can show that the hierarchical logic on which we rely, the argument a fortiori or *qol vehomer*, will not serve. For if on the basis of one set of traits which yields a given classification, we place into hierarchical order two or more items, on the basis of a different set of traits, we have either a different classification altogether, or, much more commonly, simply a different hierarchy. So the attack on the way in which the Mishnah's authorship has done its work appeals to not merely the limitations of classification solely on the basis of traits of things.   The more telling argument addresses what is, to *Listenwissenschaft*, the source of power and compelling proof: hierarchization.   That is why, throughout, we must designate the Mishnah's mode of *Listenwissenschaft* a logic of hierarchical classification. Things are not merely like or unlike, therefore following one rule or its opposite. Things also are weightier or less weighty, and that particular point of likeness of difference generates the logical force of *Listenwissenschaft*.

Sifra's authorship repeatedly demonstrates that the formation of classifications based on monothetic taxonomy, that is to say, traits that are not only common to both items but that are shared throughout both items subject to comparison and contrast, simply will not serve. For at every point at which someone alleges uniform, that is to say, monothetic likeness, Sifra's authorship will demonstrate difference. Then how to proceed? Appeal to some shared traits as a basis for classification: This is not like that, and that is not like this, but the indicative trait that both exhibit is such and so, that is to say, polythetic taxonomy. The self-evident problem in accepting differences among things and insisting, nonetheless, on their monomorphic character for purposes of comparison and contrast cannot be set aside: Who says? That is, if I can adduce in evidence for a shared classification of things only a few traits among many characteristic of each thing, then what stops me from treating all things alike?

Polythetic taxonomy opens the way to an unlimited exercise in finding what diverse things have in common and imposing, for that reason, one rule on everything.   Then the very working of *Listenwissenschaft* as a tool of analysis, differentiation, comparison, contrast, and the descriptive determination of rules yields the opposite of what is desired. Chaos, not order, a mass of exceptions, no rules, a world of examples, each subject to its own regulation, instead of a world of order and proportion, composition and stability, will result.

X. How Sifra Affirms Taxonomic Logic:
Revealed Taxonomies vs. Merely Imputed Ones

Sifra's authorship demonstrates that *Listenwissenschaft* is a self-evidently valid mode of demonstrating the truth of propositions. But *the source of the correct classification of things is Scripture and only Scripture*. Without Scripture's intervention into the taxonomy of the world, we should have no knowledge at all of which things fall into which classifications and therefore are governed by which rules. How then do we appeal to Scripture to designate the operative classifications? Here is a simple example of the alternative mode of classification, one that does not appeal to the traits of things but to the utilization of names by Scripture. What we see is how by naming things in one way, rather than in another, Scripture orders all things, classifying and, in the nature of things, also hierarchizing them. Here is one example among many of how Sifra's authorship conceives the right way of logical thought to proceed:

7. Parashat Vayyiqra Dibura Denedabah Parashah 4

V.1　A.　"...and Aaron's sons the priests shall present the blood and throw the blood [round about against the altar that is at the door of the tent of meeting]":

　　　B.　Why does Scripture make use of the word "blood" twice [instead of using a pronoun]?

　　　C.　[It is for the following purpose:] How on the basis of Scripture do you know that if blood deriving from one burnt-offering was confused with blood deriving from another burnt-offering, blood deriving from one burnt-offering with blood deriving from a beast that has been substituted therefor, blood deriving from a burnt-offering with blood deriving from an unconsecrated beast, the mixture should nonetheless be presented?

　　　D.　It is because Scripture makes use of the word "blood" twice [instead of using a pronoun].

V.2　A.　While if blood deriving from beasts in the specified classifications is to be presented, for the simple reason that if the several beasts while alive had been confused with one another, they might be offered up,

　　　B.　how do we know that even if the blood of a burnt-offering were confused with that of a beast killed as a guilt-offering, [it is to be offered up]?

　　　C.　I shall concede in the case of the mixture of the blood of a burnt-offering confused with that of a beast killed as a guilt-offering, it is to be presented, for both this one and that one fall into the classification of Most Holy Things.

　　　D.　But how do I know that if the blood of a burnt-offering were confused with the blood of a beast slaughtered in the classification of peace-offerings or of a thanksgiving-offering, [it is to be presented]?

E.   I shall concede the case of the mixture of the blood of a burnt-offering confused with that of a beast slaughtered in the classification of peace-offerings or of a thanksgiving-offering, [it is to be presented,] because the beasts in both classifications produce blood that has to be sprinkled four times.

F.   But how do I know that if the blood of a burnt-offering were confused with the blood of a beast slaughtered in the classification of a firstling or a beast that was counted as tenth or of a beast designated as a passover, [it is to be presented]?

G.   I shall concede the case of the mixture of the blood of a burnt-offering confused with that of a beast slaughtered in the classification of firstling or a beast that was counted as tenth or of a beast designated as a passover, [it is to be presented,] because Scripture uses the word "blood" two times.

H.   Then while I may make that concession, might I also suppose that if the blood of a burnt-offering was confused with the blood of beasts that had suffered an invalidation, it also may be offered up?

I.   Scripture says, "...its blood," [thus excluding such a case].

J.   Then I shall concede the case of a mixture of the blood of a valid burnt-offering with the blood of beasts that had suffered an invalidation, which blood is not valid to be presented at all.

K.   But how do I know that if such blood were mixed with the blood deriving from beasts set aside as sin-offerings to be offered on the inner altar, [it is not to be offered up]?

L.   I can concede that the blood of a burnt-offering that has been mixed with the blood deriving from beasts set aside as sin-offerings to be offered on the inner altar is not to be offered up, for the one is offered on the inner altar, and the other on the outer altar [the burnt-offering brought as a freewill-offering, under discussion here, is slaughtered at the altar "...that is at the door of the tent of meeting," not at the inner altar].

M.   But how do I know that even if the blood of a burnt-offering was confused with the blood of sin-offerings that are to be slaughtered at the outer altar, it is not to be offered up?

N.   Scripture says, "...its blood," [thus excluding such a case].

In place of the rejecting of arguments resting on classifying species into a common genus, we now demonstrate how classification really is to be carried on. It is through the imposition upon data of the categories dictated by Scripture: Scripture's use of language. That is the force of this powerful exercise. No. 1 sets the stage, simply pointing out that the use of the word "blood" twice encompasses a case in which blood in two distinct classifications is somehow confused in the process of the conduct of the cult. In such a case it is quite proper to pour out the mixture of blood deriving from distinct sources, for example, beasts that have served different, but comparable purposes. We then systemically work out the limits of that rule, showing how comparability works, then pointing to cases in which comparability is set aside. Throughout the exposition, at the crucial point we invoke the formulation of Scripture, subordinating logic or in our instance the process of classification of like species to the dictation of Scripture. I cannot imagine a more successful demonstration of what the framers wish to say.

The reason for Scripture's unique power of classification is the possibility of polythetic classification that only Scripture makes possible. Because of Scripture's provision of taxa, we are able to undertake the science of *Listenwissenschaft*, including hierarchical classification, in the right way. What can we do because we appeal to Scripture, which we cannot do if we do not rely on Scripture? It is to establish the possibility of polythetic classification. We can appeal to shared traits of otherwise distinct taxa and so transform species into a common genus for a given purpose. Only Scripture makes that initiative feasible, so Sifra's authorship maintains. What is at stake? It is the possibility of doing precisely what the framers of the Mishnah wish to do. That is to join together masses of diverse data into a single, encompassing statement, to show the rule that inheres in diverse cases. In what follows, we shall see an enormous, coherent, and beautifully articulated exercise in the comparison and contrast of many things of a single genus. The whole holds together, because Scripture makes possible the statement of all things within a single rule. That is, as we have noted, precisely what the framers of the Mishnah proposed to accomplish. Sifra's authorship maintains that only by appeal to The Torah is this fete of learning possible. If, then, we wish to understand all things all together and all at once under a single encompassing rule, we had best revert to The Torah, with its account of the rightful names, positions, and order, imputed to all things.

22. Parashat Vayyiqra Dibura Denedabah Parashah 11

I.1　A.　[With reference to M. Men. 5:5, given in boldface:] There are those [offerings which require bringing near but do not require waving, waving but not bringing near, waving and bringing near, neither waving nor bringing near: These are offering which require bringing near but do not require waving: the meal-offering of fine flour and the meal-offering prepared in the baking pan and the meal-offering prepared in the frying pan, and the meal-offering of cakes and the meal-offering of wafers, and the meal-offering of priests, and the meal-offering of an anointed priest, and the meal-offering of gentiles, and the meal-offering of women, and the meal-offering of a sinner. R. Simeon says, "The meal-offering of priests and of the anointed priest – bringing near does not apply to them, because the taking of a handful does not apply to them. And whatever is not subject to the taking of a handful is not subject to bringing near."] [Scripture] says, "When you present to the Lord a meal-offering that is made in any of these ways, it shall be brought [to the priest who shall take it up to the altar]":

B. What requires bringing near is only the handful alone. How do I know that I should encompass under the rule of bringing near the meal-offering?

C. Scripture says explicitly, "Meal-offering."

D. How do I know that I should encompass all meal-offerings?

E. Scripture says, using the accusative particle, "The meal-offering."

I.2 A. I might propose that what requires bringing near is solely the meal-offering brought as a freewill-offering.

B. How do I know that the rule encompasses an obligatory meal-offering?

C. It is a matter of logic.

D. Bringing a meal-offering as a freewill-offering and bringing a meal-offering as a matter of obligation form a single classification. Just as a meal-offering presented as a freewill-offering requires bringing near, so the same rule applies to a meal-offering of a sinner [brought as a matter of obligation], which should likewise require bringing near.

E. No, if you have stated that rule governing bringing near in the case of a freewill-offering, on which oil and frankincense have to be added, will you say the same of the meal-offering of a sinner [Lev. 5:11], which does not require oil and frankincense?

F. The meal-offering brought by a wife accused of adultery will prove to the contrary, for it does not require oil and frankincense, but it does require bringing near [as is stated explicitly at Num. 5:15].

G. No, if you have applied the requirement of bringing near to the meal-offering brought by a wife accused of adultery, which also requires waving, will you say the same of the meal-offering of a sinner, which does not have to be waved?

H. Lo, you must therefore reason by appeal to a polythetic analogy [in which not all traits pertain to all components of the category, but some traits apply to them all in common]:

I. The meal-offering brought as a freewill-offering, which requires oil and frankincense, does not in all respects conform to the traits of the meal-offering of a wife accused of adultery, which does not require oil and frankincense, and the meal-offering of the wife accused of adultery, which requires waving, does not in all respects conform to the traits of a meal-offering brought as a freewill-offering, which does not require waving.

J. But what they have in common is that they are alike in requiring the taking up of a handful and they are also alike in that they require bringing near.

K. I shall then introduce into the same classification the meal-offering of a sinner, which is equivalent to them as to the matter of the taking up of a handful, and also should be equivalent to them as to the requirement of being drawn near.

L. But might one not argue that the trait that all have in common is that all of them may be brought equally by a rich and a poor person and require drawing near, which then excludes from the common classification the meal-offering of a sinner, which does not conform

> to the rule that it may be brought equally by a rich and a poor person, [but may be brought only by a poor person,] and such an offering also should not require being brought near!

M. [The fact that the polythetic classification yields indeterminate results means failure once more, and, accordingly,] Scripture states, "Meal-offering,"

N. with this meaning: all the same are the meal-offering brought as a freewill-offering and the meal-offering of a sinner, both this and that require being brought near.

The elegant exercise draws together the various types of meal-offerings and shows that they cannot form a classification of either a monothetic or a polythetic character. Consequently, Scripture must be invoked to supply the proof for the classification of the discrete items. The important language is at H-J: these differ from those, and those from these, but what they have in common is.... Then we demonstrate, with our appeal to Scripture, the sole valid source of polythetic classification, M. And this is constant throughout Sifra.

While setting forth its critique of the Mishnah's utilization of the logic of comparison and contrast in hierarchical classification, the authorship of Sifra is careful not to criticize the Mishnah. Its position favors restating the Mishnah within the context of Scripture, not rejecting the conclusions of the Mishnah, let alone its authority. Consequently, when we find a critique of applied reason divorced from Scripture, we rarely uncover an explicit critique of the Mishnah, and when we find a citation of the Mishnah, we rarely uncover linkage to the ubiquitous principle that Scripture forms the source of all classification and hierarchy. When the Mishnah is cited by Sifra's authorship, it will be presented as part of the factual substrate of the Torah. When the logic operative throughout the Mishnah is subjected to criticism, the language of the Mishnah will rarely, if ever, be cited in context. The operative language in dealing with the critique of the applied logic of *Listenwissenschaft* as represented by the framers of the Mishnah ordinarily is, "Is it not a matter of logic?" Then the sorts of arguments against taxonomy pursued outside of the framework of Scripture's classifications will follow. When, by contrast, the authorship of Sifra wishes to introduce into the context it has already established a verbatim passage of the Mishnah, it will ordinarily, though not always, use *mikan amru*, which, in context, means, "in this connection [sages] have said." It is a simple fact that when the intent is to demolish improper reasoning, the Mishnah's rules in the Mishnah's language rarely, if ever, occur. When the authorship of Sifra wishes to incorporate paragraphs of the Mishnah into their re-presentation of The Torah, they will do so either without fanfare, as in the passage at hand, or by the neutral joining language "in this connection [sages] have said."

XI. The Rehabilitation of Hierarchical Classification:
The Torah's Taxonomy

The authorship of Sifra never called into question the self-evident validity of taxonomic logic. Its critique is addressed only to how the Mishnah's framers identify the origins of, and delineate, taxa. But that critique proves fundamental to the case that that authorship proposed to make. For, intending to demonstrate that *The Torah* was a proper noun, and that everything that was valid came to expression in the single, cogent statement of The Torah, the authorship at hand identified the fundamental issue. It is the debate over the way we know things. In insisting, in agreement with the framers of the Mishnah, that there are not only cases but also rules, not only species but also genera, the authorship of Sifra also made its case in behalf of the case for The Torah as a proper noun. This carries us to the theological foundation for Sifra's authorship's sustained critique of applied reason.

In appealing to the principle, for taxonomy, of *sola Scriptura*, I mean to set forth what I conceive really to be at stake. It is the character of The Torah and what it is, in The Torah, that we wish to discern. And the answer to that question requires theological, not merely literary and philosophical, reflection on our part. For I maintain that in their delineation of correct hierarchical logic, Sifra's authorship uncovered, within The Torah (hence by definition, written and oral components of The Torah alike) an adumbration of the working of the mind of God. That is because the premise of all discourse is that The Torah was written by God and dictated by God to Moses at Sinai. And that will in the end explain why Sifra's authorship for its part has entered into The Torah long passages of not merely clarification but active intrusion, making itself a component of the interlocutorial process. To what end we know: it was to unite the Dual Torah. But on what basis?

If Sifra had taken first place in the curriculum of Judaism, its representation of the Written Torah and the Oral Torah all together and all at once would have opened a different path altogether. For it is one thing to absorb the Torah, Oral and Written, and it is quite another to join in the processes of thought, the right way of thinking, that sustain the Torah. The authorship of Sifra proposed to regain access to the modes of thought that guided the formation of the Torah, Oral and Written alike: comparison and contrast in this way, not in that, identification of categories in one manner, not in another. Since those were the modes of thought that, in Sifra's authorship's conception, dictated the structure of intellect upon which the Torah, the united Torah, rested, a simple conclusion is the sole possible one. Now to answer the question of the basis on which Sifra's authorship represented itself as participants in, and interlocutors of, The Torah, such that they were prepared to re-present, that is to say, simply rewrite (and therefore, themselves write) The Torah.

XII. The Generative Problematic: What Is It and What Is at Stake in It?

What we see is two facts. First, beginning with Sifra, we notice that time and again an abstract issue tells the authors of the discrete compositions of which the document is made up what they wish to know about a given verse of Scripture and passage of the Mishnah. Their concern is very rarely exegetical, meaning, the explanation of the meanings of words or phrases; it is very rarely expository, meaning, in this context, the spelling out of the law at hand and how it is to be observed; it is very rarely to complement a passage with other relevant statements on that same passage. All of these traits of Mishnah commentary in the Bavli are absent in Sifra's reading of the Mishnah (and of Scripture). Rather, a single issue predominates; it is nearly always present, but spelled out only through repetition and by implication. That is what I mean by "generative problematic," what is everywhere present, at so profound a level of abstraction that the document overall coheres through recurrent exercises in response to that single question, a problematic never limited by the subject matter at hand, or even by the facts that pertain to that subject matter.

What is at stake in identifying the generative problematic of the Bavli? The answer is simple. I have maintained that the Bavli forms a coherent statement, that, wherever we are, we know why we are told the things that we are told, and what makes one thing cohere with some other, and all things with all other things. Now that conception is hardly fresh; to the contrary, just as the framers of the Bavli's Mishnah commentary rightly took for granted that all the laws of the Mishnah and of sources of equivalent authority harmoniously cohere, so all those who have studied the Bavli have understood the same premise as the beginning of all inquiry. So in general mine is a classic question: How does the document cohere? But, of course, in particular, my question is my own. To my knowledge, only a very few of those for whom the Bavli formed a principal component of the Torah ever asked in terms so abstract as these precisely what the document is all about.[2]

---

[2]Obviously the principal figure to whom I refer is Maimonides; in due course I will explain why he was fundamentally in error about the generative problematic of the Bavli, that is, why I think he misread its point and purpose.

2

A Metaproposition and Its Exposition: Analogical-Contrastive Thinking and the Problem of Dialectical Thought or When Is a List a Series?

Clearly, what we need to learn to do is identify not merely the logical premises of discourse, but the goal and purpose of a sustained inquiry, what holds a sequence of compositions together into a purposeful composition. Before I am able to propose that a single generative problematic imparts cogency to what, on the surface, form merely discrete inquiries into this and that, I have to give a single example of how I think a sustained discourse addresses a question beyond the data that are examined. For this purpose, I wish now to show a simple fact. We can indeed show that, at the deepest levels of thought, an abstract issue is present, even though, at the surface of discourse, that issue is not articulated. Once I can show that fact in one sustained and complex passage, it becomes plausible to ask whether, in other sustained and complex passages, we may identify what at the foundations holds together a variety of compositions into a cogent composite. And I shall further propose that a variety of cogent composites turn out to address in concrete terms a single issue throughout.

Entire chapters of the Bavli work in detail on accumulating evidence in behalf of a single, unarticulated but always stipulated, proposition. The Babylonian Talmud's exposition of Mishnah-tractate Zebahim 5:1-2 – Bavli Zebahim 47B-52B – in a systematic and amazingly orderly way sets forth principles of comparison and contrast within the discipline of dialectical thinking. There we find beneath the surface – but not very far – the issue of the dialectics of analogical-contrastive thought. That is, the question facing us is the logic of a series. The authors of the chapter are trying to show the logic, and limits, of a series: If A=B and B=C, then does C=A, and, if so, why? And if not, why not? To state matters in words rather than symbols, if we say something equals something else, what more are we saying, that is, what is the implication of the claim of equivalency? In its interest in finding the connection to Scripture of a rule that is set forth by the Mishnah, the Bavli's treatment of M. Zeb. 5:1-2 presents this metaproposition that encompasses numerous specific propositions: how do we make connections between rules and their point of origin. Every time we ask, "What is the source [in Scripture] for this statement," we find an answer that is left to stand. So one fundamental and ubiquitous metaproposition of the Bavli may be set forth in this language:

1. It is important to link laws that occur in one source to those that occur in another;

2. among the compilations [components of "the one whole Torah of Moses, our rabbi," in later mythic language] that enjoy canonical status [in our language], the premier is Scripture;

3. so whenever we find a statement of a rule in the Mishnah and ask for its source, the implicit criterion of success will be, "the rule is founded on language of Scripture, properly construed";

4. so, consequently, the proposition implicit in numerous propositions, common to them all and holding them all together, is this: All rules cohere, and the point of origin of nearly all of them is the written part of the Torah revealed by God to Moses at Sinai.

The particular document in which the rules now circulate does not place into a hierarchy the various rules, because they all are one; but the reason they all are one is that nearly all of them find a point of origin in the written part of the Torah; and every single one of them is harmonious in principle with each of the others – once we identify the principle implicit in the cases that make up the law. Now if we asked the framers of the Mishnah their judgment upon these allegations of one of the metapropositional planks of the platform of the Bavli, they will have found surprising only our inquiry. For, while not common or characteristic of Mishnaic discourse, each of these traits can be located therein. The Mishnah's framers sometimes explicitly cite a verse of Scripture in support of the law; they occasionally undertake the exegesis of a verse of Scripture in order to discover the law; they know the distinction between rulings of the Torah and rulings of scribes, the latter standing a cut below the former; and their heirs, in undertaking vast exercises of linkage of the Mishnah to Scripture in such documents as Sifra to Leviticus and Sifré to Deuteronomy, engage in a persistent and compelling demonstration of the same metapropositional program, point by point. And yet we cannot then assign to the authorship of our chapter (and the numerous other chapters in which a principal, recurrent concern and point of generative tension is the link of the law contained in the Mishnah or other Tannaite compilations to the law contained in Scripture and its particular wording) merely the task of saying explicitly what the framers of the Mishnah occasionally said and commonly implied.

For there is a second metaproposition in our chapter, one so profound as to demand for itself priority over all other questions and answers. It addresses the issue of the nature and structure of thought. When we understand that issue, we shall see the remarkable intellectual achievement of the authorship of the Bavli's reading of Mishnah-tractate Zebahim 5:1-2. At stake in this appreciation of what they have accomplished is the demonstration that metapropositions in the Bavli are not only particular to the problem of the documentary provenance of rules – Scripture forms the basis of nearly all rules; all rules harmonize, at their foundations in abstract principles, with all other rules. The metapropositional program turns out, as I shall now show through a reprise of the pertinent propositions of the Bavli's reading of Mishnah-tractate Zebahim 5:1-2, to be so abstract as vastly to transcend rules and their generalizations and harmonies, rising to the height of principles of thought that guide the intellect in contemplation of all being and all reality.

To grasp the metapropositional program that, in my view, defines the stakes of discourse, let me specify what I conceive to be the counterpart program, pertaining not to connecting rules to Scripture, but rather, connecting principle to (consequent) principle: how thought really takes place, which is, not in a stationary pool but in a moving stream. To state the result up front: The Mishnah portrays all things at rest, a beautifully composed set in stasis, a stage on which nothing happens. The Bavli portrays all things in motion, a world of action, in which one thing leads to some other, and nothing stands still. All of this is accomplished in a shift in the received mode of thought, and the shift is set forth in the metaproposition, fully exposed, in the reading of two paragraphs of the Mishnah. We now consider what I conceive to be the counterpart program to the one that, in my view, the Bavli's sages inherited from the Mishnah and spelled out in tedious and unending particulars. To understand what is fresh and important in the Bavli's metapropositional program concerning the nature of thought, we have to call to mind what they inherited, for what they did was to impose the stamp of their own intellect upon the intellectual heritage that the Mishnah had provided for them.

To set forth the basic theory of the framers of the Mishnah on how thought takes place, which is to say, how we may understand things and know them, we must recall a simple fact. The Mishnah teaches the age-old method of scientific thought through comparison and contrast. Like things follow like rules, unlike things, the opposite rules, and the task of thought is to show what is like something else and therefore follows the rule that governs that something else, or what is unlike something else and therefore follows the opposite of the rule that governs that something else.   So the Mishnah's mode of thought establishes connections between and among things and does so, as is clear, through the method of taxonomy, comparison and contrast, list making of like things, yielding the rule that governs all items on the list.

List making places on display the data of the like and the unlike and implicitly (ordinarily, not explicitly) then conveys the rule. The Mishnah is then a book of lists, with the implicit order, the nomothetic traits of a monothetic order, dictating the ordinarily unstated general and encompassing rule. And all this why? It is in order to make a single statement, endless times over, and to repeat in a mass of tangled detail precisely the same fundamental judgment. The framers of the Mishnah appeal solely to the traits of things. List making then defines ways of proving propositions through classification, so establishing a set of shared traits that form a rule which compels us to reach a given conclusion. Probative facts derive from the classification of data, all of which point in one direction and not in another. A catalogue of facts, for example, may be so composed that, through the regularities and indicative traits of the entries, the catalogue yields a proposition. A list of parallel items all together point to a simple conclusion; the conclusion may or may not be given at the end of the catalogue, but the catalogue – by definition – is pointed. All of the catalogued facts are taken to bear self-evident connections to one another, established by those pertinent shared traits implicit in the composition of the list, therefore also bearing meaning and pointing through the weight of evidence to an inescapable conclusion. The discrete facts then join together because of some trait common to them all. This is a mode of classification of facts to lead to an identification of what the facts have in common and – it goes without saying, an explanation of their meaning.

What is at stake in the making of lists, that is, the formation of classes of things, is the comparison and contrast of one class of things with some other, yielding at the end the account of the hierarchization of all classes of things in correct sequence and grade. The following abstract shows us through the making of connections and the drawing of conclusions the propositional and essentially philosophical mind that animates the Mishnah and makes explicit what that authorship always wants to know: the relationships, in hierarchical order, between classes of things. In the following passage, drawn from Mishnah-tractate Sanhedrin Chapter Two, the authorship wishes to say that Israel has two heads, one of state, the other of cult, the king and the high priest, respectively, and that these two offices are nearly wholly congruent with one another, with a few differences based on the particular traits of each. Broadly speaking, therefore, our exercise is one of setting forth the genus and the species. The genus is head of holy Israel. The species are king and high priest. Here are the traits in common and those not shared, and the exercise is fully exposed for what it is, an inquiry into the rules that govern, the points of regularity and order, in this minor matter, of political structure. My outline, imposed in boldface type, makes the point important in this setting. We deal with Mishnah-tractate Sanhedrin Chapter Two:

1. **The rules of the high priest: subject to the law, marital rites, conduct in bereavement**

2:1 A. A high priest judges, and [others] judge him;

   B. gives testimony, and [others] give testimony about him;

   C. performs the rite of removing the shoe [Deut. 25:7-9], and [others] perform the rite of removing the shoe with his wife.

   D. [Others] enter levirate marriage with his wife, but he does not enter into levirate marriage,

   E. because he is prohibited to marry a widow.

   F. [If] he suffers a death [in his family], he does not follow the bier.

   G. "But when [the bearers of the bier] are not visible, he is visible; when they are visible, he is not.

   H. "And he goes with them to the city gate," the words of R. Meir.

   I. R. Judah says, "He never leaves the sanctuary,

   J. "since it says, *'Nor shall he go out of the sanctuary'* (Lev. 21:12)."

   K. And when he gives comfort to others,

   L. the accepted practice is for all the people to pass one after another, and the appointed [prefect of the priests] stands between him and the people.

   M. And when he receives consolation from others,

   N. all the people say to him, "Let us be your atonement."

   O. And he says to them, "May you be blessed by Heaven."

   P. And when they provide him with the funeral meal,

   Q. all the people sit on the ground, while he sits on a stool.

2. **The rules of the king: not subject to the law, marital rites, conduct in bereavement**

2:2 A. The king does not judge, and [others] do not judge him;

   B. does not give testimony, and [others] do not give testimony about him;

C. does not perform the rite of removing the shoe, and others do not perform the rite of removing the shoe with his wife;

D. does not enter into levirate marriage, nor [do his brothers] enter levirate marriage with his wife.

E. R. Judah says, "If he wanted to perform the rite of removing the shoe or to enter into levirate marriage, his memory is a blessing."

F. They said to him, "They pay no attention to him [if he expressed the wish to do so]."

G. [Others] do not marry his widow.

H. R. Judah says, "A king may marry the widow of a king.

I. "For so we find in the case of David, that he married the widow of Saul,

J. "for it is said, *'And I gave you your master's house and your master's wives into your embrace'* (2 Sam. 12:8)."

2:3   A. [If] [the king] suffers a death in his family, he does not leave the gate of his palace.

B. R. Judah says, "If he wants to go out after the bier, he goes out,

C. "for thus we find in the case of David, that he went out after the bier of Abner,

D. "since it is said, *'And King David followed the bier'* (2 Sam. 3:31)."

E. They said to him, "This action was only to appease the people."

F. And when they provide him with the funeral meal, all the people sit on the ground, while he sits on a couch.

3. Special rules pertinent to the king because of his calling

2:4   A. [The king] calls out [the army to wage] a war fought by choice on the instructions of a court of seventy-one.

B. He [may exercise the right to] open a road for himself, and [others] may not stop him.

C. The royal road has no required measure.

D. All the people plunder and lay before him [what they have grabbed], and he takes the first portion.

E. *"He should not multiply wives to himself"* (Deut. 17:17) – only eighteen.

F. R. Judah says, "He may have as many as he wants, so long as they *do not entice him* [to abandon the Lord (Deut. 7:4)]."

G. R. Simeon says, "Even if there is only one who entices him [to abandon the Lord] – lo, this one should not marry her."

H. If so, why is it said, "He should not multiply wives to himself"?

I. Even though they should be like Abigail (1 Sam. 25:3).

J. *"He should not multiply horses to himself"* (Deut. 17:16) – only enough for his chariot.

K. *"Neither shall he greatly multiply to himself silver and gold"* (Deut. 17:16) – only enough to pay his army.

L. *"And he writes out a scroll of the Torah for himself"* (Deut. 17:17).

M. When he goes to war, he takes it out with him; when he comes back, he brings it back with him; when he is in session in court, it is with him; when he is reclining, it is before him,

N. as it is said, *"And it shall be with him, and he shall read in it all the days of his life"* (Deut. 17:19).

2:5   A.   [Others may] not ride on his horse, sit on his throne, handle his scepter.
            B.   And [others may] not watch him while he is getting a haircut, or while he is nude, or in the bathhouse,
            C.   since it is said, *"You shall surely set him as king over you"* (Deut. 17:15) – that reverence for him will be upon you.

The subordination of Scripture to the classification scheme is self-evident. Scripture supplies facts. The traits of things – kings, high priests – dictate classification categories on their own, without Scripture's dictate.

   The philosophical cast of mind is amply revealed in this essay, which in concrete terms effects a taxonomy, a study of the genus, national leader, and its two species, [1] king, [2] high priest: how are they alike, how are they not alike, and what accounts for the differences. The premise is that national leaders are alike and follow the same rule, except where they differ and follow the opposite rule from one another. But that premise also is subject to the proof effected by the survey of the data consisting of concrete rules, those systemically inert facts that here come to life for the purposes of establishing a proposition. By itself, the fact that, for example, others may not ride on his horse, bears the burden of no systemic proposition. In the context of an argument constructed for nomothetic, taxonomic purposes, the same fact is active and weighty. The whole depends upon three premises: [1] the importance of comparison and contrast, with the supposition that [2] like follows the like, and the unlike follows the opposite rule; and [3] when we classify, we also hierarchize, which yields the argument from hierarchical classification: If this, which is the lesser, follows rule X, then that, which is the greater, surely should follow rule X. And that is the whole sum and substance of the logic of *Listenwissenschaft* as the Mishnah applies that logic in a practical way.

   If I had to specify a single mode of thought that established connections between one fact and another, it is in the search for points in common and therefore also points of contrast. We seek connection between fact and fact, sentence and sentence in the subtle and balanced rhetoric of the Mishnah, by comparing and contrasting two things that are like and not alike. At the logical level, too, the Mishnah falls into the category of familiar philosophical thought. Once we seek regularities, we propose rules. What is like another thing falls under its rule, and what is not like the other falls under the opposite rule. Accordingly, as to the species of the genus, so far as they are alike, they share the same rule. So far as they are not alike, each follows a rule contrary to that governing the other. So the work of analysis is what produces connection, and therefore the drawing of conclusions derives from comparison and contrast: the *and*, the *equal*. The proposition then that forms the conclusion concerns the essential likeness of the two offices, except where they are different, but the subterranean premise is that we can explain both likeness and difference by appeal to a principle of fundamental order and unity.

To make these observations concrete, we turn to the case at hand. The important contrast comes at the outset. The high priest and king fall into a single genus, but speciation, based on traits particular to the king, then distinguishes the one from the other. Now if I further had to set forth what I conceive to form the deepest conviction at the most profound layers of thought, it is that things set in relationship always stand in that same relationship. The work of making connections and drawing conclusions produces results that are fixed and final. If we establish a connection between one set of things and another, that connection forms the end of matters – that, and not a series, by which the connection between A and B serves as a guide to a movement from C to A via B, that is, as we shall now see, the formation of not a connection but a series of things that are connected only to one another, but not to other components of the same series – which is to say, a series.

To put matters very simply, if A is like B, and B is like C, then is C like A? And if – as the received logic of the age insists! – we entertain the possibility of a series, then, and much more to the point, *precisely what are the rules of connection that form the links of the results of comparison and contrast?*

In other words, in the aftermath of classification comes not hierarchization but movement, this thing in relationship to that, that in relationship to the other, all things in movement, nothing at rest. So, if a series is possible, then how is a series composed? That is the question answered by the Bavli, the question no one in the Mishnah asked, because the Mishnah's framers contemplated a world at rest, and the Bavli's, a world in motion.

In so stating, I have leapt over each of the necessary stages of my exposition. So let us begin from the beginning. Now that the Mishnah's position is in hand, we revert to my claim that the Bavli's own statement in the chapter under discussion concerns the nature of thought. Let us first of all review the points that are made, and the sequence in which they are set forth. We begin with the point of intersection:

1.   It is important to know how to connect rules to Scripture.

2.   The principles that govern the making of connections to Scripture are those that govern making connections not between words and words ("the hermeneutical principles") but rather between one thing and something else, that is,

defining a genus and its species; so when we know how to compare and contrast, find what is like something else and what is different from something else, we know how to conduct the passage from rules to Scripture.

3. Exegetical rules tell us how to form classes of things in relationship to Scripture.

4. Dialectical rules tell us how to move from one class of things to another class of things.

To state matters in simple: What makes a list into a series? And how are we supposed to effect that transformation – that movement? Step two then marks the point of departure, and steps three and four denote the remarkable shift in the passage. We go not only from rule to generalization, or from case to principle. That, to be sure, takes place and forms an everywhere-present metaproposition, as the tedium of the remainder of the chapter showed us. Rather, we go from thinking about things and their connections (comparison and contrast) to thinking about thought itself. So what I have represented as the rules of dialectical thinking – not merely argument! – turn out to tell us how thought happens; the Bavli's reading of Mishnah-tractate Zebahim 5:1-2 forms a fundamental exercise of thought about thinking.

When we review the principal steps in the sustained and unfolding inquiry as the Bavli's commentary on M. Zeb. 5:1-2 unfolds, we realize that, in particulars and in detail, the framers of the passage have set forth a profound essay on thought. In the terms just now given, if A=B, and B=C, then does C=A? Is a series possible? Are there limits to the extension of a series? And on what basis do we construct a series? Do the media of linkage between A and B, that is, A=B, have to be the same as those that link B to C, for C to stand in the series that A has begun? These abstract questions have to become concrete before the sense of matters will emerge. So let us now review what the chapter has already told us: the sequence of points that represent the inquiry into the making of connections, which is to say, the Bavli's metapropositional statement on the character of a series. For it is the series, first this, then that, finally the third thing, and the rules that govern the movement from this, to that, to the third thing, that defines what is the center of deep thought in the Bavli's reading of the specified Mishnah paragraphs. I cite the pertinent language of my translation of the text,[1] where necessary restating what has already been given in the context of the exposition of

---

[1]This is published as *The Talmud of Babylonia. An American Translation* (Atlanta, 1991: Scholars Press for Brown Judaic Studies), XXVIII.B. *Tractate Zebahim. Chapters Four through Eight.*

the text, but I do not then repeat all of the text. The stages in the argument of the Talmud now are identified and repeated, as marked by boldface capital letters. The argument is astonishing for its sustained quality; it moves in an inexorable course, rigorously insisting on settling one question before raising the next, and consequent one.

A/II.2   E.[2]   That answer is satisfactory for him who takes the view that one may indeed derive a rule governing a prior subject from one that is given later on, but from the perspective of him who denies that fact, what is to be said?

The opening question contains the entirety of what is to follow: the conviction that anterior to conclusions and debates on fixed propositions is a premise, and the premise concerns not issues but thought itself. For what is before us is not a hermeneutical principle that guides the exegesis of Scripture, the movement from a rule back to a scriptural formulation deemed to pertain. It is a rule of how to think. And the issue is explicit: Does thought flow, or does it stand still? Does it flow backward from conclusion to a conclusion already reached? In the context of the document at hand, the issue is one of arrangements of words, that is, a literary and therefore an exegetical question. That is, then, the proposition. But the metaproposition is otherwise, though that is not yet explicit.

B/II.2   J.   But this is the reason for the position of rabbis, who declare one exempt [from having to present a suspensive guilt-offering in the case of a matter of doubt regarding acts of sacrilege]: They derive an verbal analogy to a sin-offering based on the appearance of the word 'commandments' with reference to both matters.
           N.   They take the view that one may not derive from an argument by analogy established through the use of a word in common only a limited repertoire of conclusions [but once the analogy is drawn, then all of the traits of one case apply to the other].

Here is an issue not of exegesis, therefore of hermeneutics, but of the rules of right thinking: thinking about thought. And what it concerns, as I have suggested in context, is how we establish not classes of things but linkage between and among classes of things. Let me state the centerpiece in simple words but with heavy emphasis: *Since I make connections through analogy and contrast, may I proceed to make connections beyond the limits of the original connection? And the answer is, I must proceed,*

---

[2]The reference system used in that translation is indicated; the Roman numeral, II, represents the starting point of the treatment of a Mishnah sentence; the Arabic number, 2, represents the second complete and exhaustive treatment of a subject or presentation of a proposition; the letter, E, denotes the fifth whole unit of thought ("sentence") of that presentation.

because thought does not come to rest. Comparison and contrast yield connections, which then govern.

In the language before us, once I draw an analogy, do all traits of the two classes of things that have been linked through analogy – of necessity only partial, since were the analogy entire, both classes would constitute a single class! – pertain to each class? In the present context, what we establish is the anonymous, therefore the governing rule. The norm is that once we draw an analogy, the connection established by the (mere) analogy takes over, so that we treat as analogous traits not covered by the analogy at all. The analogy establishes the connection; but then the movement of thought is such that the connection is deemed to have established a new class of things, all of them subject to one rule. The movement – the dialectic – therefore is not a mere trait of argument, if you say this, I say that, but a trait of thought: if this is the result of step A, then step B is to be taken – out from, without regard to, the limitations of step A. Thought then is continuous, always in motion, and that metaproposition states in the most abstract terms possible the prior and generative metaproposition that, when we compare classes of things, the comparison initiates a process that transcends the limits of comparison. That is to say, again with emphasis, *we can effect a series.*

C/II.2   S.   *One authority maintains that proof supplied by analogy [here: the analogy sustained by the use of "and" to join the two subjects] takes priority, and the other party maintains that the proof supplied by the demonstration of a totality of congruence among salient traits takes precedence. [Rabbis prefer the latter, Aqiba the former position.]*

T.   *Not at all! All parties concur that proof supplied by analogy [here: the analogy sustained by the use of "and" to join the two subjects] takes priority. But rabbis in this context will say to you that the rule governing the subject treated below derives from the rule governing the subject treated above, so that the guilt-offering must be worth a least two silver sheqels. This is established so that you should not argue that the doubt cannot be more stringent than the matter of certainty, and just as where there is certainty of having committed a sin, one has to present a sin-offering that may be worth even so little as a sixth of a zuz in value, so if there is a matter of doubt, the guilt-offering worth only a sixth of a zuz would suffice.*

Once the connection is made, linking an earlier rule (in Scripture's orderly exposition) to a later one, then the connection is such that movement is not only forward but backward. We have established not a connection between one thing and something else, but a series that can encompass a third thing and a fourth thing, onward – but with, or without, formal limit? This principle of right thinking that the hypothesis of the series requires is revealed by Scripture, as is made explicit once more in the following:

D/III.1   I.   *...And should you say that if Scripture had not included the matter, we should have reached the same conclusion by argument for analogy, then if that is the case, we can infer by analogy also the rule on laying on of hands....The* main point here is that, once an analogy serves, it serves everywhere an analogy can be drawn; there is no a priori that limits the power of an analogy to govern all like cases.

A series is possible once the work of thought moves beyond contrast and analogy. And it is the rule of right thought that, once we have established a comparison and a contrast, that fact validates drawing conclusions on other aspects of the classes of things that have been connected through the comparison and contrast – analogical-contrastive thinking is then not static but in motion. Is the motion perpetual? Not at all, for Scripture, for its part, has the power to place limits on a series.

E/IV.2   B.   If a matter was covered by an encompassing rule but then was singled out for some innovative purpose, you have not got the right to restore the matter to the rubric of the encompassing rule unless Scripture itself explicitly does so. [That means that the encompassing rule does not apply to an item that Scripture, for its own purposes, has singled out. The upshot is that the identified item is now exceptional in some aspect, so it is no longer subject to a common rule governing all other items in context; then the limits of analogy are set by Scripture's treatment of the items of a series. It is worth while reviewing the pertinent example:]

The series is subjected to limits, if an item in the sequence of connections that forms the series proves exceptional: this is connected to that, that to the other thing, but the other thing is other in some other way, so there the series ends.

H.   *If [you claim that the purpose of the verse is as stated and not to teach that doing the rite at the north is indispensable, as originally proposed,] then Scripture should have stated only the rule governing the rite for the one healed from the skin ailment but not the earlier version of the rule.*

I.   *Quite so – if we take the view that when something becomes the subject of a new law, it cannot then be covered by an encompassing rule that otherwise would apply, while the encompassing rule still can be derived from that special case. But if we take the view that when something becomes the subject of a new law, then it cannot be covered by an encompassing rule that otherwise would apply, and the encompassing rule also cannot be derived from that special place, then the law [Lev. 7:1-10, indicating that the guilt-offering must be killed in the north] is needed for its own purpose!*

J.   *Since Scripture has restored the matter to the rubric of the encompassing rule explicitly, that restoration has taken place.*

K.   *Said Mar Zutra b. R. Mari to Rabina, "But why not say, when Scripture restored the matter to the rubric of the encompassing rule, that was solely in regard to having to present the blood and the sacrificial parts on the altar, since the priest is necessary to perform that rite. But as to slaughtering the animal, which does not have to be done by a priest, that does not have to be done at the northern side of the altar?"*

L.   [*He said to him,*] *"If so, Scripture should say simply, 'For it is like the sin-offering.' Why say, 'Or the guilt-offering, like the sin-offering'? It is to teach, let it be like other guilt-offerings [that must be slaughtered at the northern side of the altar]."* Here again, therefore, the issue is the limits of analogy, how these are determined.

F/IV.4 A. *Raba said, "[The proposition that that which is derived on the basis of a verbal analogy does not in turn go and impart a lesson by means of a verbal analogy] derives from the following proof:*

We go over familiar ground. Raba takes the view that a series is simply not possible. Others allege that if we connect one class of things to some other by means, for example, of a verbal analogy, then making that same connection once again, where another verbal analogy connects the second class of things to yet a third, is not correct. Scripture shows that verbal analogies do not validate the making of series, and this is shown in an explicit way:

B. "It is written, 'As is taken off from the ox of the sacrifice of peace-offerings' (Lev. 4:10) [namely, the sacrificial parts of the anointed priest's bullock brought for a sin-offering] – *now for what purpose is this detail given? That the lobe of the liver and the two kidneys are to be burned on the altar [as is the case with those of the sin-offering], that fact is specified in the body of the verse itself. But the purpose is to intimate that the burning of the lobe of the liver and the two kidneys of the he-goats brought as sin-offerings for idolatry are to be derived by analogy from the bullock of the community brought on account of an inadvertent sin. That law is not explicitly stated in the passage on the bullock that is brought for an inadvertent sin, but is derived from the rule governing the bullock of the anointed priest.* 'As is taken off' *is required so that it might be treated as something written in that very passage [on the bullock of inadvertence, being superfluous in its own context], not as something derived on the basis of a verbal analogy which does not in turn go and impart a lesson by means of a verbal analogy."*

To repeat my exposition of this matter: I have two items, A and B. I claim that B is like A, therefore the rule governing A applies also to B. Now I turn forward, to C. C is not analogous to A; there are no points of congruence or (in the exegetical formulation that our authors use) verbal intersection. But C is like B. It is like B because there is an analogy by reason of verbal intersection (the same word being used in reference to C and B). The question is, may I apply to C, by reason of the verbal intersection between C and B, the lesson that I have learned in regard to B only by reason of B's similarity by reason of congruence, not verbal intersection, to A? Can a conclusion that is derived on the basis of a verbal analogy go and impart a lesson by reason of analogy to a third item? Raba now maintains that that is not the case. But the matter has gone in the other direction: a series is possible. But if a series is possible, then what limits are to be placed on the media by which a series is effected?

G/IV.5   A.   Now it is a fact that that which is derived on the basis of a verbal analogy does in turn go and impart a lesson by means of a verbal analogy, *demonstrated whether in the manner of Raba or in the manner of Rabina.*

Now we revert to our basic issue: the validity of a series. Here we move into as yet unexplored ground, which is the basis for my claim that the order of problems is dictated by an interest in a systematic presentation of the rules of right thinking. We have been exposed to the case in favor of a series: once the analogy makes the connection, then all traits of the things connected are brought into relationship with all other such traits. Scripture then provides one limit to the length of a series: a series cannot be infinite. But there is another limit proposed, and it is not scriptural but substantive, in the nature of things, a trait of thought itself. Here is the point at which I find this sustained exposition of thinking about thought simply remarkable.

B.   Is it the rule, however, that *that which is derived on the basis of a verbal analogy may in turn go and impart a lesson by means of an argument on the basis of congruence?* [Freedman: Thus the law stated in A is applied to B by analogy. Can that law then be applied to C because of congruence between B and C?]

We have proven one point. It bears a consequence. We go on to the consequence. The mode of thought is dialectical not only in form, but also in substance: If A, then B. If B, then what about C? It is one thing to have shown that if B is like A, then C, unlike A, is rendered comparable to B by a verbal analogy. But then may I take the next step and draw into the framework of B and C, joined by verbal analogy and assigned a common rule by B's congruent analogy to A, also D, E, F, and G, that is, other classes of things joined to C by verbal analogy – but not necessarily the same verbal analogy that has joined C to B? That indeed is the obvious next step to be taken, and it is now taken. It is taken in the simple words just now given, and the same point is now going to be made, in a systematic way, for each medium by which classes of things are formed and then connected to one another. Analogical-contrastive thinking therefore is not static but always in motion, since, once a connection is made, other connections may follow. If we make a connection between A and B on the basis of one set of shared traits, we may proceed to make a connection between C and A, via B, on the basis of traits shared by B and C but not by A and C. Not only so, but the same mode of thought extends to the media of connection. If I connect A to B by verbal analogy, I may connect B to other classes of things, for example, C, D, E, by other media of connection, for example, verbal analogy connects A to B, and an argument based on congruence connects B to C, and backward to A; and an argument a fortiori may connect C to D, and backward to A and B – series without end, or series that end only in the dictates of revelation, the ultimate arbiter of the classification and hierarchy of all things. What is truly impressive in what follows is the rigorous order by which each possibility is raised in its turn, the connections fore and aft, such that the framer of the whole not only makes his point in words, but also illustrates it in his own representation of matters: a series is not only possible, it is also compelling. So we see as we move forward, now with no need for further exposition, from H to M.

H/IV.6   A.   That which is learned by a verbal analogy may in turn go and impart a rule by an argument a fortiori.

I/IV.7   A.   Can that which is learned by verbal analogy in turn go and impart a rule by an analogy based on the congruence of other shared traits [but not verbal ones in context]? Once more to review: We have now linked B to C via a verbal analogy. C stands in relationship to other classes of things, but not for the same reason that it stands in relationship to B, that is, through other than verbal analogical relationships. It forms a relationship a fortiori, for instance, with D, E, and F. If something applies to C, the lesser, it surely should apply to D, the greater. So now we want to know the permissible grounds for drawing relationships – comparisons and contrasts – of classes of things. So on what basis do we move from species to species and uncover the genera of which they form a part (if they do form a part)? Is it only verbal correspondence or intersection, as has been implicit to this point? Or are there more abstract bases for the same work of genus construction (in our language: category formation and re-formation)?

J/IV.8   A.   Can a rule that is derived by analogy based on the congruence of other shared traits [but not verbal ones in context] turn around and teach a lesson through an analogy based on verbal analogy?

K/IV.9   A.   Can a rule that is derived by an analogy based on the congruence of other shared traits [but not verbal ones in context] turn around and teach a lesson through an analogy based on the congruence of [other] shared traits?

L/IV.10   A.   Can a rule that is derived by an analogy based on the congruence of other shared traits [but not verbal ones in context] go and teach a lesson through an argument a fortiori?

M/IV.10   F.   If an argument deriving from an analogy based on verbal congruence, which cannot go and, by an argument based on verbal congruence, impart its rule to some other class – *as has been shown by either Raba's or Rabina's demonstration* – nonetheless can go and by an argument a fortiori impart its rule to some other class – *as has been shown by the Tannaite authority of the household of*

R. *Ishmael* – then a rule that is derived by an argument based on analogy based on other than verbal congruence, which can for its part go and impart its lesson by an argument based on an analogy resting on verbal congruity which is like itself – *as has been shown by Rami bar Hama* – surely can in turn teach its lesson by an argument a fortiori to yet another case!

So at stake throughout is the question of how a series is composed: the media for the making of connections between one thing and something else (that is, one class of things and some other class of things, in such wise that the rules governing the one are shown by the analogy to govern the other as well). We want to know not only that a connection is made, but how it is made. And some maintain that if the connection is made between one thing and something else by means, for example, of a verbal analogy dictated by Scripture's wording, then a connection between that something else and a third thing must also be made in a manner consistent with the initial medium of connection, verbal analogy. It cannot be made by means of some other medium of connection. But the paramount position is otherwise: Dialectics affect not only argument but thought itself, because connections are made through all media by which connections are made. We now reach the end of the matter, in a set of ultimately theoretical issues:

N/IV.11 A. Can a rule that is derived by an analogy based on the congruence of other shared traits [but not verbal ones in context] go and teach a lesson through an argument constructed by analogy based on the congruence of other shared traits among two or more classifications of things?

B. *That question must stand.*

O/IV.12 A. Can a rule derived by an argument a fortiori go and teach a rule established through analogy of verbal usage?

B. The affirmative derives from an argument a fortiori:

C. If an argument deriving from an analogy based on points of other than verbal congruence, which cannot go and, by an argument based on verbal congruence, imparts its rule to some other class – *as has been shown by R. Pappa's demonstration* – then a rule that is derived by an argument a fortiori, which can be derived by an argument based on the shared verbal traits of two things – *as has been shown by the Tannaite authority of the house of R. Ishmael* – surely should be able to impart its rule to another classification of things by reason of an argument based on a verbal analogy!

D. *That position poses no problems to one who takes the view that R. Pappa's case has been made. But for one who takes the view that R. Pappa's case has not been made, what is to be said?*

E. *The question then must stand.*

P/IV.13 A. Can a rule that is derived by an argument a fortiori go and teach a lesson through an argument based on the congruence of other shared traits [but not verbal ones in context]?

B. The affirmative derives from an argument a fortiori:

C. If an argument deriving from an analogy based on points of other than verbal congruence, which cannot be derived from an argument based on verbal congruence, can impart its rule to some other class – *as has been shown by R. Yohanan's demonstration* – and can go and teach a lesson by an argument based on an analogy established through other than verbal traits – *as has been shown by Rami bar Hama* – a rule based on an argument a fortiori, which can be derived by an argument based on an analogy resting on verbal coincidence, surely should be able to impart its rule to another classification of things by reason of an argument based on an other than verbal analogy!

Q/IV.14 A. Can a rule based on an argument a fortiori turn around and teach a lesson through an argument based on an argument a fortiori?

B. Indeed so, and the affirmative derives from an argument a fortiori:

C. If an argument deriving from an analogy based on points of other than verbal congruence, which cannot be derived from an argument based on verbal congruence, can impart its rule to some other class – *as has been shown by R. Yohanan's demonstration* – and can go and teach a lesson by an argument a fortiori, as we have just pointed out, then an argument that can be derived from an analogy based on verbal congruence – *as has been shown by the Tannaite authority of the household of R. Ishmael* – surely should be able to impart its rule by an argument a fortiori!

D. But would this then represent what we are talking about, namely, a rule deriving from an argument a fortiori that has been applied to another case by means of an argument a fortiori? Surely this is nothing more than a secondary derivation produced by an argument a fortiori!

E. Rather, argue in the following way:

F. Indeed so, and the affirmative derives from an argument a fortiori:

G. If an argument based on an analogy of a verbal character which cannot be derived from another such argument based on an analogy between two classes of things that rests upon a verbal congruence – *in accordance with the proofs of either Raba or Rabina* – nonetheless can then go and impart its lesson by an argument a fortiori – *in accordance with the proof of the Tannaite authority of the household of R. Ishmael* – then an argument a fortiori, which can serve to transfer a lesson originally learned through an argument based upon verbal congruence – *in accordance with the proof of the Tannaite authority of the household of R. Ishmael* – surely should be able to impart its lesson to yet another classification of things through an argument a fortiori.

H. And this does represent what we are talking about, namely, a rule deriving from an argument a fortiori that has been applied to another case by means of an argument a fortiori.

R/IV.15 A. Can a rule based on an argument a fortiori turn around and teach a rule through an argument constructed on the basis of shared traits of an other than verbal character among two classifications of things?

B. *But that is not so. For even if we concede that that is the case there, then still the rule derives from the act of slaughter of unconsecrated beasts [Freedman].*

S/IV.16 A. Can a rule derived by an argument based on shared traits of an
             other than verbal character shared among two classes of things then
             turn around and teach a lesson by an argument based on an
             analogy of a verbal character, an analogy not of a verbal character,
             an argument a fortiori, or an argument based on shared traits?

         B. *Solve at least one of those problems by appeal to the following:*

         C. On what account have they said that if blood of an offering is left
             overnight on the altar, it is fit? Because if the sacrificial parts are
             kept overnight on the altar, they are fit. And why if the sacrificial
             parts are kept overnight on the altar are they fit? Because if the
             meat of the offering is kept overnight on the altar it is fit.
             [Freedman: Thus the rule governing the sacrificial parts is derived
             by an appeal to an argument based on shared traits of an other than
             verbal character shared among two classes of things, and that rule
             in turn is applied to the case of the blood by another such argument
             based on shared traits of an other than verbal character shared
             among two classes of things.]

         D. What about the rule governing meat that is taken outside of the
             Temple court? [If such meat is put up on the altar, it is not removed
             therefrom. Why so?]

         E. Because meat that has been taken out of the holy place is suitable
             for a high place.

         M. [Reverting to C-E:] Now can an analogy be drawn concerning
             something that has been disposed of in the proper manner for
             something that has not been disposed of in the proper manner? [If
             the sacrificial parts are kept over night, they are not taken off the
             altar, and therefore the meat kept overnight is fit; but the meat may
             be kept overnight, while the sacrificial parts may not. So, too, when
             the Temple stood, the flesh might not be taken outside, but where
             there was no Temple and only high places, the case is scarcely
             analogous!]

         N. *The Tannaite authority for this rule derives it from the augmentative
             sense, extending the rule, deriving from the formulation,* "This is the
             Torah of the burnt-offering" (Lev. 6:2). [Freedman: The verse
             teaches that all burnt-offerings, even with the defects catalogued
             here, are subject to the same rule and do not get removed from the
             altar once they have been put there; the arguments given cannot be
             sustained but still support that proposition.]

The movement from point to point, first things first, second things in
sequence, is so stunning in the precise logic of the order of issues – we
must know A before we can contemplate asking about B – that only a
brief review is called for.

   We have shown that we may move from a class of things joined to
another through analogy based on congruence, that is, from A to B,
onward to other classes of things joined to the foregoing by verbal
analogy or intersection, that is, from B to C and beyond. But can we then
move from C, linked to B via verbal analogy, to D, linked to C, but not to
A or B, by congruence, for example, comparable and shared traits of a

salient order? The issue then, is may we move forward to further classes of things by moving "backward," to a principle of linkage of classes that has served to bring us to this point, in other words, reversing the course of principles of linkage? What our framers then want to know is a very logical question: Are there fixed rules that govern the order or sequence by which we move from one class of things to another, so that, if we propose to link classes of things, we can move only from A to B by one principle (comparison and contrast of salient traits), and from B to C by a necessarily consequent and always second principle (verbal intersection); then we may move (by this theory) from C to D only by verbal intersection but not by appeal to congruence. Why not? Because, after all, if C is linked to B only by verbal intersection but not by congruence, bearing no relationship to A at all, then how can we claim that D stands in a series begun at A, if it has neither verbal connection, nor, as a matter of fact, congruence to link it to anything in the series? What is clear in this reprise is that the issue is drawn systematically, beginning to end. By simply seeing the sequence of questions, we grasp the whole: the program, the method, the order, all dictated by the inner requirements of sustained inquiry into the logic of comparison and contrast, read as a dialectical problem. The upshot may be stated now in a very few words.

A list is never a list, it is always part of a series; thought moves but does not come to rest. That metaproposition comes to formal expression at the very surface of discourse, in the ever-flowing movement of argument of the Talmud itself. That is why the framers of the Bavli never leave the Mishnah alone, allowing its formal perfection and its serene expositions of the classification of things to stand still. Rather they insist on exploring the connections among classifications of things – the connections that in their character and even in their function turn out to shift and change. The dialectic of connection takes the place of the hierarchization that, for the framers of the Mishnah, is deemed satisfactorily to portray connection in some one, set way.

The metapropositional program contributed by the Bavli's framers concerns how series are made, which is to say, whether connections yield static or dynamic results, which is to say, at the deepest layers of intellect, how thought happens. Now, at the end, we ask the framers of the Mishnah to address the question before us. And in answer, they give us silence. So we know that here we hear what is distinctive to, and the remarkable discovery of, the authorship of the Bavli. Since, it is clear, that discovery has taken place within the words of the Written Torah, and, since their deepest metaproposition maintained that the words of the Written Torah are the words of God to Moses, our rabbi, at Sinai – the words, not just the gist – we have to conclude with what I conceive to be the bedrock of the metapropositional program before us: the Torah teaches us not only what God said, but how God thinks. We know how

God thinks because the Torah reveals not only God's word, but also God's wording of God's word. And from the rules of language we move upward to the rules of logical and coherent expression; from there still higher, to rules of logical and cogent thought; and from there, upward to the rules of logic themselves. When God revealed not only the Torah, but the exact wording of the Torah, God taught us the most profound and abstract principles of how to think about thought. That claim forms the foundation of the analysis of M. Zeb. 5:1-2 at Bavli Zebahim 47B-52B. When we understand the Torah rightly, we engage in thinking about thought. And that is how we know God: thinking about thought. So Spinoza perhaps was not so heretical after all. Now that brings us to the issue of this monograph, which is, can I find a generative problematic that in a variety of unrelated passages turns out to define throughout what people want to know. For this purpose, we address passages in each of the four divisions of the Mishnah's six that are served by the Bavli.

3

The Mixed Grid in
Bavli Baba Qamma Chapter One

The thesis for testing is simple. When the Bavli's framers look at a passage of the Mishnah, one fundamental problem that will engage their attention is how the taxa of the Mishnah passage intersect with other taxa altogether. If the Mishnah paragraph (or chapter or tractate) classifies data within a given grid, the authors of the Bavli's sustained response to that paragraph will ask about other grids, proposing to place one grid atop the other, or, more accurately, to see how the two grids fit together. When the exegesis of words and phrases, sources and authorities, comes to an end,[1] then what sustains the Bavli's framers' interest in their work is a fascinating intellectual problem: turning two dimensional into three dimensional chess. That simple, but abstract, definition of matters demands a concrete example, and we turn forthwith to that task.

Our first exercise brings us to a clear, taxonomic statement: four generative classifications of causes of damages and their subdivisions. The Mishnah paragraph invites a secondary exercise in taxonomy, which is why I present it as my initial case. The relevance of what we are about to examine to the thesis I wish to propose is simple. Since I maintain that what has prompted the framer of the composite before us to ask the questions we address, rather than some other ones, is a sustained and systematic interest in how various classes of things relate to one another. This leads to the inquiry into how considerations extrinsic to these classes of things turn out to affect the definition and relationship of the classes of things onto which they are brought to bear.

---

[1] I have defined that matter in *The Bavli's Primary Discourse. Mishnah Commentary, Its Rhetorical Paradigms, and Their Theological Implications in the Talmud of Babylonia Tractate Moed Qatan* (Atlanta, 1992: Scholars Press for South Florida Studies in the History of Judaism).

1:1

A. [There are] four generative classifications of causes of damages: (1) ox (Ex. 21:35-36), (2) pit (Ex. 21:33), (3) crop-destroying beast (Ex. 22:4), and (4) conflagration (Ex. 22:5).

B. [The indicative characteristic] of the ox is not equivalent to that of the crop-destroying beast;

C. nor is that of the crop-destroying beast equivalent to that of the ox;

D. nor are this one and that one, which are animate, equivalent to fire, which is not animate;

E. nor are this one and that one, which usually [get up and] go and do damage, equivalent to a pit, which does not usually [get up and] go and do damage.

F. What they have in common is that they customarily do damage and taking care of them is your responsibility.

G. And when one [of them] has caused damage, the [owner] of that which causes the damage is liable to pay compensation for damage out of the best of his land (Ex. 22:4).

The first statement alerts us to the exegetical program of the Bavli's authorship at hand: Are there secondary causes of damages? And, if there are, how do the damages of the secondary or derivative class compare to those of the primary or generative one: clearly an exercise in secondary taxonomy.

I.1   A. Four generative causes of damages:

B. *Since the framer of the passages makes reference to* generative causes, *it is to be inferred that there are derivative ones as well.* Are the derivative causes equivalent [in effect] to the generative causes or are they not equivalent to them in effect?

C. *We have learned with reference to the Sabbath:* The generative categories of acts of labor [prohibited on the Sabbath] are forty less one [M. Shab. 7:2A]. *Since the framer of the passages makes reference to* generative categories, *it is to be inferred that there are derivative ones as well.* Are the derivative categories equivalent to the generative categories or are they not equivalent to them?

D. *Well, there is no difference between one's inadvertently carrying out an act of labor that falls into a generative category, in which case he is liable to present a sin-offering, and one's inadvertently carrying out an act of labor that falls into a derivative category of labor, in which case he is also liable to present a sin-offering. There is no difference between one's deliberately carrying out an act of labor that falls into a generative category, in which case he is liable to the death penalty through stoning, and one's deliberately carrying out an act of labor that falls into a derivative category of labor, in which case he is also liable to the death penalty through stoning.*

E. *So then what's the difference between an act that falls into the generative category and one that falls into the derivative category?*

F. *The upshot is that if one simultaneously carried out two actions that fall into the class of generative acts of labor, or two actions that fall into the*

> *classification of a derivative category, he is liable for each such action, while, if he had performed simultaneously both a generative act of labor and also a derivative of that same generative action, he is liable on only one count.*
>
> G. *And from the perspective of R. Eliezer, who imposes liability for a derivative action even when one is simultaneously liable on account of carrying out an act in the generative category, on what basis does one classify one action as generative and another as derivative [if it makes no practical difference]?*
>
> H. *Those actions that are carried out [even on the Sabbath] in the building of the tabernacle are reckoned as generative actions, and those that were not carried out on the Sabbath in the building of the tabernacle are classified as derivative.*

Clearly, the starting point of the reading of this Mishnah paragraph is precisely what I have claimed; we shall not find surprising the secondary development of the same point, specifically, a survey of other cases in which we have primary or generative and secondary or derivative taxa, and how the latter relate to the former.

I.2   A.   *With reference to uncleanness we have learned in the Mishnah:* **The generative causes of uncleanness [are] (1) the creeping thing, and (2) semen [of an adult Israelite], [2B] and (3) one who has contracted corpse uncleanness, [and (4) the leper in the days of his counting, and (5) sin-offering water of insufficient quantity to be sprinkled. Lo, these render man and vessels unclean by contact, and earthenware vessels by [presence within the vessels' contained] air space. But they do not render unclean by carrying] [M. Kel. 1:1].** And their derivatives are not equivalent to them, for while a generative cause of uncleanness imparts uncleanness to a human being and utensils, a derivative source of uncleanness imparts uncleanness to food and drink but not to a human being or utensils.

What follows is secondary expansion on these primary initiatives. We ask the theoretical questions, for example, what difference the distinction makes, what verse of Scripture yields the question at hand. In this example, I present the entire discussion. In further entries, we shall limit ourselves to the main point, which is, as we now see, that a variety of grids are here brought into juxaposition.

I.3   A.   *Here what is the upshot of the distinction at hand?*
         B.   Said R. Pappa, "There are some derivatives that are equivalent in effect to the generative cause, and there are some that are not equivalent in effect to the generative cause."

I.4   A.   *Our rabbis have taught on Tannaite authority:*
         B.   Three [of the four] generative causes of damage are stated with respect to the ox: horn, tooth, and foot.

I.5   A.   How on the basis of Scripture do we know the case of the horn?
         B.   *It is in line with that which our rabbis have taught on Tannaite authority:*

C. "If it will gore..." (Ex. 21:28) – and goring is done only with the horn, as it is said, "And Zedekiah, son of Chenaanah, made him horns of iron and said, Thus saith the Lord, with these shall you gore the Aramaeans" (1 Kgs. 22:11);

D. and it is further said, "His glory is like the firstling of his bullock, and his horns are like the horns of a unicorn; with them he shall gore the people together" (Deut. 33:17).

E. *What's the point of "and it is further said"?*

F. *Should you say that teachings on the strength of the Torah are not to be derived from teachings that derive from prophetic tradition, then come and take note:* "His glory is like the firstling of his bullock, and his horns are like the horns of a unicorn; with them he shall gore the people together" (Deut. 33:17).

G. *Yeah, well, is this really a deduction out of a scriptural prooftext? To me it looks more like a mere elucidation, showing that "goring" is something that is done by a horn.*

H. *What might you otherwise have supposed? That where Scripture makes an important distinction between an ox that was not known to gore and one that is a certified danger, that concerns a horn that is cut off [as in the case of the first of the two examples, that of 1 Kgs. 22:11], but as to one that is actually attached to the beast, all goring is classified as done by an ox that is an attested danger. Then come and take note:* "His glory is like the firstling of his bullock, and his horns are like the horns of a unicorn; with them he shall gore the people together" (Deut. 33:17).

Once the secondary taxonomic process gets underway, we shall unpack each item in succession: what are the derivatives, how they relate, the difference it makes when we recognize these derivatives, and how Scripture yields them.

I.6   A. *What are the derivatives of the horn?*

        B. Butting, biting, falling, and kicking.

        C. *How come goring is called a generative cause of damages? Because it is stated explicitly,* "If it will gore" (Ex. 21:28). *But then in reference to butting, it also is written,* "If it butts" (Ex. 21:35).

        D. *That reference to butting refers in fact to goring, as has been taught on Tannaite authority:* Scripture opens with a reference to butting [Ex. 21:35] and concludes with a reference to goring [Ex. 21:16] to tell you that in this context "butting" means "goring."

I.7   A. *Why, when the Scripture refers to injury to a human being, does it say,* "If it will gore" (Ex. 21:28), *while when Scripture refers to an ox's injuring an animal, it uses the language,* "If it will butt" (Ex. 21:35)?

        B. *A human being, who is subject to a star [planetary influence], will be injured only by [Kirzner: willful] goring, but an animal, who is not subject to a star, is injured by mere accidental butting.*

        C. *And by the way, Scripture tangentially informs us of another matter, namely, an animal that is an attested danger for a human being is an attested danger for other beasts, but an animal that is an attested danger for beasts is not necessarily an attested danger for injuring a human being.*

What is important here is the comparison of derivative classes, human and animal in this case; this question emerges only from the prior, and primary, interest in showing how the Mishnah's classes yield further ones. This same work now proceeds at a secondary level of complication.

I.8   A.   Biting: *Does this not fall into the classification of a derivative of tooth?*
       B.   *Not at all, for what characterizes injury under the classification of "tooth" is that there is pleasure that comes from doing the damage, but biting is not characterized by giving pleasure in the doing of the damage.*

I.9   A.   Falling and kicking: *Do these not fall into the classification of derivatives of foot?*
       B.   *Not at all, for what characterizes injury under the classification of "foot" is that it is quite common, while damage done by these is not so common.*

What is important in what follows is the introduction of altogether fresh considerations, that is to say, things that affect the taxa now defined, but that at the same time complicate our original taxonomy. Specifically, we want to know how the issue of intentionality interrelates with the generative classifications we have in hand: Does this form a further, autonomous point of differentiation? Since questions of the scriptural origin of taxa are integral to the generative problematic (as Sifra has shown us), I do not indent compositions or composites on that subject, regarding them as part of the sustained exposition at hand.

I.10   A.   *Now, then, as to those derivatives that are not equivalent to the generative causes [from which the derivatives come], to which R. Pappa made reference, what might they be? Should we say that he makes reference to these? Then how are they different from the generative cause? Just as horn is a classification that involves damage done with intent, one's own property, and one's responsibility for adequate guardianship, so these, too, form classifications that involve damage done with intent, one's own property, and one's responsibility for adequate guardianship. So it must follow that the derivatives of horn are equivalent to the principal, the horn, and R. Pappa must then refer to tooth and foot.*

I.11   A.   *Where in Scripture is reference made to tooth and foot? It is taught on Tannaite authority:* "And he shall send forth" (Ex. 22:4) – this refers to the foot, and so Scripture says, "That send forth the feet of the ox and the ass" (Isa. 32:20). "And it shall consume" (Ex. 22:4) – this refers to the tooth, in line with this usage: "As the tooth consumes [3A] to entirety" (1 Kgs. 14:10).

I.12   A.   The master has said: "'And he shall send forth' (Ex. 22:4) – this refers to the foot, and so Scripture says, 'That send forth the feet of the ox and the ass' (Isa. 32:20)."
       B.   *So the operative consideration is that Scripture has said, "That send forth the feet of the ox and the ass." Lo, if Scripture had not so stated, how else would you have interpreted the phrase, "And he shall send forth" (Ex. 22:4)? It could hardly refer to horn, which is written elsewhere, nor could it mean tooth, since this, too, is referred to elsewhere.*

    C.   *No, the proof nonetheless was required, for it might have entered your mind to suppose that "send forth" and "consume" refer to tooth, in the one case where there is destruction of the principal, in the other where there is no destruction of the principal, so we are informed that that is not so.*

    D.   *Now that you have established that the cited verse refers to foot in particular, then how on the basis of Scripture do we know that there is liability for damage done by the tooth in a case in which the principal has not been destroyed?*

    E.   *It would follow by analogy from the case of damage done by the foot. Just as in the case of damage done by the foot, there is no distinction to be drawn between a case in which the principal has been destroyed and one in which the principal has not been destroyed, so in the case of damage done by the tooth, there is no distinction to be drawn between a case in which the principal has been destroyed and one in which the principal has not been destroyed.*

I.13   A.   The master has said, "'And it shall consume' (Ex. 22:4) – this refers to the tooth, in line with this usage: 'As the tooth consumes to entirety' (1 Kgs. 14:10)."

    B.   *So the operative consideration is that Scripture has said, "As the tooth consumes to entirety." Lo, were it not for that statement, how might we have interpreted the phrase anyhow? It could hardly have been a reference to horn, for that is stated explicitly in Scripture, and it also could not have been a reference to foot for the same reason.*

    C.   *No, it was necessary to make that point in any event. For it might otherwise have entered your mind to suppose that both phrases speak of foot, the one referred to a case in which the beast was going along on its own, the other when the owner sent it to do damage, and so we are informed that that is not the case. [So we are informed that that is not the case.]*

    D.   *If then we have identified the matter with tooth, then how could we know that one is liable under the category of foot when the cattle went and did damage on its own?*

    E.   *The matter is treated by analogy to damage done in the category of tooth. Just as in the case of tooth we draw no distinction between a case in which the owner sent the beast out and it did damage and one in which the beast went along on its own, so in the case of foot, there is no distinction between a case in which the owner sent the beast out and one in which the beast went out on its own.*

I.14   A.   *Then let the Scripture make reference to "And he shall send forth" (Ex. 22:4) and omit "And it shall consume," which would cover the classifications of both foot and tooth? It would cover foot in line with this verse: "That send forth the feet of the ox and the ass," and it would cover tooth, in line with this verse, "And the teeth of beasts will I send upon them" (Deut. 32:24).*

    B.   *Were it not for this apparently redundant statement, I might have imagined that the intent was either the one or the other, either foot, since damage done by the foot is commonplace, or tooth, since damage done by the tooth gives pleasure.*

    C.   *Well, we still have to include them both, since, after all, which one would you exclude anyhow [in favor of the other], their being equally balanced?*

    D. *The additional clarification still is required, for you might otherwise have supposed that the liability pertains only where the damage is intentional, excluding a case in which the cattle went on its own; so we are informed that that is not the case.*

I.15 A. *What is the derivative of the generative category of tooth?*

    B. If for its own pleasure the cow rubbed itself against a wall and broke it, or spoiled produce by rolling around in it.

    C. *What distinguishes damage done by the tooth* [as a generative category] is that it is a form of damage that gives pleasure to the one that does it, it derives from what is your own property, and you are responsible to take care of it. *Well, in these cases, too, one may say the same thing, namely, here we have* a form of damage that gives pleasure to the one that does it, it derives from what is your own property, and you are responsible to take care of it.

    D. *It must follow that the derivative classes of the generative category of tooth are equivalent to the generative category itself, and when R. Pappa made his statement, he must have referred to the generative category of foot.*

I.16 A. *What is the derivative of the generative category of foot?*

    B. If the beast while moving did damage with its body or hair or with a load on it or with a bit in its mouth or with a bell around its neck.

    C. *What distinguishes damage done by the foot* [as a generative category] is that it is a form of damage that is very common, it derives from what is your own property, and you are responsible to take care of it. *Well, in these cases, too, one may say the same thing, namely, here we have* a form of damage that is very common, it derives from what is your own property, and you are responsible to take care of it.

    D. *It must follow that the derivative classes of the generative category of foot are equivalent to the generative category itself, and when R. Pappa made his statement, he must have referred to the generative category of pit.*

I.17 A. *Then what would be derivatives of the generative category of pit?*

    B. *Should I say that the generative category is a pit ten handbreadths deep, but a derivative is one nine handbreadths deep, Scripture does not make explicit reference to either one ten handbreadths deep nor to one nine handbreadths deep!*

    C. *In point of fact that is not a problem, since the All-Merciful has said, "And the dead beast shall be his" (Ex. 21:34). And, for their part, rabbis established that a pit ten handbreadths deep will cause death, one only nine handbreadths deep will cause only injury, but will not cause death.*

    D. *So what difference does that make? The one is a generative classification of pit when it comes to yielding death, the other an equally generative classification yielding injury.*

    E. *So R. Pappa's statement must speak of a stone, knife, or luggage, left in the public domain, that did damage.*

    F. *How then can we imagine damage of this kind? If they were declared ownerless and abandoned in the public domain, then from the perspective of both Rab and Samuel, they fall into the classification of pit.* [3B] *And if they were not declared ownerless and abandoned in the public domain, then from the perspective of Samuel, who has said, "All public nuisances are derived by analogy to the generative classification of pit," they fall into the classification of pit, and from the perspective of Rab, who has* held, "All of them do we derive by analogy to ox," *they fall under the classification of ox.*

G. *What is it that characterizes the pit?* It is that to begin with it is made as a possible cause of damage, it is your property, and you are responsible to watch out for it. *So of these, too, it may be said,* to begin with it is made as a possible cause of damage, it is your property, and you are responsible to watch out for it. *It therefore follows that the derivatives of pit are the same as the pit itself, and when R. Pappa made his statement, it was with reference to the derivatives of the crop-destroying beast.*

I.18   A. *So what can these derivatives of the crop-destroying beast be anyhow? From the perspective of Samuel, who has said,* "The crop-destroying beast is the same as tooth [that is, trespassing cattle]," *lo, the derivative of tooth is in the same classification as tooth [as we have already shown], and from the perspective of Rab, who has said,* "The crop-destroying beast is in fact the human being," *then what generative categories and what derivatives therefrom are to be identified with a human being! Should you allege that a human being when awake is the generative classification, and the human being when asleep is a derivative, have we not learned in the Mishnah:* **Man is perpetually an attested danger [M. B.Q. 2:6A]** *– whether awake or asleep!*

B. *So when R. Pappa made his statement, he must have referred to a human being's phlegm or snot.*

C. *Yeah, well, then, under what conditions? If the damage was done while in motion, it comes about through man's direct action, and if it does its damage after it comes to rest, then, whether from Rab's or Samuel's perspective, it falls into the classification of pit. And, it must follow, the offspring of the crop-destroying beast is in the same classification as the crop-destroying beast, so when R. Pappa made his statement, he must have been talking about the derivatives of fire.*

I.19   A. *So what are derivatives of fire? Shall we say that such would be a stone, knife, or luggage, that one left on one's roof and were blown off by an ordinary wind and caused damage? Then here, too, under what conditions? If the damage was done while in motion, then they fall into the category of fire itself. For what characterizes fire is that it derives from an external force, is your property, and is yours to guard, and these, too, are to be described in the same way, since each derives from an external force, is your property, and is yours to guard. And, it must follow, the offspring of fire are in the same classification as fire, so when R. Pappa made his statement, he must have been talking about the derivatives of foot.*

I.20   A. *Foot? Surely you're joking! Have we not already established the fact that the derivative of foot is in the same classification as the generative classification of foot itself?*

B. *At issue is the payment of half-damages done by pebbles kicked by an animal's foot, which we have learned by tradition.*

C. *And why is such damage classified as a derivative of foot?*

D. *So that compensation should be paid only from property of the highest class possessed by the defendant.*

E. *But did not Raba raise the question on this very matter? For Raba raised this question,* "Is the half-damage to be paid for damage caused by pebbles to be paid only from the body of the beast itself or from the beast property of the owner of the beast?"

F. *Well, that was a problem for Raba, but R. Pappa was quite positive about the matter.*

G. *Well, if it's a problem to Raba, then from his perspective, why would pebbles kicked by an animal's foot be classified as a derivative of foot?*

H. *So that the owner in such a case may be exempted from having to pay compensation where the damage was done in the public domain [just as damage caused by the generative category, foot, is not to be compensated if it was done in the public domain].*

We revert to our Mishnah exegesis, now defining yet another taxon and reckoning with its relationships to those already worked out.

II.1   A. **Crop-destroying beast and conflagration:**
       B. *What is the meaning of* "the crop-destroying beast"?
       C. Rab said, "The crop-destroying beast is in fact the human being."
       D. And Samuel said, "The crop-destroying beast is the same as tooth [that is, trespassing cattle]."
       E. Rab said, "The crop-destroying beast is in fact the human being," as it is written, "The watchman said, The morning comes, and also the night, if you will ask, then ask" (Isa. 21:12) [where the letters used in the word for crop-destroying beast occur].
       F. And Samuel said, "The crop-destroying beast is the same as tooth [that is, trespassing cattle]," as it is written, "How is Esau searched out, how are his hidden places sought out" (Obad. 1:6) [where the letters used in the word for crop-destroying beast occur].
       G. *And how does that verse yield the interpretation given by Samuel?*
       H. *It is in line with the translation into Aramaic given by R. Joseph, "[Kirzner:] How was Esau ransacked? How were his hidden treasures exposed?"* [Kirzner: Tooth is naturally hidden but becomes exposed in grazing.]
       I. *And how come Rab did not accept the proof of Samuel?*
       J. *He objects: "Does the Mishnah use the letters formed into the passive [which would then refer to anything that is exposed]?"*
       K. *And how come Samuel does not go along with Rab?*
       L. *He objects, "Does the Mishnah use the letters in a form that would denote mere action?"* [Kirzner: The form that is used is causative, hence with reference to tooth, which the animal exposes in grazing].
       M. *Well, let's face the fact that the scriptural verses do not decisively settle the question either in favor of the position of this master or in favor of the position of that one, so why really did Rab not concur with Samuel?*
       N. *When the Mishnah paragraph refers to ox, it covers all classifications of damage done by the ox.*
       O. *Then from Samuel's perspective, has not the Tannaite authority already covered "ox"?*

Now we come to a fine instance in which the definition of the taxa also presents an opportunity to introduce a variety of indicative traits, instead of just a few: to redefine taxa in terms of issues not present in the Mishnah statement's original list. Here, for example, we ask about whether the one that does the damage benefits from doing it, and that will form a point of distinction between one taxon and another. In what follows, that issue is joined to the issue of intent to inflict injury.

P. Said R. Judah, "When the Tannaite authority of the Mishnah paragraph referred to ox, it was to the horn, and when he referred to crop-destroying beast, it was with reference to tooth, *and this is the sense of his statement:* The indicative traits of the horn, in which instance doing damage does not give pleasure to the one who does the damage, are not the same as the indicative traits of the tooth, in which case there is pleasure to the one who does the damage, [4A] and the indicative traits of tooth, in which the intent of the beast that does the damage is not in fact to do damage, are not the same as the indicative traits of the horn, in which case the one who does the damage really does intend to do the damage he has done."

Q. Well, this point can then be derived on the strength of an argument a fortiori, as follows: If one bears responsibility for damages in the classification of tooth, in which case there is no intent to inflict injury, then in the case of damages in the classification of horn, in which case there is every intent to inflict injury, is it not an argument a fortiori that one should bear responsibility for injuries done in that way?

R. *No, it was necessary for Scripture to make explicit reference to damages done by the horn, for you might otherwise have taken for granted that one is immune for damages in the classification of the horn by analogy to the matter of damages done by one's male and female slaves. Just as a male or a female slave, though bearing every intent to do injury, do not bring upon their master liability for damages that they do, so I might have otherwise thought that the law would be the same in the case of the horn.*

S. *Said R. Ashi, "But isn't it the fact that an overriding consideration comes into play in the matter of the male and female slave, specifically,* we take account of the possibility that the master will punish the slave, and the slave may then go and burn up the standing grain of his neighbor, so from day to day this one will turn out to impose upon his master a fine of a hundred maneh? *Rather, this is the way in which the challenge is to be framed:* The indicative traits of the horn, in which case the one who does the damage really does intend to do the damage he has done, are not to be compared to the indicative traits of damages in the classification of tooth, in which case the damages are not done deliberately, nor are the indicative traits of tooth, in which case the one that does the damage gains benefit from the damage done, to be compared to the indicative traits of the damages in the classification of horn, in which case the one that does the damage gets no benefit from them [Kirzner: so neither horn nor tooth could be derived from each other]."

T. *How come foot is left out of the catalogue?*

U. The rule that whenever damage has been done, the one who has done it is liable to pay damages *encompasses the foot.*

V. *So why not so formulate the Tannaite rule as to say that in so many words?*

W. Well, said Raba, "The Tannaite formulation refers to the **ox**, encompassing the foot, and the **crop-destroying beast**, encompassing the tooth, *and this is the sense of the statement:* The indicative traits of the foot, damages in the classification of which are commonplace, are not like the indicative traits of the tooth, damages in the classification of which are not commonplace; nor are the indicative traits of damages in the classification of tooth, which benefit the one who does the damage, like the indicative traits of damages in the classification of the foot, in which case there is no benefit to the one that does the damage."

X. *How come horn is left out of the catalogue?*

Y. The rule that whenever damage has been done, the one who has done it is liable to pay damages *encompasses the horn.*

Z. *So why not so formulate the Tannaite rule as to say that in so many words?*

AA. *The Mishnah rule addresses classifications of causes of damage for which beasts to begin with are deemed habitually capable, while the Mishnah rule does not address classifications of causes of damage for which beasts to begin with are deemed innocent, but only at the end habitually capable.*

II.2   A. *So why doesn't Samuel state matters as does Rab [in explaining the meaning of* **crop-destroying beast** [Rab said, "The crop-destroying beast is in fact the human being"]?

B. *He will say to you, "If it should enter your mind that this refers to man, lo, the passage states further on:* and an ox which causes damage in the domain of the one who is injured; and (5) man [M. 1:4F-G]!"

C. *But why not include man in the initial clause anyhow?*

D. *The opening clause addresses cases of damages done by one's chattels, and it does not address the case of damages done by oneself.*

II.3   A. *And so far as Rab is concerned, does not the passage state further on:* and an ox which causes damage in the domain of the one who is injured; and (5) man [M. 1:4F-G]?

B. *Rab will say to you, "That serves the purpose of including man among those that are considered attested dangers."*

C. *Then what is the sense of the language,* [The indicative characteristic] of the ox is not equivalent to that of the crop-destroying beast...?

D. *This is the sense of that language:* The indicative characteristic of the ox, which if it kills a man imposes on the owner the necessity of paying a ransom, is not the same as the indicative trait of man, who does not impose [for example, on the owner of the slave] the obligation of paying a ransom, nor is the indicative trait of a man, who is liable to pay damages on four distinct counts, equivalent to the indicative trait of the ox, which is not liable to pay damages on four distinct counts. What they have in common is that they customarily do damage.

E. So is it customary for the ox [horn] to do damage?

F. Reference is made here to an ox that is an attested danger.

G. Well, is an ox that is an attested danger going customarily to do damage?

H. *Well, yes, since it has been declared an attested danger, it is assumed customarily to do damage!*

I. Well, is it customary for man to do damage?

J.   When he is sleeping.

K.   Are you saying that when man is asleep, he customarily does damage?

L.   *Since he stretches out his legs or curls them up, he really does customarily do damage in such a way.*

M.   And taking care of them is your responsibility: Is not the care of a human being exclusively his or her own responsibility? [How can we say, taking care of them is your responsibility? How can this refer to man, as Rab maintains?]

N.   *In accord with your contrary view, lo, Qarna has repeated as his Tannaite formulation:* [There are] four generative causes of damages, and man is one of them. But is not the care of a human being exclusively his or her own responsibility?

O.   *Rather, it is in accord with the manner in which R. Abbahu instructed the Tannaite authority to frame matters:* "Taking care of a human being [not to inflict damage] is his or her responsibility," [4B] *and here, too,* taking care of a human being [not to inflict damage] is his or her responsibility.

II.4   A.   *Objected R. Mari, "But maybe* crop-destroying beast *really refers to water that does damage, in line with the verse:* 'As when the melting fire burns, fire causes water to bubble' (Isa. 54:1) [in which the consonants used in crop-destroying beast recur]."

B.   Does the verse say, "Water bubbles"? What it says is, "Fire causes bubbling."

C.   *Objected R. Zebid, "But maybe* crop-destroying beast *really refers to fire, since fire is the referent of the cited verse?"*

D.   If that were so, how would you deal with the repetition, crop-destroying beast and fire?! *If you should propose that "fire" stands in apposition to "crop-destroying beast," then instead of four classifications of generative causes, there would be only three, and if you suggest that ox stands for two distinct classifications, then what will be the sense of the statement,* nor are this one and that one, which are animate? *How is fire animate?! And what will be the sense of the concluding part of the same clause,* equivalent to fire?

Having completed our work on the four classes, we now ask whether there are not a great many more, thirteen in all. But there is a shift in meaning here, since what we now understand by "generative cause of damage" shades over into "categories of compensation," that is, compensation under a number of counts; and that represents a considerable move beyond the matter of categories of causes of damages. Once that taxonomic process has gotten under way, we are not limited to our original basis for differentation at all.

II.5   A.   *R. Oshaia repeated as a Tannaite formulation:* There are thirteen generative causes of damages, including unpaid bailee, borrower, paid bailee, one who rents; compensation paid for depreciation, pain, healing, loss of time, humiliation; *and the four enumerated in our Mishnah paragraph. That makes up thirteen. Now how come the Tannaite authority of our paragraph listed four and not the others?*

B. *From Samuel's perspective there is no problem in answering that question, since the Mishnah speaks only of damage committed by one's chattel, not that committed by one's person, but as to Rab, [who has held that the crop-destroying beast refers to man,] why not include these items?*

C. *By speaking of man, the framer of the passage has encompassed every kind of damage done by man.*

D. *Yeah, well, then how come R. Oshaia's version does not make reference to man?*

E. *There is a distinction to be drawn between types of damage that man does: one is damage done by man to man, the other, damage done by man to chattel [and these latter are specified, for example, pain, healing, and so on].*

F. *If so, then why not draw the same distinction among damages done by ox: one is damage done by an ox to chattel, the other, damage done by an ox to a human being?*

G. *How are these parallel? There is no problem in explaining how the distinction pertains to man, since if a man damages chattel, he pays for depreciation but not the other four kinds of classes of damages, but if he does damage to a human being, he has to pay the other four types of compensation, but how can an ox be treated in this way, since damage done by it to either man or chattel is the same and involves only one kind of damage [namely, depreciation]?*

H. *Well what about unpaid bailee, borrower, paid bailee, one who rents? These all are in the framework of a man who does damage to chattel, and yet they are included in R. Oshaia's reckoning.*

I. Damage done by a person directly and damage done indirectly are kept distinct by him.

II.6 A. *R. Hiyya taught as his Tannaite version of the passage before us:* There are twenty-four generative causes of damages, including double payment [for theft], fourfold or fivefold payment, theft, robbery, a conspiracy to give false evidence, rape, seduction, slander, one who imparts uncleanness to someone else's property, one who renders someone else's property doubtfully tithed produce, and one who renders someone else's wine into libation wine [in all three cases diminishing their value], *and the thirteen enumerated by R. Oshaia, twenty-four in all.*

B. *How come R. Oshaia did not reckon these others?*

C. *He addressed classifications of damages involving civil liability but not with extrajudicial penalties.*

D. *So why not include theft and robbery, which also form civil liabilities?*

E. *They fall under the classifications of unpaid bailee and borrower.*

F. *Well, why didn't R. Hiyya include them in those classifications?*

G. *He dealt with each on its own, since in the one case possession of the chattel comes into one's hands lawfully, in the other [theft, robbery], it is in violation of a prohibition.*

H. [5A] Well, a conspiracy to give false evidence *is classified as a civil liability, so why not [have Oshaia] include that item?*

I. *He concurs with R. Aqiba, who said, "A conspiracy of witnesses is not required to pay compensation on the basis of their own testimony."* [Kirzner: "Liability for false evidence is penal in nature and cannot consequently be created by confession."]

J.   *If he concurs with R. Aqiba, then why not distinguish in the classification of ox and identify two distinct classifications of damage, the damage done by an ox to chattel, and the damage done by an ox to a human being, for have we not learned in the Mishnah:* R. Aqiba says, "Also: An ox deemed harmless [which injured] a man – [the owner] pays full damages for the excess" [M. B.Q. 3:8K]?

K.   *As a matter of fact, R. Aqiba himself has vitiated the force of that distinction, for it has been taught on Tannaite authority:* R. Aqiba says, "Might one suppose that even a beast deemed harmless who did injury to a human being – the owner should have to pay compensation from land of the highest quality? Scripture states, 'This judgment shall be done to it' (Ex. 21:31), meaning that the liability to damages should be limited to the value of the corpus of the beast that is formerly deemed harmless, and not out of any other source."

L.   *What about rape, seduction, and slander, which also fall under the classification of civil liabilities, why should R. Oshaia not include these as well?*

M.   *What can you mean? If it was for liability to depreciation, he's got that on his list, and if it's for liability to suffering, he has that in the classification of pain, and if it is humiliation, he's got that in the classification of degradation; and if it's for deterioration, he's got that under depreciation. So what can you have in mind?*

N.   The extrajudicial penalty involved in these items.

O.   *[Oshaia] was not reckoning with extrajudicial penalties.*

P.   *[And how come Oshaia omitted from his list]* one who imparts uncleanness to someone else's property, one who renders someone else's property doubtfully tithed produce, and one who renders someone else's wine into libation wine [in all three cases diminishing their value]? *These, too, involve a civil liability!*

Q.   *Well, what do you think about injury that is intangible? If you classify it as injury, then he has included in his list the classification of depreciation; and if you maintain that it is not classified as civil damage, then any liability would fall into the classification of an extrajudicial penalty, with which, as we saw, R. Oshaia is not dealing here.*

R.   *Shall we then maintain that R. Hiyya takes the position that intangible injury is not classified as depreciation and a matter of civil liability? For if he maintained that such was classified as a civil liability, lo, he has specified in his list depreciation?*

S.   *What he did was specify in his Tannaite formulation tangible damages and then he went on and specified intangible damages as well.*

II.7   A.   *Now we can well understand why our Tannaite authority has specified the number of classifications of generative causes of damages, since it was to include the number of classifications reckoned by R. Oshaia, and, of course, R. Oshaia specified as his Tannaite formulation the number of damages, so as to include the much larger number conceived by R. Hiyya. But what is accomplished by the exclusive number reckoned by R. Hiyya?*

B.   *That serves to exclude the cases of one who squeals [to the government, and so causes loss to an Israelite] and one who by his improper intentionality spoils the offering of someone and renders it null.*

C.   *Well, why not include them?*

D. *Well, there is no problem in explaining why he has not counted in his classifications the matter of the priest who by his improper intentionality spoils someone's offering, since our Tannaite compilation is not dealing with Holy Things anyhow. But what reason can there be for omitted reference to one who squeals?*

E. *That matter is exceptional, since it involves a mere verbal assault, and he is not dealing with verbal assaults?*

F. *Well, if he's not dealing with verbal assaults, then what about the matter of slander, which is nothing other than a verbal assault, and he has included it in his Tannaite formulation!*

G. *That is a verbal assault involving a concrete action.*

H. *Well, then, what about the conspiracy to give false testimony? Here, too, we have a verbal assault without any concrete action, and yet he has included it on his list!*

I. *Well, in that case, you are dealing with something that may not involve a concrete action, but Scripture itself has classified it as a concrete action, in the language:* "You shall do to him as he proposed to do to his brother" (Deut. 19:19).

II.8 A. *Now there is no problem in understanding why our Tannaite authority has specified generative categories, since he maintains that there are also derivative ones. But from the perspectives of R. Hiyya and R. Oshaia, if we speak of generative categories, bearing the implication that there might be derivative ones, then what might these be?*

B. Said R. Abbahu, "So far as the requirement that damages be paid out of the best of one's real estate, all of them are classified as generative classifications. *How come? We treat as a verbal analogy references in common to* 'instead,' 'compensation,' 'payment,' and 'money'" (Ex. 21:36, Ex. 21:32, Ex. 22:8, and Ex. 21:34, respectively). [Kirzner: One of these four terms occurs with each of the four categories of damage specified in the Mishnah, and likewise with each of the kinds of damage enumerated by Oshaia and Hiyya, thus teaching uniformity in regard to the mode of payment in them all.]

What follows is routine and narrowly exegetical, and so it gives us a good insight into how the process is shaped when large-scale issues are not at stake. All we want to know is what a sentence means; the answer is worked out in terms of how one class of things relates to some other, that is, can we deduce the rule of one class of things from the rule governing another, analogous one?

III.1 A. **[The indicative characteristic] of the ox is not equivalent to that of the crop-destroying beast:**

B. *What is the sense of this statement?*

C. *Said R. Zebid in the name of Raba,* "This is the sense of the statement: If someone should maintain, 'Let Scripture explicitly make reference to only one kind of damage, and you may deduce the liability for the other,' the answer is given, 'The rule governing one kind of damage cannot be deduced from any other.'"

Here is yet another example in which we make sense of a statement by appeal to our primary concern. What we wish to know we find out by appeal to our generative question. To put it differently, before we ask a question, we know why we are asking it, what we wish to discover, and how we shall know that we are right when we do find the answer – all of this in less than a hundred words!

IV.1   A.   **Nor are this one and that one, which are animate, equivalent to fire, which is not animate:**
       B.   *What is the sense of this statement?*
       C.   *Said R. Mesharshayya in the name of Raba, "This is the sense of the statement:* [5B] *If someone should say, 'Let Scripture explicitly make reference to only two of the three kinds of damage [ox and crop-destroying beast], and you may deduce the liability for the remaining one,' the answer is given,* [Nor are this one and that one, which are animate, equivalent to fire, which is not animate,] *so even from two kinds of damage we cannot deduce the rule governing a third."*

IV.2   A.   *Said Raba, "If you include pit and any other classification of damage, all the others will then be derived by analogy [via the feature common to pit and any other classification of damage], except for the case of horn. Horn is exceptional, in that all the other kinds of damage are classified as attested dangers to begin with [except for damage done by a goring ox, where the distinction between an attested danger and an ox deemed harmless is drawn].*
       B.   *"But within the view that damage done by the horn is a weightier matter since in that case the beast had every intention to do damage, then even the classification of horn could be deduced. And, in that case, for what definitive purpose did Scripture find it necessary to make explicit reference to each such classification?"*

What follows is a fine example of introducing further points of taxonomic differentiation into what is up to now a fairly simple, single-dimensional grid. Now we want to know about such distinctions as Scripture's between a beast deemed harmless and one that is an attested danger; public and private domain; animate and inanimate objects (or sources of damage); classifications of damages defined by the counts under which compensation is made, rather than the counts under which damages may be distinguished from one another. What is interesting is that the Mishnah has made a set of distinctions, for example, get up and go do damage versus not doing so, that the Bavli has absorbed, but then proposed to augment. How far we have moved, now, from the simple point that the various taxa have in common: What they have in common is that they customarily do damage and taking care of them is your responsibility! Instead, we find other points in common, but also other points of distinction.

C. [1] Horn: to make the distinction between the beast deemed harmless and that one that is an attested danger;
D. [2] tooth and foot: to exempt the owner from damage that was done within these classifications in public domain;
E. [3] pit: to exempt the owner from damage done to inanimate objects;
F. and from the perspective of R. Judah, who takes the view that one is liable for damage done to inanimate objects by a pit one has dug, it is to exempt one from liability to death caused by it to man;
G. [4] man: to impose upon him the four additional classifications of compensation to be paid for damage done by a human being to another human being;
H. [5] fire: to make one immune for damage done to objects that were hidden away [and not known by the person who kindled the fire] by a fire one has kindled;
I. *and according to R. Judah, who maintains that one is liable to damage done by fire to hidden objects, what purpose is served?*
J. *[6A] It is to encompass under the rule damage done by fire lapping his neighbor's ploughed field and grazing his stones.*

The Mishnah sentence now proceeds to compare and contrast our several generative categories, and this is accomplished time and again by introducing what one might call subordinate considerations, but what I have called a distinct set of grids: other taxic indicators besides the main ones. In this way we subdivide our categories.

V.1   A. **What they have in common is that they customarily do damage and taking care of them is your responsibility:**
B. *So what is encompassed by this generalization?*
C. Said Abbayye, "It is to encompass the stone, knife, and bundle that one left on his rooftop, which fell by the action of a seasonal breeze and did injury."
D. *Under what conditions? If the damage was done while in motion, then they fall into the category of fire itself. For what characterizes fire is that it derives from an external force, is your property, and is yours to guard, and these, too, are to be described in the same way, since each derives from an external force, is your property, and is yours to guard. So it must follow that the damage was done after these things came to rest.*
E. *Well, if the damage was done after they came to rest, then how can we imagine damage of this kind? If they were declared ownerless and abandoned in the public domain, then from the perspective of both Rab and Samuel, they fall into the classification of pit.*
F. *What is it that characterizes the pit? It is that* to begin with it is made as a possible cause of damage, it is your property, and you are responsible to watch out for it. *So of these, too, it may be said,* to begin with it is made as a possible cause of damage, it is your property, and you are responsible to watch out for it. *It therefore follows that they were not declared ownerless and abandoned in the public domain.*
G. *But then from the perspective of Samuel, who has said, "All public nuisances are derived by analogy to the generative classification of pit," they fall into the classification of pit [and from the perspective of Rab,*

who has held, "All of them do we derive by analogy to ox," they fall under the classification of ox].

H.   *In point of fact, they have not been declared ownerless property, but they still are not to be classified along with the pit.* For the indicative traits of the pit are that no external force is involved with it, *and you must say in the case of these that an external force is involved in it. [The stone, knife, and luggage are indeed to be characterized in that way.]*

I.   But that fire [carried by an external force, the wind, but nonetheless imposing liability for compensation] is a refutation for that reasoning.

J.   The indicative trait of fire is that it is routine for it to go along and do damage.

K.   A pit will prove the contrary, and we have come full circle.

V.2 A.   **[What they have in common is that they customarily do damage and taking care of them is your responsibility:** *So what is encompassed by this generalization:]* Raba said, "Encompassed is a pit [Kirzner: a nuisance] that is moved around by the feet of man or beast."

B.   *If they were declared ownerless and abandoned in the public domain, then from the perspective of both Rab and Samuel, they fall into the classification of pit.*

C.   *What is it that characterizes the pit? It is that* to begin with it is made as a possible cause of damage, it is your property, and you are responsible to watch out for it. *So of these, too, it may be said,* to begin with it is made as a possible cause of damage, it is your property, and you are responsible to watch out for it. *It therefore follows that they were not declared ownerless and abandoned in the public domain.*

D.   *But then from the perspective of Samuel, who has said, "All public nuisances are derived by analogy to the generative classification of pit," they fall into the classification of pit [and from the perspective of Rab, who has held, "All of them do we derive by analogy to ox," they fall under the classification of ox].*

E.   *In point of fact, they have been declared ownerless property, but they still are not to be classified along with the pit.* For the indicative trait of the pit is that the sole cause of damage is that one has made the pit. *But how can you say the same in the case of this nuisance, making the nuisance by itself is not the direct cause of the damage [but the man or beast who moved it from place to place is the cause]?*

F.   *The classification of ox then proves the contrary.*

G.   The distinctive trait of the ox is that it routinely goes along and causes damage [which does not apply here].

H.   The pit proves the contrary.

I.   We have come full circle. The indicative trait of the one is not the same thing as the indicative trait of the other.

The foregoing is a fine example, among many, in which polythetic classification replaces monothetic classification. If we have traits characteristic of two items, may we then impute them to the third of the same class, even if all three items are not entirely uniform in their definitive traits?

V.3   A. *R. Adda bar Ahba said, "It serves to encompass that which has been taught in the following Tannaite formulation:* All those of whom they have spoken, who open up their gutters or sweep out the dust of their cellars into the public domain, in the dry season have no right to do so, but in the rainy season, have every right to do so. But even though they do so with every right, nonetheless, if what they have done causes damage, they are liable to pay compensation."

B. *Well, how can we imagine such a case? If these things do damage as he goes along and sweeps them, then the damage that they do is a direct result of his own action. So it must be after they have come to rest, but in that case, how can we imagine the case? If they were declared ownerless and abandoned in the public domain, then from the perspective of both Rab and Samuel, they fall into the classification of pit.*

C. *What is it that characterizes the pit? It is that* to begin with it is made as a possible cause of damage, it is your property, and you are responsible to watch out for it. *So of these, too, it may be said,* to begin with it is made as a possible cause of damage, it is your property, and you are responsible to watch out for it. *It therefore follows that they were not declared ownerless and abandoned in the public domain.*

D. *But then from the perspective of Samuel, who has said, "All public nuisances are derived by analogy to the generative classification of pit," they fall into the classification of pit [and from the perspective of Rab, who has held, "All of them do we derive by analogy to ox," they fall under the classification of ox].*

E. *In point of fact, they have been declared ownerless property, but they still are not to be classified along with the pit.* For the indicative trait of the pit is that one makes it without the right to do so. *But how can you say the same in the case of this nuisance, since the one who made it had every right to do so?*

F. [6B] The classification of ox then proves the contrary.

G. The distinctive trait of the ox is that it routinely goes along and causes damage [which does not apply here].

H. The pit proves the contrary.

I. We have come full circle. The indicative trait of the one is not the same thing as the indicative trait of the other. [Kirzner: And liability can be deduced only from the common aspects.]

V.4   A. *Rabina said, "It serves to encompass that which has been taught in the following Tannaite formulation:* The wall or the tree which fell down into public domain and inflicted injury – [the owner] is exempt from having to pay compensation. [If] they gave him time to cut down the tree or to tear down the wall, and they fell down during that interval, [the owner] is exempt. [If they fell down] after that time, [the owner] is liable [M. B.M. 10:4F-K]."

B. *Well, how can we imagine such a case? If these things do damage as he goes along and sweeps them, then the damage that they do is a direct result of his own action. So it must be after they have come to rest, but in that case, how can we imagine the case? If they were declared ownerless and abandoned in the public domain, then from the perspective of both Rab and Samuel, they fall into the classification of pit.*

C. *What is it that characterizes the pit? It is that* it commonly does damage, it is your property, and you are responsible to watch out for it. *So of these, too, it may be said,* it commonly does damage, it is your property, and you are responsible to watch out for it.

D. *But if they were not declared ownerless and abandoned in the public domain, then from the perspective of Samuel, who has said,* "All public nuisances are derived by analogy to the generative classification of pit," *they fall into the classification of pit [and from the perspective of Rab, who has held,* "All of them do we derive by analogy to ox," *they fall under the classification of ox].*

E. *In point of fact, they have been declared ownerless property, but they still are not to be classified along with the pit.* For the indicative trait of the pit to begin with is that making it serves as a cause of injury. *But how can you say the same in the case of those things that, from the moment they are made, are causes of injury?*

F. The classification of ox then proves the contrary.

G. The distinctive trait of the ox is that it routinely goes along and causes damage [which does not apply here].

H. The pit proves the contrary.

I. We have come full circle. The indicative trait of the one is not the same thing as the indicative trait of the other. [Kirzner: And liability can be deduced only from the common aspects.]

We come now to interests other than the exposition of the generative categories and the complexities inherent in them. The entire set of opening pages has focused on this one matter. To see the proportion of the whole devoted to that exposition, we now indent what is not.

VI.1   A.   **And when one [of them] has caused damage, the [owner] of that which causes the damage is liable:**

        B.   *The Mishnaic word choice is odd, and should be accountable [HYYB] and not liable [HB]!*

        C.   *Said R. Judah said Rab, "This Tannaite authority comes from Jerusalem and uses the [Kirzner:] easier form [the contraction]."*

What is interesting in what follows is how the mode of exegetical inquiry takes over and produces points of differentiation to generate secondary questions.

VII.1   A.   **Out of the best of his land (Ex. 22:4):**

        B.   *Our rabbis have taught on Tannaite authority:*

        C.   "Of the best of his field and of the best of his vineyard shall he make restitution" (Ex. 22:4) –

        D.   [as to the reference of "his,"] "This refers to the field of the injured party or the vineyard of the injured party," the words of R. Ishmael.

        E.   R. Aqiba says, "The purpose of Scripture is solely to indicate that damages are to be paid out of the real estate of the best quality [belonging to the defendant], even more so for damage to property that has been consecrated to the Temple."

Once we have introduced a fresh taxic system – injured party, party responsible for the injury – we forthwith take up intersecting grids:

property of varying quality, assigned to injuries of varying character. It would be hard to find a better, simple instance in which one grid is superimposed on another to yield an entire exegetical program. Truly has it been said that the history of religion is the exegesis of exegesis. I can imagine no more acute instance than the following secondary development of the simple inquiry with which we commence:

VII.2   A. *And from R. Ishmael's perspective, if the defendant has damaged the quality of the best property, he would pay from the best, but if he damaged real estate of the worst property, would he still pay from the best?*

        B. *Said R. Idi bar Abin, "Here with what sort of a case do we deal? It would be one in which he damaged a furrow among several furrows, and it is not known whether the furrow that he damaged was the best or the worst. In that case he compensates for the best."*

        C. *Said Raba, "Well, if we knew for sure that he damaged the worst, he would pay only for the worst, and now that we don't know for sure whether the furrow he damaged was of the best or the worst quality, why should he pay for the best? The one who bears the burden of proof is the plaintiff."*

        D. *Rather, said R. Aha bar Jacob, "Here with what sort of a case do we deal? It is one in which the best of the estate of the injured party is as good as the worst of the property of the defendant's property, and what is at issue among the two Tannaite authorities is this: R. Ishmael takes the view that the quality of the land that is paid in compensation is valued in relationship to what is owned by the injured party, and R. Aqiba says that the quality of the real estate of the defendant is what has to be assessed in determining compensation."*

VII.3   A. What is the scriptural basis for the position of R. Ishmael?

        B. We find a reference to the word "field" in both parts of the verse ["Of the best of his field" (Ex. 22:4), "If a man cause a field or a vineyard to be eaten" (Ex. 22:4)]. Just as in the earlier usage reference is made to the property of the injured party, so in the latter clause it refers to the property of the injured party.

        C. And R. Aqiba?

        D. "Of the best of his field and of the best of his vineyard shall he make restitution" (Ex. 22:4) *clearly speaks of the person who does the paying.*

        E. And R. Ishmael?

        F. *The verbal analogy just now drawn and the sense of the verse of Scripture itself both serve to make the point. The verbal analogy makes the point [that the quality of the land is assessed in the context of the estate of the injured party], and the clear sense of Scripture makes its point as well, which is to deal with a case in which the defendant's estate is made up of real estate of good quality and of bad quality, and the injured party's estate likewise is made up of land of good and bad quality, but the worst of the defendant's estate is not so good as the best of the property of the injured party; in this case, the defendant pays out of the real property of his estate that is of the better quality, since he has not got the right to say to him, "Come and be paid out of land of bad quality" [which is below the quality of the estate of the plaintiff (Kirzner)], but he is entitled to the land of the better quality.*

VII.4   A.   R. Aqiba says, "The purpose of Scripture is solely to indicate that damages are to be paid out of the real estate of the best quality [belonging to the defendant], even more so to property that has been consecrated to the Temple": *What is the purpose of that concluding clause*, even more so to property that has been consecrated to the Temple? *If we say that we speak of a case in which an ox belonging to a common person gored an ox consecrated to the sanctuary, in fact does not Scripture say, "The ox of one's neighbor," so excluding liability for damage done to consecrated property?*

        B.   Then it would deal with a case in which someone said, "Lo, incumbent on me is a maneh to be paid for the upkeep of the Temple," *in which case the Temple treasurer may collect from land of the highest quality.*

        C.   But the Temple treasurer should not be in a better position than an ordinary creditor, [7A] and an ordinary creditor collects only from land of middling quality.

        D.   *And, moreover, should you maintain that R. Aqiba takes the view that a creditor may collect what is owing to him even from property of the highest quality, one may pose the following challenge then to the implicit analogy:* What characterizes the common creditor is that he also has a strong claim in the matter of torts, but will you say the same of the Temple treasury, which has no strong claim in the matter of torts?

        E.   *In point of fact we really do deal with a case in which an ox belonging to a common person gored an ox consecrated to the sanctuary, and as to the question that you raised, namely, in fact does not Scripture say, "The ox of one's neighbor," so excluding liability for damage done to consecrated property, R. Aqiba concurs with the position of R. Simeon b. Menassia, for it has been taught on Tannaite authority:* R. Simeon b. Menassia says, "An ox belonging to the sanctuary that gored an ox of a common person – the sanctuary is exempt from paying damages. An ox of a common person that gored an ox belonging to the sanctuary, whether the ox was assumed harmless or an attested danger – the owner pays full damages."

        F.   *If that is the case, then with reference to the dispute of R. Ishmael and R. Aqiba, how do you know that at issue between them is a case in which the best of the injured party's land is of the quality of the worst of the defendant's? Perhaps all parties concur that we make our estimate based on the quality of the property of the injured party, but what is at issue here is the dispute between R. Simeon b. Menassia and rabbis. R. Aqiba concurs with R. Simeon b. Menassia, and R. Ishmael agrees with rabbis?*

        G.   *If so, then what is the meaning of the statement,* R. Aqiba says, "The purpose of Scripture is solely to indicate that damages are to be paid out of the real estate of the best quality [belonging to the defendant]"? *And, moreover, what is the sense of* "even more so to property that has been consecrated to the Temple"? *Furthermore, lo,* said R. Ashi, "It has been explicitly stated in a Tannaite formulation in this regard: '"Of the best of his field and the best of his vineyard shall he make restitution" (Ex. 22:4) – it is to be the best of the field of the injured party, and the best of the vineyard of the injured party,' the words of R. Ishmael. R. Aqiba says, '"...the best of the field" of the one who did the damage, and "the best of the vineyard" of the one who did the damage.'" [So that proposal is null.]

The next components of the present composite generate yet further points of distinction, for example, payment is made with the defendant's full intentionality and consent, the other [the former] a case in which it is against his will [and solely by court order]:

VII.5   A. Abbayye pointed out to Raba the following contradiction: "It is written, 'Of the best of his field and the best of his vineyard shall he make restitution' (Ex. 22:4), so one may then conclude that compensation must be only out of the best of one's property, not out of anything of lesser quality. *But has it not further been taught on Tannaite authority: '...he should return' (Ex. 21:34) – encompassing whatever has monetary value, even bran?"*

       B. *"That really does not form a contradiction. The one speaks of a case in which payment is made with the defendant's full intentionality and consent, the other [the former] a case in which it is against his will [and solely by court order]."*

       C. *Said Ulla b. R. Ilai, "Note that the language of Scripture itself yields such an inference: '...restitution shall be paid...' (Ex. 21:34), that is, even against his will."*

       D. *Said to him Abbayye, "Are the letters given consonants so that one must read them as '...shall be paid...'? The letters standing on their own may be read, '...he shall pay...,' meaning, with the defendant's full intentionality and consent."*

       E. *Rather, said Abbayye, "It is in line with what the master said in that which has been taught on Tannaite authority:* In the case of someone who possessed houses, fields, and vineyards, but is not able to sell them [to realize the cash he needs for his day-to-day expenses], they provide him with food out of poor man's tithe up to half the value of his property [Kirzner: to enable him to sell his property for half its value, which, it is assumed, he can realize any time]. *Now reflecting on that statement, the master asked: 'What sort of case can be in hand? If everybody's land was depressed, and his, too, was depressed, then why not give him even more than half the value of his estate, since the depression of prices is universal? Then if it is a case in which everybody's land reflated, but his, because he had to go and get some cash, fell, then* [7B] *one should not give him even a minimal value* [his property really being worth the money, but his own circumstance preventing him from realizing its value (Kirzner)]!' *Rather, the master said, 'The rule pertains to a case in which, in the month of Nisan [spring] property is worth more, in Tishri [fall] less. In general everybody waits until Nisan to put their property on the market, but this one, since he is in need of money, is ready to sell at the prevailing mark to even half of the anticipated price. So he is given half, since, it is the way of real estate to drop to half its value, but it is not the way of real estate to fall below half its value.' Now here, too, with reference to compensation for damages, the law is that the injured party is to be paid out of property of the best quality. But if the injured party said to him, 'Give me land of middling quality but more of it,' the defendant has the right to reply, 'If you take the land in accord with the law of what's coming to you, take it at the present valuation; but otherwise, you'll have to take it in accord with the higher price that will be coming later on.'"* [Kirzner: "He shall return," introducing payment in kind, authorizes calculation on the higher price anticipated whenever the plaintiff prefers a quality different from that assigned to him by law.]

F.   *Objected R. Aha bar Jacob, "If so, you have diminished the claim of plaintiffs for damages to be paid of land of middling and poor quality. For the All-Merciful has said, 'Out of the best' (Ex. 22:4), but you have then said that even from land of middling and poor quality, payment may not be exacted!"*

G.   *Rather, said R. Aha bar Jacob, "If there is any pertinent analogy [to the case of the rule governing poor person's tithe to an estate holder], we should draw that analogy to the case of paying a creditor. For as a matter of right he is to be paid out of land of middling quality. But if he said to the debtor, 'Give me land of middling quality but more of it,' the defendant has the right to reply, 'If you take the land in accord with the law of what's coming to you, take it at the present valuation; but otherwise, you'll have to take it in accord with the higher price that will be coming later on.'"*

H.   *Objected R. Aha b. R. Iqa, "If so, you will close the door in the face of borrowers. For the creditor may say to him, 'If I had my money in hand, I could go and buy land at the present prices, but now that my money is with you, I can only buy land in accordance with the higher prices that are anticipated later on!'"*

I.   *Rather, said R. Aha b. R. Iqa, "If there is any pertinent analogy [to the case of the rule governing a poor person's tithe to an estate holder], we should draw that analogy to the case of paying a marriage contract. For as a matter of right it is to be paid out of land of the poorest quality. But if he said to the debtor, 'Give me land of middling quality but less of it,' the defendant has the right to reply, 'If you take the land in accord with the law of what's coming to you, take it at the present valuation; but otherwise, you'll have to take it in accord with the higher price that will be coming later on.'"*

J.   *One way or the other, there is still a problem!*

K.   *Said Raba, "Whatever is paid over has to fall into the class of the best quality of its class"* [thus bran would have to be the best type of bran].

L.   But Scripture says, "The best of his field" [and that means, the best of land, not the best of anything else]!

M.   *Anyhow, when R. Pappa and R. Huna b. R. Joshua came from the household of their master, they explained as follows: "Anything may be 'best.' If they were not to be sold here, they could be sold somewhere else, except for land, so that is where payment has to be made out of the best, so that possible buyers may leap for the chance of buying it."*

What follows is not required by the sustained formation of mixed grids, but is a footnote to the foregoing. In other presentations, I would have indented what follows to signal that it is a footnote or an appendix; in the present case, I treat it as integral to the passage that is footnoted.

VII.6 A. *R. Samuel bar Abba from Iqronayya asked R. Abba, "When they estimate the value of property, is the calculation based on what the defendant owns, or upon what people in general own? Now as a matter of fact, that question is not addressed to the position of R. Ishmael, for he maintains that the calculation is based on the value of the property of the injured party pure and simple; where the question is raised, it can be only within the position of R. Aqiba, who has said that we make the estimate based on the property of the defendant in the case. Now what is the answer? When Scripture says, '...the best of his field,' is the intent only to exclude from the calculation the property of the injured party, or perhaps it is meant to exclude from consideration even the quality of property in general?"*

B. *He said to him, "Scripture has said, '...the best of his field,' and do you really want to maintain that the sense is, the calculation is based on the value of property in general?"*

C. *He objected,* "If the defendant possesses only property of the finest quality, then all plaintiffs are paid out of property of the finest quality; if he has only property of middling quality, then all plaintiffs are paid out of property of middling quality; if he has only property of the poorest quality, all of them are paid out of property of the poorest quality. If he had property of the finest, middling, and poorest quality, then damages are compensated out of property of the finest quality; debts are collected out of property of middling quality; and the collection of a marriage settlement for a wife is made out of property of the poorest quality. If he had only property of the finest and middling quality, then damages are compensated out of property of the finest quality, and debts and a woman's marriage settlement are collected out of property of middling quality. If he had only property of middling and of the poorest quality, then damages and debts are paid out of property of middling quality, and a woman's marriage settlement out of property of the poorest quality. [8A] If he had only property of the finest and the poorest quality, then compensation for damages is paid out of property of the finest quality, and debts and a woman's marriage contract are paid out of property of the poorest quality. *Now the intermediate clause of the passage in any event is explicit,* If he had only property of middling and of the poorest quality, then damages and debts are paid out of property of middling quality, and a woman's marriage settlement out of property of the poorest quality. *Now if matters were as you say, that* they make the estimate in terms of the property of the defendant, then why not treat the middling property of the defendant as property of the finest quality [since relative to what he owns, that is just what it is], and then assign the creditor to the class of property of the poorest quality?"

D. *Here with what sort of case do we deal?* It is one in which the defendant had owned property of the best quality, but he had sold it, and so said R. Hisda, "It is one in which the defendant had owned property of the best quality, but he had sold it." *And that stands to reason, for the further clause explicitly formulates the Tannaite rule in this language:* If he had only property of middling and of the poorest quality, then damages and debts are paid out of property of middling quality, and a woman's marriage settlement out of property of the poorest quality. *These would contradict one another, unless we draw the inference that* in the one case, the defendant had owned property of the best quality, but he had sold it, and in the other case, he did not have property of the highest quality, which he had sold. *Or, if you prefer, I shall explain, in both cases the man did not have property of the best quality that he had sold, but there still is no contradiction. The one speaks of a case in which this man's property of middling quality was equivalent in value to real estate of the highest quality in general, and the other speaks of a case in which the middling property of this man was not equivalent in value to real estate of the highest quality in general. And if you prefer, I shall explain that both rules refer to a situation in which the defendant's real estate of middling quality was equivalent in value to middling property in general, but subject to dispute is the following: One party maintains* that they assess the value in terms of his property, *and the other party maintains* that they estimate the value in terms of generally prevailing standards.

E. *Rabina said, "What is under dispute is what Ulla said, for* said Ulla, 'By the strict law of the Torah, a creditor should be paid out of land of the poorest quality, since it is said, "You shall stand outside, and the man to whom you lend shall bring forth the pledge outside to you" (Deut. 24:11). Now in general, people would bring outside the worst of his possessions. So how come the creditor for loans is paid out of land of middling quality? It is so as not to close the door in the face of borrowers.' *Now the one authority accepts this ordinance stated by Ulla, and the other does not accept it."*

Yet another activity of category formation asks about the comparative rights of diverse claimants to a piece of property; it is relevant because one is owed damages, and the rest follows. In some ways what follows is asymmetrical to the foregoing; but it is comfortably tied to it and fits very well.

VII.7 A. *Our rabbis have taught on Tannaite authority:*
       B. If someone [who was a debtor for damages, a loan, and a marriage settlement] sold all of his land to someone else, or all of it to three other persons simultaneously, all of them assume the status of the original owner of the field. If he sold land to them sequentially, all of the claimants come and collect from the last of the land to be sold. If that does not suffice, they collect from the land sold before that. If that does not suffice, they collect from the land sold before that."
       C. "If someone [who was a debtor for damages, a loan, and a marriage settlement] sold all of his land to someone else" – *how are we to imagine such a case? Should we say that all of the land was transferred at one moment [in a single deed]? But if he sold it to three persons, in which case one could maintain that one of them came prior to another, you have maintained that* all of them assume the status of the original owner of the field, *can there be any question at all of the rule that applies if he sold all the property to one person? So it is obvious that we deal with a case in which the sale of the lands was sequential. But then how are we*

going to differentiate [so that one purchaser is in a less secure legal position than another]?

D. It is because each one of them may say to him, "I left you a spot for collecting what is owing to you."

E. *Well, then, why can't the purchaser who bought the land all by himself but by deeds of different dates likewise assign the burden of payment to the property purchased last, saying, "When I acquired title to the earlier purchases, I was careful to leave you plenty of land to collect from"?*

F. Here with what sort of a situation do we deal? It is one in which he purchased land of the finest quality at the end of the purchased property, and so said R. Sheshet, "It is one in which he purchased land of the finest quality at the end of the purchased property."

G. *Well, if that's the case, then why can't all the creditors come and get paid out of land of the best quality [which is the land that was bought last in sequence]?*

H. Because the defendant may say to them, "If you shut up and collect what is coming to you by law, take it, but if not, I will assign the deed of the property of the worst quality to the original owner, so all of you will be paid out of that."

I. *If so, [8B] why not say the same in the matter of those who are owed compensation for damages? Rather, with what sort of a case do we deal here? It is one in which the seller of the land has died, and his heirs are not personally liable to pay [there being no real estate left in the inherited estate (Kirzner)], the original liability [assumed with the property when it was purchased] remains on the purchaser [Kirzner: for even by transferring the worst quality to the heirs, he would not escape any liability affecting him]. Now he could not say, "If you shut up and collect what is coming to you by law, take it, but if not, I will assign the deed of the property of the worst quality to the original owner, so all of you will be paid out of that." [Kirzner: The liability upon him will not thereby be affected, so why should they not resort to the best property that was purchased?]*

J. *Rather, the reason that the creditors cannot be paid out of land of the finest quality is that he may say to them, "What is the reason that the rabbis have ordained, 'Property that has been sold by a debtor cannot be attached if he still has other property subject to his own disposition'? It is for my sake. But here, I am not interested in taking advantage of this ordinance of the rabbis."*

K. *That is in line with what Raba said, for said Raba, "Whoever says, 'I am not interested in taking advantage of the ordinance of rabbis in such a case,' is listened to."*

L. *What is the sense of in such a case?*

M. *It is in line with what R. Huna said, for said R. Huna, "A woman has the power to say to her husband, 'I shall not accept maintenance from you, and I do not want you to benefit from the work that I do.'"*

From the present perspective, what follows is not required; we have finished the final touches on the foregoing composite. But from any other perspective but the one at hand, what follows is integral; that is why I do not indent it.

VII.8   A.   *It is obvious that* if the purchaser of a property [who has successively bought the estate of a debtor, with the last of the purchases being the property of the highest quality (Kirzner)] has sold over property of a middling and a poor quality but kept for himself property of the best quality, *then all of the classes of claimants may come and collect what is owing to them out of land of the finest quality, for that property was acquired by him at the end, and since he no longer possesses property of the medium and the poorest quality, he cannot say to the creditors, "Collect from the land of the medium or poorest quality, since I do not wish to take advantage of the rabbinic enactment."* But if he had sold off the land of the best quality and kept land of the medium and the worst quality, *what is the law?*

         B.   *Abbayye considered ruling, "Let all of them come and collect from the land of the highest quality"* [Kirzner: since nothing else of the same estate is with him to be offered to the creditors].

         C.   Said to him Raba, "Has not the first one sold to the second one [property with the stipulation] 'all rights connected therewith that may accrue to him'? *So just as when the creditors come to claim from the initial purchaser, he can pay them out of land of the medium or worst quality, without regard to the fact that when the medium and the worst quality lands were purchased by him, the original seller still had property of the highest quality, and in spite of the ordinance that* properties that have been sold off cannot be attached from a purchaser when the original debtor still has property that he has not disposed of. *The reason is that the purchaser has the right to say he does not wish to take advantage of the rabbinic ordinance, and so the next purchaser has the same right to say to the creditors, 'Take your payment out of real estate of the middling or poorest quality.' For the one who purchased from the purchaser had entered the sale only with the clear understanding that any right that the one from whom he buys the land may possess in the context of the purchase also is assigned to him."*

VII.9   A.   Said Raba, "In a case in which Reuben sold all of his fields to Simeon, and Simeon went and sold one field to Levi, and a creditor of Reuben came to collect what was owing to him, if he wanted, he may collect from this party, and if he wanted, he may collect from that party. *But we have stated that rule only if he has sold land of middling quality. But if he sold land of the highest and of the lowest quality, that is not the case. For Levi may say, 'I was careful to purchase land of the highest and of the lowest quality, which is to say, property that is not available for you to collect what is owing to you.' And we have stated that rule only in a case in which he did not leave himself land of middling quality of a similar kind, in which case he cannot plead,* 'I leave you a place for collecting from Simeon.' *But if Levi did leave with Simeon land of medium quality of a similar character, the creditor may not attach the land of Levi, since he may quite properly reply,* 'I left you plenty of land with Simeon for you to collect what is owing to you.'"

VII.10   A.   *Abayye said, "Reuben sold a field to Simeon with a guarantee [against seizure by Reuben's creditors], and a creditor of Reuben came and went and seized the field from [Simeon] – Reuben may go and sue the creditor, and the creditor cannot say to Reuben, 'I have no business to do with you.' For Reuben may say to the creditor, 'What you seized from Simeon comes back on me [since I shall have to refund the purchase money. I am concerned with the action against Simeon and can stop you from seizing his land because of my counterclaim].'"*

        B.   *Some say, "Even if the field is sold without a guarantee, for [Reuben] may say to him, 'I don't want Simeon to have a complaint against me.'"*

        C.   And said Abayye, "Reuben sold a field to Simeon without a guarantee [against seizure by Reuben's creditors], **[9A]** and claimants came forth, contesting Reuben's title to the field and right to sell the land – Simeon may retract on the sale prior to his taking possession of it, but once he has taken possession of the land, he has not got the right to retract on the sale. *How come? Reuben may say to Simeon [in declining to cancel the sale], 'You went and bought a bag that is sealed with knots. [You agreed to the sale without examining my title, and you have to live with it.] Now you've got it!'"*

        D.   *At what point is the act of taking possession complete? When the buyer has set foot on the landmarks.*

        E.   *That is the case only if the field had been sold without a guarantee. But if it was sold with a guarantee, that is not the case. But some say, "Even if the field had been sold with a guarantee also, [Simeon may not retract on the sale,] for Reuben may claim, 'Show me the document that legalizes the seizure of the field and then I shall pay you back the purchase price. [I don't have to refund your money until the court has given a decision on the legality of the seizure and given you a right to have your money returned (Daiches, Baba Mesia).]'"*

The exposition of the Mishnah is willy-nilly an exposition of the taxa that the Mishnah has defined. What follows therefore presents no surprises. Not only so, but we immediately see a further point of differentiation – ready cash as against real or movable property. That other grid has now to come into relationship with the existing ones.

VIII.1   A.   **[And when one [of them] has caused damage, the [owner] of that which causes the damage is liable to pay compensation for damage out of the best of his land:]** R. Huna said, "He may pay compensation either in ready cash or with the best of his landed estate."

        B.   *R. Nahman objected to R. Huna, "'He shall return' (Ex. 21:34) – this serves to encompass even what has monetary value, even bran."*

        C.   *Here with what case do we deal? It is one in which he has nothing else.*

        D.   *Well, if he has nothing else, it's obvious that he can pay any way he can!*

        E.   *Well, what might you otherwise have supposed? We might say to him, "Go and take the trouble and sell the bran and pay him off in ready cash"? So we are informed that that is not the case.*

VIII.2   A.   Said R. Assi, "As to ready cash, lo, it is in the same category as real estate."

B.   *For what legal purpose? If we say that it has to do with payment in terms of the best of his property, that is precisely what R. Huna has just told us. Rather, it is to deal with a case of the following character:* Two brothers divided an estate, and one of them took real estate, the other ready cash, and a creditor of the deceased came and collected what was owing from real estate. *The other then may go and collect half of the value of the debt he has paid in behalf of his father out of the ready cash that the brother has collected from the estate.*

C.   *So what else is new?! Is one a son and the other not a son?!*

D.   *There are those who say quite the opposite: The other brother may say to him, "But that is precisely why I took my share in ready cash; and if that money were stolen from me, I would not have been able to be compensated by you. And it was precisely for the same reason that you took land, even though, if the land were seized from you, you could not come and collect reparations from me."*

E.   *Rather, the pertinence of the statement is to the following case:* Two brothers divided an estate, and a creditor of the deceased father came and collected what was owing to him from one of them. [The other can pay him back in either ready cash or land.]

F.   *But lo, R. Assi already said this once, for it has been stated:* Two brothers divided an estate, and a creditor came and attached the share of one of them – Rab said, "The original division of the estate is null."

G.   And Samuel said, "He has waived his share."

H.   R. Assi said, "The portion is compensated either a quarter in land or a quarter in money."

I.   Rab said, "The original division of the estate is null": *He takes the view that brothers who have divided an estate remain co-heirs no matter what.*

J.   And Samuel said, "He has waived his share": *He takes the view that brothers who have divided an estate are in the status of purchasers, specifically, like purchasers who have made the deal without the right of claiming an indemnity in such a case as this.*

K.   R. Assi said, "The portion is compensated either a quarter in land or a quarter in money": *He takes the view that it is a matter of doubt whether brothers who have divided an estate remain co-heirs no matter what or whether brothers who have divided an estate are in the status of purchasers. That is why compensation is either a quarter in land or a quarter in money.*

L.   *So what can be the meaning of the statement,* "As to ready cash, lo, it is in the same category as real estate"? *This has to do with the matter of compensation out of the best of one's property.*

M.   *So isn't this the same thing that R. Huna said?*

N.   *Phrase matters as,* "And so did R. Assi say."

VIII.3   A.   Said R. Huna, "In a matter of a religious duty, one may go up a third."

B.   *What is the meaning of a third? [9B] One can hardly say, a third of one's entire household property, since, if it then happened that one had to perform three religious duties at pretty much the same time, it would mean giving up all of his possessions!*

      C.   Rather, said R. Zira, "This has to do with carrying out a religious duty in the best possible way, in which case, one goes up to a third more than the anticipated expense in carrying out the duty."

VIII.4   A.   *R. Ashi raised this question: "Is it a third calculated within the ordinary expense, or a third calculated from the aggregate [33 percent or 50 percent]?"*

      B.   *That question stands.*

VIII.5   A.   *In the West they said in the name of R. Zira,* "Up to a third comes out of the person's own resources. To do more than a third, it must come from what belongs to the Holy One, blessed be He."

What is important for the present purpose requires only a brief restatement. Nearly the entire long and sustained composite, which holds together remarkably well, is devoted to the task of showing the relationships between a number of distinct sets of categories, that is, one set, A, B, C, D, located in relationship to another, 1, 2, 3, 4, and yet a third, *, #, ß, and Ó. Even in that limited framework of three intersecting grids, we see how the 64 possible classifications are formulated in a single expansive grid, that is to say, that three-dimensional chess match to which I alluded in the preface.

Let me briefly review what we have seen. We open with a sizable exercise in explaining the language of our Mishnah paragraph, in line with the same usage in other Mishnah paragraphs, I.1-3. No. 4 then turns to the amplification of the Mishnah's statement by appeal to other Tannaite materials; we start with a complement that locates in Scripture the generative categories that are before us. This complement forms an integral part in the exposition of No. 3, and the entire composite goes from No. 3 through No. 20. That the whole is a continuous, beautifully crafted composite, shaped into a single coherent and unfolding statement, is beyond all doubt. II.1-4 gloss the Mishnah's word choices. This leads into a first-rate exercise in Mishnah criticism, dealing both with the formulation and the underlying logic. Then, in the continuing analysis of the problem introduced at II.1, we have other versions of the opening statement of the Mishnah tractate, those of Oshaia and Hiyya, Nos. 5-6, further expounded at Nos. 7-8. III.1, IV.1 go through the same process of Mishnah exegesis, explaining the implication of the Mishnah's formulation. No. 2 continues the foregoing. V.1-4 once more address the exegesis of the language of the Mishnah, asking a familiar question; each entry follows a single, well-crafted form. VI.1 adds a minor gloss to the Mishnah's language. VII.1 adds a Tannaite complement to the Mishnah's rule. Nos. 2-4 provide a talmud to the foregoing. Nos. 5, 6 address the same problem in a fresh way. Nos. 7, 8-11 carry forward the issues of No. 6. VIII.1, 2+3-5 implicitly treat the same matter.

Our Mishnah paragraph will now set forth two grids. The first has to do with my responsibility for damages. If I am liable for damages done by my property, I am liable to make compensation in various ways and through various media of payment. The second has to do with the location in which the damages have taken place, for example, property that belongs to Heaven, to an Israelite, and to gentiles; property that is not owned at all; and so on. The Mishnah paragraph itself demands that these two grids be formed into an interstitial construct. No wonder, then, that the Bavli's framers pursue the question in ever more complex and subtle ways, making distinction after distinction, or, in my language, imposing grid upon grid.

1:2

A. In the case of anything of which I am liable to take care, I am deemed to render possible whatever damage it may do.

B. [If] I am deemed to have rendered possible part of the damage it may do,

C. I am liable for compensation as if [I have] made possible all of the damage it may do.

D. (1) Property which is not subject to the law of sacrilege, (2) property belonging to members of the covenant [Israelites], (3) property that is held in ownership,

E. and that is located in any place other than in the domain which is in the ownership of the one who has caused the damage,

F. or in the domain which is shared by the one who suffers injury and the one who causes injury –

G. when one has caused damage [under any of the aforelisted circumstances],

H. [the owner of] that one which has caused the damage is liable to pay compensation for damage out of the best of his land.

I.1   A. Our rabbis have taught on Tannaite authority:

B. In the case of anything of which I am liable to take care, I am deemed to render possible whatever damage it may do.

C. How so?

My first distinction is between a person assumed to bear responsibility and one not, to whom I assign my responsibilities. Immediately I am required to introduce distinctions already established, for example, my several generative categories of damages. Now what that means is simple. The fact that M. 1:1 has introduced those categories defines for the Bavli exegete what he wishes to know at M. 1:2, which is how the categories of M. 1:1 intersect with those of M. 1:2, or, once more, the mixing of grids.

D. In the case of an ox or a pit that one has handed over to a deaf-mute, an insane person, or a minor, which did damage, one is liable to pay compensation, which is not the case with fire.

E. With what sort of case do we deal? If it is the case of an ox that was chained or a pit that was covered up, corresponding to the case of fire in a hot coal, then what distinguishes the one from the other? So we must be dealing with a case of an ox that was not tied up and a pit that was not covered up. But, then, this is comparable to the case of a a flaming fire. Then the language, which is not the case with fire, would mean that one is not liable to pay compensation. But lo, said R. Simeon b. Laqish in the name of Hezekiah, "They have declared one is exempt from having to pay compensation only if he handed over to a deaf-mute, insane person, or minor, a coal, which the guard has then blown upon [making it a flame, which then kindled other things]. But if he handed over what was an already glowing flame, there is full liability, since the danger was clear and present."

F. In point of fact, we deal with an ox that was tied up or a pit that was covered up. And as to the statement, "Corresponding to the case of fire in a hot coal, then what distinguishes the one from the other?" here is the answer: It would be quite usual for an ox to loosen itself, and for a pit to get uncovered, but as to a hot coal, the longer you leave it alone, the cooler it gets.

G. And from the perspective of R. Yohanan, who has said, "Even when a flaming fire has been handed over to him, one is still exempt, here, too, the ox could have been untied and the pit uncovered, so why should we differentiate the one from the other?"

H. In the case of the fire, it is how the deaf-mute handles the fire that makes damage, while in the case of the ox and the pit, nothing that the deaf-mute does is going to cause the damage.

As if the foregoing did not make my point with power, what follows shows again how skilled are our exegetes of the law (whether framers of Tannaite statements or analysts thereof) in bringing together a variety of differentiated categories. Now we deal with the comparison of generative categories, on the one side, of ox and pit, with the comparison of types of compensation, on the other side.

I.2 A. Our rabbis have taught on Tannaite authority:
B. A more stringent rule pertains to the ox than to the pit, and a more stringent rule pertains to the pit than to the ox.
C. A more stringent rule pertains to the ox than to the pit, in that on account of an ox's killing a man, the owner has to pay a ransom and is liable to paying thirty sheqels if the ox kills a slave. When the case against the ox has been completed, the ox may no longer be used in any beneficial manner. It is routine for the ox to move about and cause damage. None of this pertains to the pit.
D. And a more stringent rule pertains to the pit than to the ox, in that to begin with, the pit is made to do damage; it is to begin with an attested danger, which is not the case with an ox.
E. [10A] A more stringent rule pertains to the ox than to fire, and a more stringent rule pertains to fire than to the ox.
F. A more stringent rule pertains to the ox than to fire, in that on account of an ox's killing a man, the owner has to pay a ransom and is liable to paying thirty sheqels if the ox kills a slave. When the case against the ox has been completed, the ox may no longer be

used in any beneficial manner. If one handed it over to a deaf-mute, an insane person, or a minor, one is liable, which is not the case for fire.

G. And a more stringent rule pertains to fire than to the ox, in that fire is an attested danger to begin with, which is not the case for the ox.

H. A more stringent rule applies to fire than to the pit, and a more stringent rule applies to the pit than to fire.

I. A more stringent rule applies to the pit than to fire, for to begin with it is made to cause damage. If one handed it over to the guardianship of a deaf-mute, insane person, or minor, he is liable for the damage that may be caused, which is not the case with fire.

J. A more stringent rule applies to fire than to the pit, for it is the way of fire to go along and do damage, and it is an attested danger to consume both what is suitable for it and what is not suitable for it, which is not the case with a pit.

I.3 A. *Why not include in the Tannaite formulation:* A more strict rule applies to the ox than to the pit, for the owner of the ox is liable for damage done to utensils [inanimate objects], which is not the case with the pit?

B. *Lo, who is the authority behind this anonymous rule? It is R. Judah, who declares the owner liable for damages done to utensils in the case of a pit.*

C. *If you really think it is R. Judah, then let me cite the concluding statement to you:* A more stringent rule applies to fire than to the pit, for it is the way of fire to go along and do damage, and it is an attested danger to consume both what is suitable for it and what is not suitable for it, which is not the case with a pit! *Now what might fall into the classification of* what is suitable for it? Wood. *And what might fall into the classification of* what is not suitable for it? Utensils – which is not the case with a pit! *Now if this really is R. Judah, lo, you have maintained that* R. Judah holds one responsible for the pit's damages to utensils. *So in hand must be the position of rabbis, and the Tannaite framer of the passage set matters forth but omitted reference to some items.*

D. *Well, then, what else has he left out, if he has left out this item?*

E. He omitted reference to one's liability to pay for damages done by one's fire to goods that are hidden.

F. *If you prefer, I shall say that in point of fact the passage does set forth the view of R. Judah, and what might fall into the classification of* what is not suitable for it? *It is not to encompass under the rule utensils, but rather, to encompass a case in which* the fire did damage by lapping at the neighbor's ploughed furrow and grazing the stones.

G. *Objected R. Ashi, "Well then why not formulate the Tannaite statement in this way:* A more strict rule applies to the ox than to the pit, for in the case of an ox the owner is liable for damage done to consecrated animals that were not fit for the altar, and that is not the case for the pit? *Now if you maintain that before us is the position of rabbis, there is no problem, for having omitted one possible entry, they will also have omitted this other. But if you maintain that before us is the position of R. Judah, then what else has he left out, along with the item at hand?"*

H. He has left out the case of one's ox's trampling newly broken land [which a pit cannot do].

I. *If you maintain that the further omission is the case of one's ox's trampling newly broken land, that is not a good example of an omission, for this is covered when the framer says in so many words, for it is the way of fire to go along and do damage!*

II.1 A. **[If] I am deemed to have rendered possible part of the damage it may do, I am liable for compensation as if [I have] made possible all of the damage it may do:**

B. *Our rabbis have taught on Tannaite authority:*

Here comes a new grid: how deep the pit, on the one side, the differentiation of responsibility, on the other. Specifically, what if I have not done all the damage; what if my act on its own would have caused none, but joined to someone else's, causes damage? That is, once more, a distinction that raises a set of questions the initial statement hardly demands, opening new paths of inquiry altogether: the mixed grid of whole versus partial responsibility; direct versus only proximate responsibility, and the like, or, in terms Greco-Roman philosophy developed, the issue of causation.

C. **[If] I am deemed to have rendered possible part of the damage it may do, I am liable for compensation as if [I have] made possible all of the damage it may do:** How so?

D. He who digs a pit nine cubits deep, and someone else comes along and finishes it to ten – the latter is liable [having completed the pit so that it can kill someone].

E. *That does not accord with the position of Rabbi, for it has been taught on Tannaite authority:* He who digs a pit nine cubits deep, and someone else comes along and finishes it to ten – the latter is liable.

F. Rabbi says, "We go after the latter in the case of death, but after both of them in the case of damages."

G. R. Pappa said, "The passage before us refers to death and represents the view of all parties."

H. *There are those who set matters forth as follows: May one say that this does not accord with the position of Rabbi?*

I. Said R. Pappa, "The passage before us refers to death and represents the view of all parties."

J. *Objected R. Zira, "Well, aren't there any other examples? Lo, there is the case of* one's handing over one's ox to five persons, one of whom was careless, so that the ox did damage – that one bears the liability. *Now how can we imagine such a case? If it is a case in which, were it not for that one man, the ox would not have been cared for at all, then it's self-evident that that is the one who is responsible for damages! So it is a case in which, even without that one, the ox would have been subject to control. But, then, what has that man done to warrant having to pay damages all by himself?"*

K. *Objected R. Sheshet, "Lo, there is the case of someone who adds twigs to a fire."*

L. **[10B]** *Well, what sort of a case can be in mind? If it were a case in which, without him, the fire would not have spread, then obviously he is entirely* culpable. *If without his cooperation the fire would have spread, then what has he done anyhow to deserve culpability?*

M.   *Objected R. Pappa,* "Lo, there is that which has been taught on Tannaite authority: If there were five people sitting on a bench and they did not break it, but someone else came along and sat down on it with them and they broke it, only the last person is liable – *assuming he was as fat as Pappa bar Abba. Now what sort of case can be in mind? If we should say that if without him the bench would not have broken, then that statement is obvious. So it has to be a case in which without that man the bench would have broken anyhow. So what did he do to warrant being held liable?"*

N.   *One way or the other, how in the world can this Tannaite formulation be worked out?*

O.   *It is necessary to cover a case in which, without the newcomer, the bench would have broken after a couple of hours, while now it broke after only one. So the other five sitting on the bench may say to him, "If it weren't for you, we could have sat a bit more on the bench and then gotten up."*

P.   *So why can't he say to him, "If it weren't for you, the bench would never have broken on my account at all"?*

Q.   *The rule is necessary to cover a case in which he never actually sat down on the bench but only leaned on the people sitting there, and the bench broke.*

R.   *So obviously he's liable! What else is new?*

S.   *Well, you might have supposed that the damage done by someone's secondary effects is not the same as that done by the person himself. So we are informed that one is responsible for what happens through secondary effects as much as for what he himself does, for whenever one personally causes damage, his secondary effects are involved.*

II.2   A.   *Are there no other examples? Lo, there is that which has been taught on Tannaite authority:* If ten people hit someone with ten sticks, whether simultaneously or sequentially, and the man died, all of them are exempt. R. Judah b. Betera says, "If they did it sequentially, then the last one is liable, since he [Kirzner:] was the immediate cause of the death."

B.   *We're not dealing here with murder cases.*

C.   *Or, if you prefer, we're not dealing with laws that are subject to dispute.*

D.   *Oh we're not, aren't we? Then didn't we just establish the fact that the passage does not accord with Rabbi?*

E.   *As a matter of fact, while we are prepared to establish that the Mishnah paragraph is not in accord with Rabbi but is in accord with rabbis, we are not prepared to establish that it is in accord with R. Judah b. Betera and not in accord with rabbis [since we prefer to assign the Mishnah's rules to the majority of sages' opinion].*

III.1   A.   I am liable for compensation as if [I have] made possible all of the damage it may do:

B.   *The language that is used is not,* I am liable for making up the damage, *but,* I am liable for compensation. *That has been set forth as a Tannaite rule, for our rabbis have taught on Tannaite authority:* I am liable for compensation – this teaches that the owner has to take care of the disposition of the carcass [receiving the proceeds as part payment] [T. B.Q. 1:1E-F].

C. *What is the scriptural basis for this ruling?*
D. Said R. Ammi, "Said Scripture, 'He who kills a beast shall make it good' (Lev. 24:18) – the letters of the word 'shall make it good' can be read 'he shall complete its deficiency.'"
E. R. Kahana said, "From here: 'If it be torn in pieces, let him bring compensation up to the value of the carcass; he shall not make good that which was torn' (Ex. 22:12) – 'up to' the value of the carcass he pays, but for the carcass itself he does not have to pay."
F. Hezekiah said, "From here: 'And the dead shall be his own' (Ex. 21:36) – referring to the owner of the beast."
G. And so the Tannaite authority of the household of Hezekiah: "'And the dead shall be his own' (Ex. 21:36) – referring to the owner of the beast. You say that it is to the injured party, but perhaps it refers to the party responsible for the injury? You may state, 'That is not the case.'"
H. *What is the meaning of* "that is not the case"?
I. *Said Abbayye, "If it should enter your mind that the carcass is going to belong to the party responsible for the injury, then why didn't the All-Merciful stop when it had finished saying, 'He shall surely pay ox for ox' (Ex. 21:36)? What is the point of adding, 'And the dead shall be his own' (Ex. 21:36)? This shows that the Scripture speaks [when it says, his own], of the injured party."*

We appeal to the grid of distinctions before us to account for the requirement of a variety of proofs of propositions; one proof could not serve all propositions, for the reasons now given. This is beyond any reasonable doubt an exercise deriving solely from the prior interest in differentiation of sets of data, then multiple grounds for differentiation of those same sets of data.

III.2　A. *And the various verses of Scripture that have been cited all are necessary. For had Scripture stated only,* "He who kills a beast shall make it good" (Lev. 24:18), *I might have supposed that the reason for the ruling was that it is an unusual event [for someone to kill a beast intending to cause his neighbor harm], but if an animal was torn to pieces by a wild beast, which is pretty common, I might have taken the opposite view* [Kirzner: in the interest of the plaintiff].
　　B. *And if Scripture had made reference only to that which is torn* ["If it be torn in pieces, let him bring compensation up to the value of the carcass; he shall not make good that which was torn" (Ex. 22:12)], *I might have supposed that the operative consideration is that the damage was done not by the bailee but by an indirect cause, but if a man killed the beast, where the damage was done by a direct agency, I might have taken the opposite view.*
　　C. *And if Scripture had made reference to both of these cases, I might have supposed that the one is special because it is infrequent, and the other is exceptional because it deals with indirect agency. But the damage to which the language,* "And the dead shall be his own" (Ex. 21:36), *refers, being both frequent and the result of direct action, would be subject to an opposite rule.*

D. *And if Scripture had given us only, "And the dead shall be his own"* (Ex. 21:36), *I might have appealed to the explanation that the damage has been done only by the man's own possession, while if the damage was done by the man's own person [as is the case at Lev. 24:18 and Ex. 22:12], I might have supposed otherwise. So all of the verses of Scripture are required.*

III.3　　A. *Said R. Kahana to Rab[a], "So the operative consideration is that Scripture has said, 'And the dead shall be his own' (Ex. 21:36). Lo, if it were not for that statement, I would have thought that the carcass should belong to the party responsible for the damage. Then it must follow that, if there were in the hands of the person responsible for the damage a number of such carcasses, he has the right to pay the injured party with them, for the master has said, '"He shall return"* (Ex. 21:34) – even payment in kind, even bran,' *so what question can there be about doing so with the carcass of his own animal!"*

B. *The verse is required to cover a case in which the carcass has decreased in value [and the injured party is going to suffer that loss, since from the moment the beast was gored, the carcass is assigned to him].*

III.4　　A. *May we say that at issue between the following Tannaite authorities is the question of the decrease in the value of the carcass? For it has been taught on Tannaite authority:* "If it be torn in pieces, let him bring it for testimony" (Ex. 22:12) – [11A] "let him bring it for testimony" *that it was torn by accident and so exempt himself from having to pay damages. Abba Saul says,* "Let him bring the torn animal to court." *Is this not what is at issue, namely, one authority takes the view that the decreased value of the carcass is assigned to the injured party, and the other party maintains that it is assigned to the party responsible for the injury?*

B. *Not at all. All parties take the position that it is assigned to the injured party, but what is at issue here is the responsibility for bringing up the carcass from the pit, in line with that which has been taught on Tannaite authority:* Others say, "How on the basis of Scripture do we know that the owner of the pit is responsible to raise up the ox from his pit? Scripture says, 'Money shall he return to the owner, and the dead beast...' (Ex. 21:34) [that is, he shall return both money and the dead beast, which he is then responsible to recover]."

C. *Said Abbayye to Raba, "So as to the trouble of dealing with the carcass, what are we talking about? If the value of the carcass in the pit is a zuz, and if it is on the bank of the pit it is worth four zuz, then is he not taking the trouble of bringing up the carcass only in his own interest anyhow?"*

D. *He said to him, "The rule is required to cover a case in which when in the pit the carcass is worth a zuz, and on the banks it is also worth a zuz."*

E. *Is such a case possible?*

F. *It certainly is, for people say, "A beam in town is worth a zuz, and a beam in the field is worth a zuz."*

III.5　　A. Said Samuel, "They do not make an estimate in the case of a thief or a robber [the guilty party having to pay in full for the original value of the damaged article (Kirzner)] but they do so for compensation for damages [the carcass going back to the injured party]. And I say that the same is the case for borrowing, and Abba [Rab] agrees with me."

B. *The question was raised: "Is this the sense of what he said, 'So, too, in the* case of borrowing, they make an estimate, and Abba agrees with me'? *Or perhaps this is the sense of what he said: 'And I say, even in* the case of a borrower they do not make an estimate, and Abba agrees with me'?"

C. *Come and take note: There was the case of someone who borrowed an axe* from his neighbor and broke it. *The case came before Rab. He said to him,* "Go pay him for the originally sound axe." *Does this not show that the* law of assessment does not apply to borrowing [since the responsible party *does not get to deduct the value of the sherds of the ax]?*

D. *To the contrary, since R. Kahana and R. Assi said to Rab, "Is this the* rule?" *and Rab shut up, it must follow that they did in fact make an* assessment [of the remnants of the axe, and they deducted their value from *the compensation to be paid].*

III.6 A. *It has been stated:*

B. Said Ulla said R. Eleazar, "They make an estimate [of the value of the remnant of a stolen object] in the case of a thief or a robber [who then pays compensation for the rest of the loss, deducting the value of the remnant of the stolen object, which the original owner gets back as part of his compensation]."

C. R. Pappa said, "They do not make such an estimate."

D. And the decided law is that they do not make such an estimate in the case of a thief or a robber, but in the case of a borrower they do make such an estimate, in accord with the position of R. Kahana and R. Assi.

III.7 A. And said Ulla said R. Eleazar, "In a case in which the placenta emerges partly on one day, partly on the next, they count the days of uncleanness [decreed at Lev. 12:1ff.] from the first day."

B. *Said to him, "Now what are you thinking? That this yields a* stringent ruling? *Well, it's a stringent ruling that yields a lenient* one, because you have not only declared her unclean as of the first *day, but you have declared her clean also as of the first day."*

C. *Rather, said Raba, "We take account of the possibility that the first* day [is unclean], but the actual counting begins on the second day."

D. *What's your point? That there is no placenta that does not contain* part of the foetus? *That we have already learned as a Tannaite* statement: **An afterbirth, part of which emerged, is prohibited to be eaten. It is a token of [the birth of] an offspring in a woman, and the token of [the birth of] an offspring in a beast [M. Hul. 4:7E-F].**

E. *Had I had to derive the rule only from the Mishnah paragraph, I* might have supposed [11B] *that it is entirely conceivable that there* can be a placenta that does not contain part of the foetus, but that sages made a decree concerning a case in which part of the placenta came forth because of the case in which the whole of it came forth. So we are informed that that consideration is not in play.

III.8 A. And said Ulla said R. Eleazar, "A firstborn that perished within the first thirty days of birth – they do not redeem him."

B. And so taught Rammi bar Hama as a Tannaite statement: "'You shall surely redeem' (Num. 18:15) – might one think that

is the case even if he perished within the first thirty days of
birth? Scripture says, '...but...,' as exclusionary language."

What follows shows how questions are provoked by distinctions and
the relationship between or among what is distinguished. No. 8 raises
the distinction between big and small beasts, on the one side, and modes
of acquisition, on the other. No. 9 distinguishes between heirs of an
estate and their clothing, on the one side, and their heirs and their
clothing, on the other. No. 10 asks about the distinction between a paid
and an unpaid bailee. How these several compositions fit into the larger
talmud before us is not an issue; what is important for my argument is
only that each distinction is shown to make a difference, all differences
shown to yield new distinctions, and it is through that ongoing,
dialectical process that the analytical program holding the whole
together unfolds. I wonder whether Greco-Roman philosophical writing
yields a counterpart of sustained, practical reason and applied logic.

III.9   A.   And said Ulla said R. Eleazar, "A large beast is acquired through
             the act of drawing."
        B.   *But we have learned in the Mishnah that that is through an act of delivery!*
        C.   He made that statement in accord with the position of the Tannaite
             authority of the following: And sages say, "This and that [large,
             small beasts alike] are acquired through drawing." R. Simeon says,
             "This and that are acquired through lifting up the beast."

III.10 A.   And said Ulla said R. Eleazar, "Brothers who divide an estate
             among themselves – whatever they are wearing is assessed in the
             value of the estate, but what is worn by their sons and daughters is
             not assessed as part of the estate."
        B.   Said R. Pappa, "Sometimes even what they are wearing is not
             assessed in the value of the estate. *You would find such a case in the
             instance of the eldest of the sons, [who is spared this degrading procedure,]
             since the rest of them would concur that what he says should be treated
             with respect.*"

III.11 A.   And said Ulla said R. Eleazar, "A bailee who handed over the
             bailment to another bailee is exempt from further liability. *Now that
             is beyond question when it comes to the case of an unpaid bailee who
             handed over his bailment to a paid bailee, for in that case, the quality of the
             guardianship of the bailment is improved. But even if a paid bailee hands
             over the bailment to an unpaid one, where the quality of guardianship
             diminishes, he is still not liable, for he has transferred the bailment in any
             event to a responsible party.*"
        B.   Raba said, "A bailee who entrusted [the bailment] to another bailee
             is liable. *There is no issue in respect to a paid bailee who handed the
             bailment over to an unpaid bailee, in which case he has diminished the
             standard of care of the bailment. But even in the case of an unpaid bailee
             who handed the beast over to a paid bailee, in which case he has improved
             the conditions of the bailment, he remains liable. What is the reason? He
             may say to him, 'You are credible to me when you take an oath, but the
             other party is not credible to me when he takes an oath.'*"

One of the category formations that a legal system for a slave-holding society generates is the distinction between realty and personalty, that is, what we would call real estate and property for which we have no name at all, namely, human beings. Here, as we see as No. 11 shades into No. 12, the relationship between the categories of wealth, real and personal, leads to a set of comparisons and contrasts.

III.12   A.   And said Ulla said R. Eleazar, "The decided law is that to collect a debt the creditor may attach the slaves of the debtor."

B.   *Said R. Nahman to Ulla, "Did R. Eleazar make this statement even with reference to attaching the slaves of an estate?"*

C.   *"No, only from him."*

D.   *"Well if it was only with reference to him, then one can collect a debt even by seizing the cloak on his back! [So why bother to make such a statement anyhow?]"*

E.   *"Here with what case do we deal? It is one in which the slave was mortgaged for the debt, in line with what Raba said. For* said Raba, 'If one mortgaged one's slave and then sold him, the creditor can collect by attaching the slave. If he mortgaged his ox and sold it, the creditor cannot collect from it. *What's the difference? In the one case, the matter is publicly known, but in the other, the matter is not going to be publicly known [so the creditor has no way of knowing what has happened].*"

F.   [12A] *After [Nahman] left, Ulla said to them, "This is what R. Eleazar said, '...even with reference to attaching the slaves of an estate.'"*

G.   *[Hearing about this reversion,] said R. Nahman, "Ulla spoke disingenuously."*

H.   *There was a case in Nehardea, and the judges of Nehardea attached the slaves in the hands of the heirs to pay a debt of the deceased.*

I.   *There was a case in Pumbedita and R. Hana bar Bizna attached the slaves in the hands of the heirs to pay a debt of the deceased.*

J.   *Said to them R. Nahman, "Go, retract your rulings, and if not, then we are going to attach your houses [to compensate the parties whom your incorrect rulings have damaged]."*

K.   *Said Raba to R. Nahman, "And lo, there is Ulla, there is R. Eleazar, there are the judges of Nehardea, there is R. Hana bar Bizna. So what authorities do you claim to evoke in support of your position?"*

L.   *He said to him, "Well, as a matter of fact, we know a Tannaite formulation, for Abimi stated as a Tannaite formulation: 'A prosbol [nullifying the remission of debts in the Sabbatical Year] applies to real estate but it does not apply to slaves. Movables are acquired along with real estate but are not acquired along with slaves.' [So slaves are in a different category from real estate, just as I have said.]"*

III.13   A.   *May we say that the same issue is what is under debate in the following Tannaite dispute: If one party sold to another slaves and real estate, if the purchaser has acquired possession of the slaves, he has not acquired possession of the real estate. If he acquired possession of the real estate, he has not acquired possession of the slaves. If the sale involved real estate and movables, if he acquired possession of* the real estate, he has acquired possession of the movables. If he has acquired possession of the movables, he has not acquired possession of the real estate. If the sale involved slaves and movables, if he acquired possession of the slaves, he has not acquired possession of the movables. If he acquired possession of the movables, he has acquired possession of the slaves. *And lo, it has been taught on Tannaite authority: If he has acquired possession of the slaves, he also has acquired possession of the movables. Now is this not what is at issue between the two formulations of the rule, namely, one authority takes the view that slaves are in the classification of real estate, and the other authority maintains that slaves are in the classification of movables?*

B. Said R. Iqa b. R. Ammi, *"All parties concur that slaves are in the classification of real estate. When the latter formulation tells us that, if he has acquired possession of the slaves, he also has acquired possession of the movables, that poses no problem. But when the other, prior formulation states that there has been no valid act of acquisition, that is because the kind of real estate that we require is what bears the same indicative traits as the walled cities of Judah, which are utterly immovable. For we have learned in the Mishnah:* **Property for which there is security is acquired through money, writ, and usucaption. And that for which there is no security is acquired only by an act of drawing [from one place to another]. Property for which there is no security is acquired along with property for which there is security through money, writ, and usucaption. And property for which there is no security imposes the need for an oath on property for which there is security [M. Qid. 1:5]."**

C. *What is the scriptural basis for this ruling?*

D. Said Hezekiah, "Said Scripture, 'And their father gave them great gifts of silver and of gold and of precious things with fortified cities in Judah' (2 Chr. 21:3)."

E. *There are those who say, said R. Iqa b. R. Ammi, "All parties concur that slaves are in the classification of movables. When the latter formulation tells us that, if he has not acquired possession, that poses no problem. But when the other, prior formulation states that there has been a valid act of acquisition, that is because the movables that were acquired were actually worn by the slave."*

F. *But even if they were actually worn by him, what difference does that make? What he is is just a walking courtyard, and a walking courtyard does not effect ownership [of its contents for the person who acquires it]. And if you say that the rule refers to a case in which he is standing still, lo, said Raba, "In any case in which, if something were in motion, it would not effect transfer of ownership, if the same thing is standing still or sitting down, it also does not effect transfer of ownership."*

G. *The law refers to a case in which the slave was in stocks.*

H. *But has it not been taught in the cited Tannaite formulation: If one acquired ownership of the land, he has acquired ownership of the slaves?*

I. *That speaks of a case in which the slaves were standing within the limits of the real estate.*

J.   Is there then the inference that the reason that acquisition has not been effected is a case in which the slaves were not standing within the limits of the real estate that was acquired? Then that poses no problem to this formulation of the view of R. Iqa b. R. Ammi that slaves are classified as movables. That explains why, if they are standing in the property, the transfer is effected for them as well as for the real estate, but if not, then it is not effected. But in line with the formulation, "Slaves are classified as real estate," what difference does it make to me whether they were standing in the real estate when it was acquired, or whether they were not there? Lo, said Samuel, "If one has sold to someone ten fields in two states, once one has made acquisition of one of them, he has acquired them all"!

K.   Well, in accord with your version of matters, namely, "Slaves are classified as real estate," then what difference does it make to me whether the slaves were standing within the property or not?! [12B] Lo, we have as established fact that we do not require the slaves to be gathered on the land anyhow. So what is there to be said? It is only that there is a distinction to be drawn between movables that are in fact in motion and movables that in fact cannot be moved about. And here, too, we maintain that there is a distinction to be drawn between immovables that are in fact in motion and immovables that in fact cannot be moved about. Specifically, slaves are now conceived to be in the classification of real estate that is movable, while the ten fields, the land is conceived to be one integrated plot.

We revert to the Mishnah paragraph's own taxic structure, explained above; we proceed to expound another component of it and how that square of the grid relates to other squares of the same grid; only then do we turn to the superimposition of another grid altogether.

IV.1   A.   **Property which is not subject to the law of sacrilege:**
        B.   It is specifically property that is not at that moment subject to the law of sacrilege that is excluded from the rule at hand, lo, if it is property that has been consecrated [but is not yet subject to the law of sacrilege] is not exempt from the rule at hand. So who is the Tannaite authority behind that position?
        C.   Said R. Yohanan, "In the case of Lesser Holy Things, it is the view of R. Yosé the Galilean, who has said that they are classified as the property of the owner. For so it has been taught on Tannaite authority: '"If a soul sin and commit an act of sacrilege against the Lord and lie to his neighbor" (Lev. 5:21) – this extends the law to Lesser Holy Things, which are classified as the property of the neighbor,' the words of R. Yosé the Galilean." [Kirzner: For example, peace-offerings belong partly to the Lord and partly to the neighbor, parts burnt on the altar, parts consumed.]
        D.   But lo, we have learned in the Mishnah: **He [who was a priest] who betroths a woman with his share [of the priestly gifts], whether they were Most Holy Things or Lesser Holy Things – she is not betrothed [M. Qid. 2:8A-B].** Now do we have to say that that rule does not accord with the position of R. Yosé the Galilean?
        E.   Well, you may even maintain that that does accord with the position of R. Yosé the Galilean. When R. Yosé the Galilean made his ruling, it

*concerned animals that had been consecrated but were still alive, but in the
cases of Holy Things that had been slaughtered, even R. Yosé the Galilean
concurs that when those who have a right to eat the flesh acquire that
right, it is from the table of the Most High that they have acquired that
right.*

F.   *Well, then, when the beast is alive, does he actually take the view that the
consecrated beast in the case of Lesser Holy Things is private property?
Lo, we have learned in the Mishnah:* [As to] the firstling [the first
calves of the year's herd]: (1) They [the priests] sell it [when the
animal is] unblemished [and] alive; (2) and [when the animal is]
blemished, [whether it is] alive or slaughtered. (3) And they give
it as a token of betrothal to women. They do not deconsecrate
[produce in the status of] second tithe with (1) a poorly minted
coin nor with (2) coin that is not [currently] circulating, nor with
(3) money that is not in one's possession [M. M.S. 1:2]. *And said
R. Nahman said Rabbah bar Abbuha, "This rule pertains only to a
firstling at this time* [after the destruction of the Temple], *for, since it
is not suitable to be offered up, the priests have a right of ownership in it;
but in the time that the sanctuary was standing, when the beast was
suitable for an offering, that was not the case"* [Kirzner: the priests
would not have had in it a proprietary right nor have been able to
use it for the betrothal of a woman]. *And objected Raba to R. Nahman,
""'If a soul sin and commit an act of sacrilege against the Lord and
lie to his neighbor"* (Lev. 5:21) – this extends the law to Lesser Holy
Things, which are classified as the property of the neighbor,' the
words of R. Yosé the Galilean." *And Rabina replied, "[They are
considered private property] only in the case of a firstling born outside of
the Land, along the lines of the position of R. Simeon, who has said, 'If
firstlings were brought, unblemished, from abroad, they may be
offered up.'"* So *that is the case only if they actually had been brought to
the country, but if they were not brought there, there was no requirement
to bring them there to begin with for that purpose* [so they are merely the
private property of the priests]. *Now if it really is the position of R. Yosé
the Galilean that they are private property when they are alive,* [13A] *then
why did Rabina not simply say, "This represents the position of R. Yosé
the Galilean, the other, the position of rabbis"?* [Yosé would then
maintain that the firstling is the private property of the priests;
Nahman's statement that a firstling is not private property
represents the position of his opposition (Kirzner).]

G.   *Do you make reference to the priestly gifts? The priestly gifts are
exceptional* [even Yosé regards them in no way as the private
property of the priest, and all rabbis concur on the same point,
which is why Rabina could not appeal to the distinction between
Yosé's and rabbis' opinions on the matter (Kirzner)], *for, when people
gain their entitlement to them, it is from the table of the Most High that
they gain that entitlement* [Kirzner: even while the firstling is still
alive].

Here come footnotes to the foregoing, not indented for reasons
already given.

IV.2 A. *Reverting to the body of the prior composition:*
B. *"'If a soul sin and* commit an act of sacrilege against the Lord and lie to his neighbor' (Lev. 5:21) – this extends the law to Lesser Holy Things, which are classified as the property of the neighbor," the words of R. Yosé the Galilean.
C. Ben Azzai says, "That phrase serves to encompass peace-offerings."
D. Abba Yosé b. Dosetai says, "Ben Azzai made that statement solely with reference to a firstling."

IV.3 A. The master has said, "Ben Azzai says, 'That phrase serves to encompass peace-offerings'":
B. *What is this meant to eliminate? If we say it is meant to eliminate the firstling [from the classification of property that is subject to compensation for damages], now if peace-offerings, on which the owner has to lay hands, which have to be accompanied by libations, and the breast and thigh of which have to be waved, are classified as private property, is there any question that the firstling will be classified as private property [since these rites do not pertain to him]?*
C. *Rather, said R. Yohanan, "It is meant to eliminate tithe [of cattle, which is not private property,] in line with that which has been taught on Tannaite authority: 'With respect to a firstling, Scripture states, "You shall not redeem" (Num. 18:17), bearing the implication that it may be sold* [if the animal is blemished, the owner may sell it as a firstling to a priest, since Scripture only forbids redeeming it but not selling it (Miller, *Temurah*)]. *Scripture states with respect to an animal that has been designated as tithe, "You shall not redeem" (Lev. 27:28), that means, it may not be sold alive or dead, unblemished or blemished."'*
D. *Rabina repeats the foregoing with respect to the concluding clause of the cited passage:* "Abba Yosé b. Dosetai says, 'Ben Azzai made that statement solely with reference to a firstling.'" *What is this meant to eliminate? If we say it is meant to eliminate the peace-offerings [from the classification of property that is subject to compensation for damages], now if the firstling, which is sanctified from the womb, is deemed to be the property of the owner, then can there be any question about peace-offerings?*
E. *Rather, said R. Yohanan, "It is meant to eliminate tithe [of cattle, which is not private property,] in line with that which has been taught on Tannaite authority: 'With respect to a firstling, Scripture states, "You shall not redeem" (Num. 18:17), bearing the implication that it may be sold* [if the animal is blemished, the owner may sell it as a firstling to a priest, since Scripture only forbids redeeming it but not selling it (Miller, *Temurah*)]. *Scripture states with respect to an animal that has been designated as tithe, "You shall not redeem" (Lev. 27:28), that means, it may not be sold alive or dead, unblemished or blemished."'*
F. *But he has said, "The firstling alone"!* [This then excludes everything else, even peace-offerings (Kirzner).]
G. *That is a problem.*

IV.4 A. *Raba said, "What is the meaning of* property which is not subject to the law of sacrilege? *This means,* property which does not to begin with fall into the category to which the law of sacrilege applies to begin with. *And what might that be? It is property belonging to a common person."*

B.   Well then, why not just say, "Property belonging to a common person"?

C.   *So that's a problem.*

IV.5   A.   Said R. Abbai, "In the case of an animal designated as peace-offerings that inflicted damage [while still deemed harmless, so that the damages must be collected only out of the value of the body of the beast itself (Kirzner)], the injured party collects what is owing only from the meat of the beast, but he cannot collect what is owing out of the value of the sacrificial parts."

B.   *So what else is new! The sacrificial parts belong to the Most High!*

C.   *No, the ruling is required to indicate that one does not collect from the meat in proportion to what is due from the sacrificial parts.*

D.   *In accord with whose principle would such a position be set forth anyhow? It cannot be in accord with the position of rabbis, for that would then be obvious. They maintain that, if there is no possibility of collecting what is owing from one party, there is then no occasion to make it up from the other party. And it cannot be held that it accords with R. Nathan [who says that the beast is not private property], for he holds that if one cannot collect from one party, one may still collect from the other party anyhow.*

E.   *If you prefer, I shall explain that, in point of fact, it is in accord with R. Nathan, but if you like, I can also explain that it is in accord with rabbis.*

F.   *If you like, I can explain that it is in accord with rabbis: The position of rabbis pertains when there are two distinct agencies that are responsible for having done the damage, but if the damage was done by one agency, the injured party may still be able to require payment from wherever he can get it. And if you like, you may say that the ruling accords with R. Nathan, for it is only in a case in which one ox pushed another's ox into a pit that the owner of the injured ox may say to the owner of the pit, "I found my ox in your pit; whatever is not paid to me by your co-defendant will be paid by you." [13B] But here, could the injured party say, "The meat did the damage and the sacrificial parts did no damage"?!*

IV.6   A.   Said Raba, "An animal designated as a thanksgiving-offering that did damage – the injured party collects from the meat of the animal, but he may not collect from the bread-offering that has been designated to go along with it."

B.   *The bread-offering! So what else is new!*

C.   *Well, it was because of the concluding part of the same rule that it was necessary to make that statement, namely:* The injured party eats the bread, and the one who is going to achieve atonement through his animal then has to present the bread-offering. [That is, the party who presents the animal also produces the bread-offering that goes with it.]

D.   *So what else is new!*

E.   *What might you otherwise have said? Since the bread-offering is required to validate the sacrifice, the party responsible for the injury may say to the plaintiff, "Should you eat the meat and I bring the bread?" So we are informed that that is not so, but the bread-offering is an obligation for the original owner of the sacrifice.*

We proceed to the definition of the Mishnah's taxa.

V.1   A.   **Property belonging to members of the covenant [Israelites]:**

       B.   *What is excluded by this qualification?* *If it is to exclude a gentile, lo, that is later on made explicit:* **An ox belonging to an Israelite which gored an ox belonging to a gentile – [the Israelite owner] is exempt [M. 4:3A-B].**

       C.   *The Tannaite authority here lays out the principle and there articulates it.*

VI.1   A.   **Property that is held in ownership:**

       B.   *What is excluded by this qualification?*

       C.   *Said R. Judah, "It is to exclude a case in which [there are two defendants, and]* one says, 'Your ox did the damage,' and the other says, 'Your ox did the damage.'"

       D.   *Well, is this not explicitly stated below:* If there were two oxen pursuing a third, and this party claims, "Your ox did the damage," and that party claims, "Your ox did the damage," both parties are exempt from having to pay compensation?

       E.   *The Tannaite authority here lays out the principle and there articulates it.*

VI.2   A.   *In a Tannaite formulation it has been stated:* What is excluded is ownerless property.

       B.   *How shall we imagine such a situation? If we say that an ox belonging to us has gored an ownerless ox, against whom is there to lay claim? And if it is an ownerless ox that gored an ox belonging to one of us, then why not just go and seize the ownerless ox that has done the damage?*

       C.   *The rule speaks of a case in which someone else went and acquired the ownerless beast [and in line with the Mishnah's qualification, the injured party gets nothing].*

VI.3   A.   *Rabina said, "The phrase is meant to exclude this case:* An ox gored, and then the owner sanctified it, or the ox gored, and then the owner declared it free for all."

       B.   *So, too, it has been taught on Tannaite authority:*

       C.   Furthermore said R. Judah, "Even if an ox gored and afterward the owner declared it sanctified, or it gored and afterward the owner declared it free for all, the owner is exempt, in line with this verse: 'And if it has been testified to his owner, and he has not kept it in, but it has killed a man or a woman, the ox shall be stoned' (Ex. 21:29). That is the case only where the conditions that prevail at the time of the killing are the same as those that prevail at the time of the court appearance [that is, the beast must be private property throughout the process]."

       D.   *Well, would we not then require that the same conditions prevail at the time of the final verdict? Lo, the verse itself, saying, "The ox shall be stoned," speaks of the time of the final verdict!*

       E.   *Formulate the matter in this way:* That is the case only where the conditions that prevail at the time of the killing are the same as those that prevail at the time of the court appearance and at the time of the final verdict.

VII.1 A.   **And that is located in any place other than in the domain which is in the ownership of the one who has caused the damage:**

       B.   *That is because the defendant may argue against the plaintiff, "What was your ox doing on my property?"*

VIII.1   A.   Or in the domain which is shared by the one who suffers injury and the one who causes injury:

The following in just a few sentences draws together these grids:

1.   a courtyard owned by partners other than the person responsible for the damages vs. one in which the defendant is an owner ["any situation in which the injured party has domain and the party responsible for the injury does not have domain"]
2.   the classifications of tooth and foot
3.   a paid bailee and a borrower, an unpaid bailee or a hirer,
4.   negligence as against deliberate action

B.   Said R. Hisda said Abimi, "In the case of a courtyard owned by partners, liability is incurred for damages caused under the generative classifications of tooth and foot, *and this is the sense of the Mishnah's statement:* And that is located in any place other than in the domain which is in the ownership of the one who has caused the damage, in which case the defendant is exempt; but in the domain which is shared by the one who suffers injury and the one who causes injury, ...[the owner of] that one which has caused the damage is liable to pay compensation for damage."

C.   But R. Eleazar said, "No liability is incurred for damages caused under the generative classifications of tooth and foot, *and this is the sense of the Mishnah's statement:* ...Except for that which is located in any place other than in the domain which is in the ownership of the one who has caused the damage, or in the domain which is shared by the one who suffers injury and the one who causes injury – where there is also an exception. But when one has otherwise caused damage, [the owner of] that one which has caused the damage is liable to pay compensation."

D.   *That statement encompasses damage in the classification of the generative category of horn* [Kirzner: for which there is liability even in public domain].

E.   *That position poses no problems to Samuel, but from the perspective of Rab, who has said, "The Tannaite authority has made reference to ox with the intention of encompassing all kinds of damage that an ox may do,"* what is encompassed by the clause, when one has otherwise caused damage, [the owner of] that one which has caused the damage is liable to pay compensation?

F.   *It was meant to encompass that concerning which our rabbis have taught on Tannaite authority:* ...When one has otherwise caused damage, [the owner of] that one which has caused the damage is liable to pay compensation is meant to encompass liability for a paid bailee and a borrower, an unpaid bailee or a hirer, in the case in which any one of these has an animal as a bailment that did damage; then the ox that was presumed innocent pays half-damages, and the ox that was an attested danger pays damages. But if a wall broke open at night or robbers took the beast by force, and then it went out and did damages, they are exempt.

VIII.2   A.   The master has said: "When one has otherwise caused damage, [the owner of] that one which has caused the damage is liable to pay compensation is meant to encompass liability for a paid bailee and a borrower, an unpaid bailee or a hirer, in the case in which any one of these has an animal as a bailment that did damage; then the ox that was presumed innocent pays half-damages, and the ox that was an attested danger pays damages...":

B.   *Now how are we to imagine such a case? If we should say that the ox belonging to the lender did injury to the ox that belonged to the borrower, why cannot the lender say to the borrower, "If my ox had done damage to someone else's, you would have had to pay compensation" [since the borrower is responsible for any damage an ox he has borrowed may do], so now that my ox has done damage to your ox, how can you claim compensation from me?" And if the ox of the borrower did injury to the ox of the lender, why cannot the lender say to the borrower, "If my ox had been injured by anybody else's, you would have had to compensate me for the full value of my ox. Now that your ox has done the damage, how can you pay me half-damages?"*

C.   *In point of fact, we deal with a case in which the ox of the lender did injury to the ox of the borrower. But here with what sort of a case do we deal? It is one in which the borrower had taken upon himself responsibility for the body of the ox [14A] but not for any damage that the ox may do to a third party.*

D.   *Yeah – well what about the rest of the story:* But if a wall broke open at night or robbers took the beast by force, and then it went out and did damages, they are exempt? *Then if it happened by day, he would have been responsible! Yet you just said that he did not take responsibility for any damage that the ox might do to a third party.*

E.   *This is the sense of the statement:* But if he accepted responsibility for damage that it might do, he would be liable to pay compensation. But if a wall broke open at night or robbers took the beast by force, and then it went out and did damages, they are exempt.

VIII.3   A.   [But R. Eleazar said, "No liability is incurred for damages caused under the generative classifications of tooth and foot":] *Is that so? But did not R. Joseph teach as a Tannaite statement:* "In the case of a jointly owned courtyard or an inn, there is liability for damages that fall into the classification or tooth and foot." *Does this not refute R. Eleazar's position?*

B.   *R. Eleazar may say to you, "But do you really think that no one dissents from that Tannaite formulation? But has it not been taught on Tannaite authority:* Four general principles did R. Simeon b. Eleazar state in connection with damages: In any situation in which the injured party has domain and the party responsible for the injury does not have domain, the party responsible for the injury is liable to pay the full damages for injury he has caused. If the party responsible for the injury has domain and the injured party does not, the former is exempt from all obligation for compensation for damages. If this one and that one both enjoy rights of domain, for instance, a courtyard belonging to partners, or a valley, as to damage done by tooth or leg, the party responsible for the injury is exempt. As to damage done by goring, pushing, biting, lying down, or kicking, a beast that is an attested danger imposes upon the owner the obligation to pay full damages, and one that had been deemed harmless imposes upon the owner the obligation to pay half-damages. In any situation in which neither this party nor that party has domain, for instance, a courtyard that belongs to neither party, for damage done by tooth or leg, the owner pays full damages; and as to damage done by goring, pushing, biting, lying down, or kicking, a beast that is an attested danger imposes upon the owner the obligation to pay full damages, and one that had been deemed harmless imposes upon the owner the obligation to pay half-damages" [T. B.Q. 1:9]. *So in any event, the passage is explicit:* If this one and that one both enjoy rights of domain, for instance, a courtyard belonging to partners, or a valley, as to damage done by tooth or leg, the party responsible for the injury is exempt! *So the passages in the names of Tannaite authorities do contradict one another."*

C.   *When that latter formulation was set forth, it was meant to make exclusive reference to a courtyard that was designated for the plaintiff and the defendant whether for use for storing produce or for tying up oxen. The formulation cited by R. Joseph, by contrast, referred to a courtyard that was designated for use for storing produce, but not for tying up oxen. So with respect to damage done by tooth, the premises were regarded in effect as the domain of the plaintiff alone [there being no right to tie up cattle there]. You may find in the language of the formulation support for that view, for here we find a reference that is explicit:* an inn. In the other formulation, by contrast, the comparison is drawn to "a jointly owned valley."

D.   *That's decisive proof.*

E.   *Objected R. Zira, "While, if the courtyard is designated for the produce of both parties, lo, we require that the condition be met, 'And it feed in another man's field' (Ex. 22:4), which condition has not been met in this case!"*

F.   *Said to him Abbayye, "Since it is not designated for use for oxen, it falls into the category of a field belonging to a third party."*

G.   *Said R. Aha of Difti to Rabina, "May we then say that since the Tannaite formulations do not differ on this matter, so, too, the Amoraic formulations also do not differ?"* [Kirzner: Hisda deals with a case where the keeping of cattle has not been permitted, Eleazar with one in which the premises may be used for that purpose also.]

H.   *He said to him, "Quite so."*

I.   *But if you prefer to think that they do differ, then what is at issue between them is the question raised by R. Zira and the solution proposed by Abbayye* [Kirzner: Hisda concurs with Abbayye, Eleazar concurs with Zira].

VIII.4   A.   *Reverting to the body of the foregoing:* Four general principles did R. Simeon b. Eleazar state in connection with damages: In any situation in which the injured party has domain and the party responsible for the injury does not have domain, the party responsible for the injury is liable in all.

B.   *Now the language that is used is not "for all [kinds of damages]" but "liable in all" – meaning, for the whole of the damage. Now is this not in accord with R. Tarfon, who takes the view,* "Damage varying from the norm that is done by horn in the premises of the injured party will be compensated in full"?

C. *But then what about what comes later on:* In any situation in which neither this party nor that party has domain, for instance, a courtyard that belongs to neither party, there is liability for damage done by tooth or foot! *Now what can be the meaning of neither this party nor that party has domain? If we say that* neither this party nor that party has domain, but someone else does, *for there has to be compliance with the condition,* "And it feed in another man's field" (Ex. 22:4) [the field must belong to the plaintiff], *and that condition has not been met here. So it is obvious that the sense of neither this party nor that party has domain is, it is owned only by the plaintiff. And yet it states at the end,* a beast that is an attested danger imposes upon the owner the obligation to pay full damages, and one that had been deemed harmless imposes upon the owner the obligation to pay half-damages. *Now that accords with the view of rabbis, who maintain,* "Damage varying from the norm that is done by horn in the premises of the injured party will be compensated only by half-damages." *So are we going to end up in the position of having the opening clause accord with the view of R. Tarfon and the closing one with rabbis?*

D. *Yes indeed. For lo, Samuel said to R. Judah,* "Sharp wit! Ignore the Tannaite formulation and accept my position that the opening clause accords with the view of R. Tarfon and the closing one with rabbis."

E. *Rabina in the name of Raba said,* "The whole really represents the position of R. Tarfon. And what is the meaning of the language, neither this party nor that party has domain? Neither this party nor that party has domain with respect to storing produce, *but all the same are this party and that party with respect to tying up oxen. So with reference to damage done by the tooth, the produce belongs to the injured party, but with regard to damages done by the horn, it is regarded as public domain."*

F. *Well, if that's the case, then how can you say that there are four classifications, when there are only three?* [Kirzner: In principle they are only three in number, exclusively the plaintiff's premises, exclusively the defendants, and partnership premises.]

G. Said R. Nahman bar Isaac, [14B] "There are three comprehensive principles, applying to four distinct situations [Kirzner: partnership premises may be subdivided into two, where both have the right to keep produce and cattle and where the right to keep produce is exclusively the plaintiffs]."

Once more, we see that the entire exposition finds cogency in a single thought problem, which is, how distinct grids interrelate. The sizable, yet rather derivative unit at the end, in which four distinct grids are introduced, three of them of considerable generative force in the composite, shows us a routine example of the process. Let me now briefly summarize what we have seen. I.1 commences with a Tannaite complement to the Mishnah's rule. After a talmudic reading of that passage, we proceed, at No. 2, to a second Tannaite complement, this one, too, accorded its own, considerable talmud, at No. 3. II.1-2 complement the Mishnah's statement with a concrete case, illustrating the principle of the Mishnah and investigating its implications and logic. We end up with a very good example illustrating the rather subtle rule of the Mishnah. III.1 finds the scriptural authority behind the Mishnah's ruling. Nos. 2, 3, 4 provide a talmud to No. 1. Nos. 5-6 continue the inquiry into how damages are assessed in the present matter, all thus extending the Mishnah's rule and amplifying it. Nos. 7-12+13 are tacked onto No. 6 because they form a composite made up of materials that share the same named authorities. IV.1 finds the authority behind the Mishnah's rule, a common mode of Mishnah exegesis. Nos. 2-3 provide an appendix to the foregoing. No. 4 provides another amplification of the language of the Mishnah. At Nos. 5, 6 we have a secondary problem in amplification of the Mishnah's rule. V.1, VI.1-3 ask the same question of Mishnah exegesis. VII.1 then explains the reasoning behind the Mishnah's rule. VIII.1, with its talmud at Nos. 2, 3 (for 1.C), and its appendix at No. 4, a talmud for 3.B, provides an important qualification for the Mishnah's rule.

1:3

A. Assessment [of the compensation for an injury to be paid] is in terms of ready cash [but may be paid in kind – that is,] in what is worth money.

B. [Assessment of the compensation for an injury to be paid is] before a court.

C. [Assessment of the compensation for an injury to be paid is] on the basis of evidence given by witnesses who are freemen and members of the covenant.

D. Women fall into the category of [parties to suits concerning] damages.

E. And the one who suffers damages and the one who causes damages [may share] in the compensation.

Since by this point readers may ask themselves whether this process that has predominated, so sensible and obvious and necessary, is just natural to the task of the document, that is, the Bavli's task of Mishnah exegesis. So, as though to address the very question I bring to the document, our framers shift into a different mode, even while dealing with another grid. The mode is simple: the exegesis of words and phrases. I indent what is not grid analysis, and the alternative modes of exegesis become visually apparent.

I.1   A.   [Assessment [of the compensation for an injury to be paid] is in terms of ready cash:] *What is the meaning of* in terms of ready cash?

	B.	Said R. Judah, "This evaluation is to be reckoned only in specie."
	C.	*That is in line with what our rabbis have taught as a Tannaite statement:* In the case of a cow that did damage to a garment and the garment also did damage to the cow, they do not rule, "Let the cow be handed over for the cloak that it has damaged, and let the cloak be handed over in compensation for the injury done to the cow." But they estimate their value in ready cash [T. B.Q. 1:2B].
II.1	A.	But may be paid in kind – that is, in what is worth money:
	B.	*That is in line with what our rabbis have taught on Tannaite authority:* In what is worth money – this teaches that the court makes an evaluation only of immovable property. If there is movable property that has been seized by the one who has been injured, they make an estimate in settlement of his claim from that property [T. B.Q. 1:2D-F].
II.2	A.	The master has said, "In what is worth money – this teaches that the court makes an evaluation only of immovable property":
	B.	*How is this to be inferred?*
	C.	Said Rabbah bar Ulla, "It must be something that is fully worth what is paid for it in cash."
	D.	*What might this mean?*
	E.	Something that is not subject to the law of deception. [Kirzner: Money's worth would thus mean, property which could not be said to be worth less than the price paid for it, and is thus never subject to the law of deception; this holds good with immovable property.]
	F.	*Well, slaves and bonds also are not subject to the law of deception!*
	G.	Rather, said Rabbah bar Ulla, "It must be something that may be purchased with ready cash."
	H.	*Well, slaves and bonds also are purchased with ready cash.*
	I.	*Rather, said R. Ashi, "What 'worth money' means is, worth money but not actually money, but all of these are things that are equivalent in themselves to ready cash."*
II.3	A.	*To R. Huna b. R. Joshua, R. Judah bar Hinena pointed out the following contradiction: "A Tannaite formulation states,* In what is worth money – this teaches that the court makes an evaluation only of immovable property. *But has it not further been taught on Tannaite authority: "'...he should return" (Ex. 21:34) – encompassing whatever has monetary value, even bran'?"*
	B.	*In the former instance with what situation do we deal? It is a case of heirs* [who have to pay only out of the real estate but not out of slaves or other property (Kirzner)].
	C.	*If you claim we are dealing with heirs to an estate, then notice the concluding part of the same statement:* If there is movable property that has been seized by the one who has been injured, they make an estimate in settlement of his claim from that property [T. B.Q. 1:2D-F]! *But if we are dealing with heirs, how is the court going to collect payment for him out of them?*

D.   *It is in line with that which Raba said R. Nahman said, "It is a case in which the plaintiff seized the property while the original defendant was alive." Here, too, the seizure was while the defendant was still alive.*

III.1   A.   **[Assessment of the compensation for an injury to be paid is] before a court** [Kirzner: meaning, payment in kind is made out of possessions that are in the presence of the court, not disposed of]:

B.   That then excludes the case of one who first sells off his property and then goes to court.

C.   *Does that not then yield the inference that,* where one has borrowed money and then sold off his property before going to court, the court cannot collect the debt out of an estate that has been disposed of? [That is an impossible inference.]

D.   The purpose of the text is to exclude a court of laymen [this, in the presence of the court, means, only by qualified judges (Kirzner)].

IV.1   A.   **[Assessment of the compensation for an injury to be paid is] on the basis of evidence given by witnesses who are freemen and members of the covenant:**

B.   That then excludes the case of one who confesses an act that is subject to an extrajudicial fine [in which case he is exempt from the fine], but afterward witnesses came along [and testified he had done what he had confessed; that makes no difference, he remains exempt from the extrajudicial sanction].

C.   *That inference poses no problem to him who says that in* the case of one who confesses an act that is subject to an extrajudicial fine [in which case he is exempt from the fine], but afterward witnesses came along [and testified he had done what he had confessed; that makes no difference, he remains exempt from the extrajudicial sanction]. *But from the perspective of him who says that in* the case of one who confesses an act that is subject to an extrajudicial fine [in which case he is exempt from the fine], but afterward witnesses came along [and testified he had done what he had confessed], he is liable, *what is to be said?*

D.   *It is the conclusion of the passage that is necessary,* [15A] *namely* **witnesses who are freemen and members of the covenant. Who are freemen** *serves to exclude slaves;* **And members of the covenant** *serves to exclude gentiles. And it was necessary to make these exclusions explicit, for had we been given the rule only concerning the slave, we might have thought that he was excluded only because he has no identifiable parentage, but a gentile, who has identifiable parentage, I might have said is not excluded; and had we been given only the case of the gentile, I might have thought that he is excluded because he is not subject to the commandments, but a slave, who is subject to the commandments, I might have thought was not excluded. So it was necessary to specify both.*

V.1   A.   **Women fall into the category of [parties to suits concerning] damages:**

B.   *What is the scriptural basis for this ruling?*

C. Said R. Judah said Rab, *and so, too, has a Tannaite authority of the household of R. Ishmael stated,* "'When a man or a woman commits any sin that men commit' (Num. 5:6). In this language, Scripture has treated the woman as comparable to the man for the purpose of all the penalties that are imposed by the Torah."

D. The household of R. Eleazar repeated as its Tannaite formulation: "'Now these are the ordinances that you shall set before them' (Ex. 21:1) – in this language, Scripture has treated the woman as comparable to the man for the purpose of all the laws that are imposed by the Torah."

E. The household of Hezekiah and R. Yosé the Galilean presented as a Tannaite formulation, "Said Scripture, 'It has killed a man or a woman' (Ex. 21:1) – in this language, Scripture has treated the woman as comparable to the man for the purpose of all the forms of the death penalty that are specified in the Torah."

F. *And all three proofs are required to make the point. For had we heard only the initial one, we might have thought that it is in that area in particular that the All-Merciful has taken pity on a woman, so that she will have a means of atonement, but so far as civil laws in general, a man, who is engaged in business transactions, would be subject to the law, but I might have thought that a woman is not.*

G. *And had we been given the rule concerning the civil law, I might have thought that that is so that a woman should have a way of making a living, but as to atonement, since a man is responsible to carry out the religious duties, he would be given the means of making atonement for sin, but a woman, who is not responsible for keeping [all] religious duties, is not under the law.*

H. *And had we been given these two, the one because of making atonement, the other because of making a living, but as to the matter of manslaughter, a man, who is subject to the religious duty of paying a ransom in the case of manslaughter, would be subject to the law, but a woman would not.*

I. *And had we been given the matter of ransom, it might have been thought because in that matter, it is because a soul has perished, but as to these other matters, in which there is no issue of a soul's having perished, I might have thought that that was not the case. So all of them are required.*

Here we have dealt with taxa but not with the interplay of grids of taxa. The next composite reminds us of the alternative I maintain bears emblematic character in the document overall: a mark of how its framers think, of what tells them what they wish to know. What we have now to do is classify interstitial damages, that is, half-damages, paid under circumstances that we need not here define. What we want to know is how to classify a classification of damages in relationship to another classification, civil as against extrajudicial sanctions.

VI.1 A. **And the one who suffers damages and the one who causes damages [may share] in the compensation:**

B. *It has been stated:*

C. *Half-damages –*

D. *R. Pappa said, "They are classified as civil damages."*

E. *R. Huna b. R. Joshua said, "They fall into the classification of an extrajudicial sanction."*

F. *R. Pappa said, "They are classified as civil damages": He takes the view that oxen under ordinary circumstances are not assumed to be properly guarded, and therefore as a matter of law, the owner should have to pay full damages, but it is the All-Merciful who has taken pity on his situation, since up to that point his ox has not yet been placed under a warning.*

G. *R. Huna b. R. Joshua said, "They fall into the classification of an extrajudicial sanction": He takes the view that oxen under ordinary circumstances are assumed to be properly guarded, and therefore, as a matter of law, the owner should not have to pay any damages at all. But it is the All-Merciful that has imposed an extrajudicial sanction on him so that he will take good care of his oxen.*

H. *We have learned in the Mishnah:* **And the one who suffers damages and the one who causes damages [may share] in the compensation.** *Now from the perspective of him who has said, "They are classified as civil damages," that is why the plaintiff, getting only half of what is coming to him, is involved in the payment. But from the perspective of him who maintains, "They fall into the classification of an extrajudicial sanction," since, after all, this payment really does not belong to the plaintiff at all, how can he be involved in the payment?*

I. *The reference is required to cover a case in which the loss derives from the decrease in the value of the carcass of the beast [which the injured party suffers].*

J. *As to the decrease in the value of the carcass of the beast [which the injured party suffers], lo, that is covered by the prior statement, namely,* I am liable for compensation as if [I have] made possible all of the damage it may do – this teaches that the owner has to take care of the disposition of the carcass [receiving the proceeds as part payment] [T. B.Q. 1:1E-F].

K. *The one statement speaks of a beast that was deemed harmless, the other a beast that was an attested danger. And it was necessary to make the same point in both cases, for had we been given the rule concerning the beast that was deemed harmless, we might have supposed that the reason for the rule is that the owner has not yet been subjected to a warning to watch out for his ox. But in the case of an ox, in which the owner had been warned, I might have said that that is not the case. And had we been given the rule covering the beast that was an attested danger, the operative consideration would have been that he pays the whole of the damages, but as to the beast that was deemed innocent, I might not have thought that the same rule applied. So both rules are required.*

L. *Come and take note:* **What is the difference between what is deemed harmless and an attested danger? But if that which is deemed harmless [causes damage], [the owner] pays half of the value of the damage which has been caused, [with liability limited to the value of the] carcass [of the beast which has caused the damage]. But [if that which is] an attested danger [causes damage], [the owner] pays the whole of the value of the damage which has been** caused from the best property [he may own, and his liability is by no means limited to the value of the animal which has done the damage] [M. 1:4K-N]. *Now if it were the fact that liability for half-damages is an extrajudicial sanction, why not add to the foregoing* the following point of difference: The owner of the beast that was deemed harmless will not have to pay if he confesses to the matter on his own, while the owner of a beast that was an attested danger has to pay if he confesses on his own.

M. *The Tannaite authority left out items from his list.*

N. *Yeah, well, if he left out items from his list, what else did he leave off?*

O. *He left out the matter of the half-ransom for manslaughter [which does not have to be paid by the owner of the beast that was deemed harmless; the owner of the beast that was an attested danger pays full ransom].*

P. *That is no real omission, since the Mishnah may accord with the position of R. Yosé the Galilean, who takes the view that the owner of the beast deemed harmless does pay half-liability as a ransom.*

Q. *Come and take note:* [15B] "My ox killed Mr. So-and-so," or "...Mr. So-and-so's ox" – lo, this one pays compensation on the strength of his own testimony. *Now does this not refer to the case of an ox that was deemed harmless?* [Kirzner: And if the liability is created by admission, it proves that it is not an extrajudicial penalty but a civil penalty.]

R. No, it refers to an ox that was an attested danger.

S. *Then what is the rule in the case of a beast that was deemed harmless? Is it not the fact that, here, too, he would not pay if he himself confessed the facts?*

T. If so, why include further on, "My ox killed Mr. So-and-so's slave" – he does not have to pay on the strength of his own confession. *Why not just formulate matters covering both cases by saying the rule in this language:* Under what circumstances? In the case of an ox that was an attested danger. But in the case of an ox that was thought to be harmless, he does not pay on the strength of his own confession?

U. *The whole of the passage speaks of an ox that was an attested danger.*

V. *Come and take note:* This is the governing principle. In any case in which the payment exceeds the value of the actual damages, one does not pay on the strength of his own confession. *Would this then not yield the inference that in cases where payment is less than the actual damage, liability comes about even by one's own confession?*

W. *Not at all.* No, that is the case only when the payment is the same as the amount of the damage done. But what is the law where the payment is less than the value of the damage done? Would it be the fact that confession does not establish liability? If so, why state, This is the governing principle. In any case in which the payment exceeds the value of the actual damages, one does not pay on the strength of his own confession? *Why not use this language:* This is the governing principle. In any case in which the payment is not exactly the same as the amount of the damages..., *and that would bear the inference of payment being less or more.*

X. *That's a solid refutation. Nonetheless, the decided law is that half-damages fall into the classification of an extrajudicial sanction.*

Y.   Can you have a case in which there is a refutation, but what is refuted stands as the decided law?

Z.   Well, as a matter of fact, you can, for what constitutes the refutation anyhow? It is only that the Tannaite formulation does not say, "...where the payment does not correspond exactly to the amount of the damages." But that is not entirely precise, since there is liability for half-damages in the case of pebbles [that an animal kicks], which in accord to the law that has been received as a tradition is classified as civil. And it is on that account that the proposed formulation is not the one that was adopted.

AA. Now that you have reached the position that liability for half-damages is an extrajudicial sanction, lo, if a dog ate a lamb or a cat ate a hen, which is regarded as an unusual occasion, and we do not in Babylonia collect extrajudicial penalties, [so these should not be actionable cases in Babylonia,] on condition that the lambs or chickens were big, but if they were little, it would be a commonplace event [and then would be a civil damage under the classification of tooth]. Now if the injured party had seized property of the one responsible for the injury, we would not take the property back from him. And if the injured party were to say, "Set a fixed time, so that I may go to the Land of Israel, and plead my case," we do set a fixed time, and if the other party did not go along for the trip, we excommunicate him. Now, one way or the other, we should excommunicate him until he removes the source of the damage, in line with what R. Nathan said. For it has been taught on Tannaite authority: R. Nathan says, "How on the basis of Scripture do we know that someone should not raise a vicious dog in his house or maintain a shaky ladder in his house? 'You shall not bring blood upon your house' (Deut. 22:8)."

The wonderful final unit shows us the difference between what our authors produce in explanation of words and phrases, that is, clarification of inert facts, and how they take a question of mixing grids and through that inquiry sustain a wide-ranging and profound analysis: the difference is between reporting facts and solving problems.

Briefly to review the structure of the whole: I.1, II.1 appeal to Tannaite clarifications of the rule given by the Mishnah. Nos. 2, 3 further analyze the materials of No. 1. III.1 corrects a possible, false interpretation of the Mishnah's rule. IV.1 goes through the same exercise. V.1 finds a scriptural basis for the Mishnah's ruling. VI.1 presents an analysis of the Mishnah's topic, utilizing the Mishnah's rule in the course of the argument.

1:4A-J

A.   [There are] five [deemed] harmless, and five [deemed] attested dangers.

B.   A domesticated beast is not regarded as an attested danger in regard to [1] butting, (2) pushing, (3) biting, (4) lying down, or (5) kicking.

C. (1) A tooth is deemed an attested danger in regard to eating what is suitable for [eating].

D. (2) The leg is deemed an attested danger in regard to breaking something as it walks along.

E. (3) And an ox which is an attested danger [so far as goring is concerned];

F. (4) and an ox which causes damage in the domain of the one who is injured;

G. and (5) man.

H. (1) A wolf, (2) lion, (3) bear, (4) leopard, (5) panther, and (6) a serpent – lo, these are attested dangers.

I. R. Eliezer says, "When they are trained, they are not attested dangers.

J. "But the serpent is always an attested danger."

Once more the Mishnah's grid is immediately subjected to a superimposition, now of a grid distinguishing damages done in the property of the injured party from those done in the property of the defendant, on the one side, or in public domain, on the other; then there is the grid involving different levels and forms of compensation, for example, half-damages vs. whole damages. Then there is the grid distinguishing damages that are to be foreseen and prevented and damages that cannot be foreseen; the latter are also to be compensated, but not in the way the former are. Then there will still be the Mishnah's grid: what is an attested danger as against what is not; this grid will be mixed with the grid defined by types of sources of injury, foot, etc.; modes of inflicting damage, for example, butting, pushing, and so on.

I.1   A. *Since the passage of the Mishnah has stated,* A tooth is deemed an attested danger in regard to eating what is suitable for [eating], *it must be inferred that we deal with the courtyard belonging to the injured party* [Kirzner: for otherwise there is no liability in the case of tooth]. *And it is further stated here,* A domesticated beast is not regarded as an attested danger in regard to [1] butting, (2) pushing, (3) biting, (4) lying down, or (5) kicking, *with the inference that the compensation will not be for the entirety of the damages but only the half-damages. In accord with whom is this ruling? It is in accord with the position of rabbis, who maintain,* if damage that is of an unusual character is done, even on the premises of the injured party, only half-damages are paid. *Now go on to the end of the same passage:* (3) And an ox which is an attested danger [so far as goring is concerned]; (4) and an ox which causes damage in the domain of the one who is injured; and (5) man. *This accords with the view of R. Tarfon, who has said,* "Damage varying from the norm that is done by horn in the premises of the injured party will be compensated in full." *So are we left with a situation in which the opening clause of the passage accords with the rabbis and the concluding clause is in accord with the view of R. Tarfon!?*

B. Yes indeed, for did not Samuel say to R. Judah, "Sharp wit! Ignore the
   Tannaite formulation and accept my position that the opening clause
   accords with the view of R. Tarfon and the closing one with rabbis."

C. R. Eleazar in the name of Rab said, [16A] "The whole really represents the
   position of R. Tarfon. The opening clause refers to a courtyard that is
   reserved for produce for one of them, while both this one and that one may
   use it for oxen. Now in regard to damages in the classification of tooth,
   therefore, the courtyard is held to belong to the injured party. With respect
   to injuries that fall into the classification of horn, it is regarded as public
   domain." [Kirzner: Both plaintiff and defendant had the right to
   keep their cattle there.]

D. Said R. Kahana, "I repeated this tradition before R. Zebid of Nehardea, and
   he said to me, 'Can you really establish this passage wholly in accord with
   the position of R. Tarfon? Is it not taught in the Mishnah: A tooth is
   deemed an attested danger in regard to eating what is suitable for
   [eating]? If it is suitable for it, then that is the case, but if it is not
   suitable for it, then that is not the case. But were it R. Tarfon who was
   responsible for what is before us, has he not said, "Damage varying
   from the norm that is done by horn in the premises of the injured
   party will be compensated in full"?' So, in point of fact, the passage
   represents the position of rabbis, but it suffers from a lacuna, and this is
   how it should read: [There are] five [deemed] harmless, but if the
   owner is warned in their regard, then they are deemed to be
   attested dangers. And the tooth and foot are deemed to be attested
   dangers to begin with. And in what regard are they deemed to
   have been attested as dangers? In the courtyard of the injured
   party." [Kirzner: The ox doing damage on the plaintiff's premises
   refers to tooth and not to horn.]

E. To this proposition objected Rabina, "We have as our Tannaite
   formulation below, An ox which causes damage in the domain of the
   one who is injured [M. 1:4F] – how so? [If it gored, pushed, bit,
   lay down, or kicked [= M. 1:4B], in the public domain, the owner
   pays half of the value of the damages the ox has caused. If it did
   so in the domain of the injured party, R. Tarfon says, 'The owner
   pays the full value of the damages the ox has caused.' And sages
   say, 'Half of the value'] [M. 2:5]. Now if you maintain that this
   damage has been covered in the passage before us, that is why the passage
   then adds, how so? But if you hold the view that this is a kind of damage
   that has not been dealt with, then how could the passage proceed as it does,
   how so?"

F. Rather, said Rabina, "The passage presents us with a lacuna, and this is
   how it should read: [There are] five [deemed] harmless, but if they
   are subjected to a warning, then all five of them are then classified
   as attested dangers. And the tooth and foot are held to be attested
   dangers to begin with. And this is the way in which the ox is an
   attested danger. And as to the ox that does damages in the domain
   of the injured party, there is a dispute between R. Tarfon and rabbis.
   There are, moreover, other classifications of those that are attested
   dangers in the same category as these: (1) A wolf, (2) lion, (3) bear,
   (4) leopard, (5) panther, and (6) a serpent – lo, these are attested
   dangers."

G. *So, too, it has been taught on Tannaite authority:* **[There are] five [deemed] harmless, but if they are subjected to a warning, then all five of them are then classified as attested dangers. And the tooth and foot are held to be attested dangers to begin with. And this is the way in which the ox is an attested danger. And as to the ox that does damages in the domain of the injured party, there is a dispute between R. Tarfon and rabbis.** There are, moreover, other classifications of those that are attested dangers in the same category as these: **(1) A wolf, (2) lion, (3) bear, (4) leopard, (5) panther, and (6) a serpent – lo, these are attested dangers.**

H. *There are those who reached this conclusion by raising the following objection: We have learned in the Mishnah:* **[There are] five [deemed] harmless, and five [deemed] attested dangers.** *But are there no more? Lo, there are* **(1) a wolf, (2) lion, (3) bear, (4) leopard, (5) panther, and (6) a serpent – lo, these are attested dangers.** *And in this regard it is set forth as follows: Said Rabina, "The passage presents us with a lacuna, and this is how it should read:* **[There are] five [deemed] harmless, but if they are subjected to a warning, then all five of them are then classified as attested dangers. And the tooth and foot are held to be attested dangers to begin with. And this is the way in which the ox is an attested danger. And as to the ox that does damages in the domain of the injured party, there is a dispute between R. Tarfon and rabbis.** There are, moreover, other classifications of those that are attested dangers in the same category as these: **(1) A wolf, (2) lion, (3) bear, (4) leopard, (5) panther, and (6) a serpent – lo, these are attested dangers."**

II.1 A. **A domesticated beast is not regarded as an attested danger in regard to butting, (2) pushing, (3) biting, (4) lying down, or (5) kicking:**

B. Said R. Eleazar, "That is the rule only in the case of big jugs. But in the case of small jugs, *that is a routine occurrence.*"

C. *May we say that the following supports his view:* A beast is deemed an attested danger to walk in its normal way or to break things or to crush a person, animal, or utensils?

D. *But maybe this refers to doing so from the side.*

E. *There are those who state the matter in the following way: Said R. Eleazar, "Do not state this rule in such a way that it pertains only to big jugs, in which case this would not be the ox's usual practice, but in regard to little jugs, which it would be usual for him to break, the rule applies; but even in the case of little jugs, it also is not usual for him to do that."*

F. *An objection was raised:* A beast is deemed an attested danger to walk in its normal way or to break things or to crush a person, animal, or utensils.

G. *Said R. Eleazar, "But maybe this refers to doing so from the side."*

H. *There are those who to begin with raise this as an objection: We have learned in the Mishnah:* **not regarded as an attested danger...lying down.**

I. *But has it not been taught on Tannaite authority:* A beast is deemed an attested danger to walk in its normal way or to break things or to crush a person, animal, or utensils?

J.   Said R. Eleazar, "That is no problem. The one speaks of big jugs, the other, of little ones."

III.1   A.   (1) A wolf, (2) lion, (3) bear, (4) leopard, (5) panther, and (6) a serpent – lo, these are attested dangers:

   B.   What is the definition of a panther?

   C.   Said R. Judah, "A jumper."

   D.   What is a jumper?

   E.   Said R. Joseph, "A hyena."

   F.   An objection was raised: R. Meir says, "Also a many-colored one" [a hyena]. R. Eleazar says, "Also a snake." Now R. Joseph has said that the jumper is a hyena!

   G.   That is no problem, the one speaks of a male, the other, a female, as has been taught on Tannaite authority: [Kirzner:] A male hyena after seven years turns into a bat, a bat after seven years turns into an arpad-bat, an arpad-bat after seven years turns into a kimmosh-thorn, a kimmosh-thorn after seven years turns into a thorn, a thorn after seven years turns into a demon. The spine of a man after seven years turns into a snake. But that is the case only if he did not bow when he recited the benediction, "We give thanks to you."

III.2   A.   A master has said: R. Meir says, "Also a many-colored one" [a hyena]. [16B] R. Eleazar says, "Also a snake."

   B.   But have we not learned in the Mishnah: R. Eliezer says, "When they are trained, they are not attested dangers. But the serpent is always an attested danger"?

   C.   Read: the snake [alone] [Kirzner: only the snake, excluding the hyena and the other animals on the list].

III.3   A.   Said Samuel, "In the case of a lion in public domain, if it seized and ate an animal, the owner is exempt, but if it tore the animal to pieces and ate it, he is liable.

   B.   "If it seized and ate an animal, the owner is exempt: Since it is its way to seize, it is as though an animal ate fruit and vegetable, so it is classified as damage in the category of tooth in public domain, and there is an exemption from the requirement of paying damages.

   C.   "But if it tore the animal to pieces and ate it, he is liable: This is not the ordinary custom of a lion [Kirzner: and it falls into the category of horn, which is not immune even in public domain]."

   D.   Is that to imply that it is unusual for a lion to tear at its prey? But it is written, "The lion did tear in pieces enough for his whelps" (Nah. 2:13)!

   E.   It is usual only when it is for the sake of the whelps.

   F.   But what about the next clause, "And strangled for his lionesses" (Nah. 2:13).

   G.   It is usual only for the sake of the lionesses.

   H.   "And filled his holes with prey" (Nah. 2:13)?

   I.   It is usual only when it is done to preserve the prey in his holes.

   J.   "And his dens with ravin"?

   K.   It is usual only when it is done to preserve the prey in his dens.

   L.   But has it not been taught on Tannaite authority: So, too, if a wild animal went into the courtyard of the injured party and tore up a beast and ate up the meat, the owner has to pay full damages?

M. *Here with what sort of a case do we deal? It is one in which* he tore up the animal to preserve it.
N. *But lo, it is taught,* ate up the meat!
O. *It changed its mind and ate it up after all.*
P. *Yeah, and how would we know what it was thinking? And in the matter of Samuel's ruling, why not assume the same thing anyhow?*
Q. *Said R. Nahman, "The passages have to be interpreted to deal with diverse cases, namely,* if it either tears to pieces for the purpose of preservation, or seizes and eats the meat, the payment must be full damages."
R. *Rabina said, "When Samuel made his statement, he dealt with a tame lion, and it was within the framework of the position of R. Eleazar, who said, 'That is not the usual thing for a tame lion to do.'"*
S. *Well, then, even in the case of the lion's seizing, the same rule should apply and there should be liability!*
T. *What Rabina said does not pertain to what Samuel said, but rather to the Tannaite formulation, which, then, we have to assume treats a tame lion and takes the view of R. Eleazar that such a lion does not usually do that sort of thing.*
U. *Then why not pay only half-damages?*
V. *The owner of the lion was warned that the beast was an attested danger.*
W. *If so, then why present this formulation with regard to the secondary classifications of tooth, while it should be presented in regard to the secondary classifications of horn?*
X. *That's a good question.*

The analysis of the implications of the Mishnah paragraph, and how they conflict, is well executed at I.1. II.1 provides a minor clarification of the rule of the Mishnah. III.1+2 gloss the Mishnah's language. No. 3 adds a refinement to the law.

1:4K-N

K. What is the difference between what is deemed harmless and an attested danger?
L. But if that which is deemed harmless [causes damage], [the owner] pays half of the value of the damage which has been caused,
M. [with liability limited to the value of the] carcass [of the beast which has caused the damage].
N. But [if that which is] an attested danger [causes damage], [the owner] pays the whole of the value of the damage which has been caused from the best property [he may own, and his liability is by no means limited to the value of the animal which has done the damage].

There is no reason for us to wonder where our exegetes learned how to think in the way they do. The Mishnah authors taught them everything they needed to know. Here is how the Mishnah statement itself shows the interplay of these grids: (1) attested danger versus what is assumed harmless; (2) full damages versus half-damages; (3)

compensation from property of various classifications. The exegetes here rightly begin by pointing out that the several categories at hand are dictated by the Torah itself.

I.1   A.   [**The best property:**] *What is the meaning of* **the best property?**
       B.   Said R. Eleazar, "The best of the estate of the defendant: 'And Hezekiah slept with his father, and they buried him in the best of the sepulchres of the sons of David' (2 Chr. 32:33)."
       C.   And R. Eleazar said, "'In the best...' means, near the best of the family, David and Solomon."

I.2   A.   "And they buried him in his own sepulchres, which he had made for himself in the city of David, and laid him in the bed that was filled with sweet odors and diverse kinds of spices" (2 Chr. 16:14):
       B.   *What is the meaning of* "with sweet odors and diverse kinds of spices"?
       C.   R. Eleazar said, "Just that."
       D.   R. Samuel bar Nahmani said, "Spices such that whoever smells them becomes lustful."

I.3   A.   "For they have dug a ditch to take me and hid snares for my feet" (Jer. 18:22) –
       B.   R. Eleazar said, "They suspected him of having sexual relations with a whore."
       C.   Samuel bar Nahmani said, "They suspected him of having sexual relations with a married woman."
       D.   *Now with respect to the position of the one who has said, "They suspected him of having sexual relations with a whore," that is in line with how it is written, "For a harlot is a deep ditch" (Prov. 23:27). But from the perspective of him who said, "They suspected him of having sexual relations with a married woman," what is the connection between the term "ditch" and "a married woman"?*
       E.   *Well, is a married woman not a whore under such circumstances?*
       F.   *Now with respect to the position of the one who has said, "They suspected him of having sexual relations with a married woman," Scripture thereafter states, "Yet Lord you know all their counsel against me to slay me" (Jer. 18:23). But from the perspective of him who said, "They suspected him of having sexual relations with a whore," how did they propose to slay him? [They did not accuse him of a sin punishable by death.]*
       G.   They threw him into a pit of mud.

I.4   A.   *Raba interpreted, "What is the meaning of the verse, 'But let them be overthrown before you; deal thus with them in the time of your anger' (Jer. 18:23)?* Said Jeremiah before the Holy One, blessed be He, 'Lord of the world, even when they do acts of righteousness, make them stumble through people who are unworthy of the charity, so that they will not receive a reward for the good that they do.'"

I.5   A.   "And they did him honor at his death" (2 Chr. 32:33) – this teaches that they called a session [for Torah study] at his grave.

	B.	There was a dispute in that regard between R. Nathan and rabbis. One said, "It was for three days," [17A] and the other said, "It was for seven days."
	C.	And some say, "For thirty days."
I.6	A.	*Our rabbis have taught on Tannaite authority:*
	B.	"'And they did him honor at his death' (2 Chr. 32:33) – this refers to Hezekiah, king of Judah, before whom thirty-six thousand soldiers marched forth with bare shoulders," the words of R. Judah.
	C.	Said to him R. Nehemiah, "But didn't they do the same before Ahab? But what they did as a special honor was to place a stroll of the Torah on his bier, saying, 'This one carried out what is written in that.'"
	D.	*Don't we do the same thing at this time, too?*
	E.	*We carry it forth, but we do not put it on the bier.*
	F.	*If you prefer, we put it on the bier, but we do not use the language, "This one carried out what is written in that."*
I.7	A.	*Said Rabbah bar bar Hanna, "I was following R. Yohanan to ask him about this tradition, when he went into a privy. I put the matter before him [when he came out], but he did not answer my question until he had washed his hands, put his prayer boxes containing verses of Scripture back on, and recited the benediction. Then he said to us, 'We even do use the language, "This one carried out what is written in that," we do not say, "He taught the Torah...."'"*
	B.	But did not a master say, "Great is the study of the Torah, for study brings about practice"?
	C.	*There is no contradiction, the one speaks of studying the Torah, the other, teaching the Torah.*
I.8	A.	*Said R. Yohanan in the name of R. Simeon b. Yohai, "What is the meaning of the verse of Scripture, 'Happy are you who sow beside all waters, that send forth the feet of the ox and the ass' (Isa. 32:20)?* Whoever is devoted to the Torah and to doing deeds of grace, has the merit of inheriting two tribes: 'Blessed are you that sow.' And 'sowing' speaks of acts of charity, 'Sow to yourselves in charity, reap in kindness' (Hos. 10:12). Water stands for the Torah: 'Everyone that thirsts, come to the water' (Isa. 55:1)."
	B.	"He is worthy of the inheritance of two tribes," Joseph: "Joseph is a fruitful bough, whose branches run over the wall" (Gen. 49:22); and Issachar, "Issachar is a strong ass" (Gen. 49:14).
	C.	Some say, "His enemies will fall before him: 'With them he shall push the people together to the ends of the earth' (Deut. 33:17)."
	D.	"He is worthy of understanding like Issachar, which were men who had understanding of the times, to know what Israel ought to do" (1 Chr. 12:32).

Where the Mishnah does our work, the Bavli has nothing to do. I.1 defines a term of the Mishnah. This bears in its wake the composite of Nos. 2-8. So much for a complete and amazingly coherent chapter of the Bavli. On to another example of the same sustained effort at bringing into relationship sets, or grids, of differentiations, moving from one set, that is, two that yield four subdivisions, to two sets, four that yield sixteen, and even the cubic set, eight that yield sixty-four.

4

The Mixed Grid in Bavli Shabbat Chapter One

My claim to have identified a principal generative problematic that explains for us how, beyond the thin exegesis of words and phrases, the Bavli forms a thick exegesis of concepts, categories, and their interplay calls for another large example. What I have now to show is that my initial example in fact exemplifies a larger phenomenon. Were my example to stand only for itself, with the mode of thought particular to the case at hand, then my larger hypothesis could scarcely claim attention. So I shall now demonstrate that, in response to entirely unrelated materials, the same hermeneutic produces a structurally exact parallel to the one that operates in Bavli Baba Qamma Chapter One. For that purpose, I move to a different range of data altogether. The interests of the Mishnah's division of appointed times bear little in common with those of its division of damages. The former concerns itself with the interplay between time and space, the latter, the relationships among persons and things. The former proves abstract, the latter concrete; the former, practical and material, the latter, intellectual and intangible. And yet, we shall now see, the same fundamental problematic, a concern for how distinct grids may be brought into relationship with one another, provokes the same analysis; the same basic structures replicate themselves. Everything changes except for the main thing, and that, in the end, tells us how a generative problematic imposes itself on a vast range of discrete problems and makes of them all one, recurrent analytical problem.

1:1

A. [Acts of] transporting objects from one domain to another [which violate] the Sabbath are (1) two, which [indeed] are four [for one

who is] inside, and (2) two which are four [for one who is]
outside.

B.   How so?

C.   [If on the Sabbath] the beggar stands outside and the householder
inside,

D.   [and] the beggar stuck his hand inside and put [a beggar's bowl]
into the hand of the householder,

E.   or if he took [something] from inside it and brought it out,

F.   the beggar is liable, the householder is exempt.

G.   [If] the householder stuck his hand outside and put [something]
into the hand of the beggar,

H.   or if he took [something] from it and brought it inside,

I.   the householder is liable, and the beggar is exempt.

J.   [If] the beggar stuck his hand inside, and the householder took
[something] from it,

K.   or if [the householder] put something in it and he [the beggar]
removed it –

L.   both of them are exempt.

M.   [If] the householder put his hand outside and the beggar took
[something] from it,

N.   or if [the beggar] put something into it and [the householder]
brought it back inside –

O.   both of them are exempt.

The issue of the Mishnah paragraph is the interplay of two domains,
public and private. The first point of concern is the parallel to be drawn
between the claim that two domains yield four divisions here, and the
counterpart claims of exactly the same order that are set forth in other
contexts altogether. That is not a problem of parallels (for example,
harmonizing what appear to be conflicting statements), nor is it a
problem of mere exegesis of words and phrases; it is not an exegetical
problem at all. It is a problem identified, and solved, by appeal to the
hermeneutic I have claimed operative.

I.1   A.   [...are (1) two, which [indeed] are four:] *We have learned in the
Mishnah there:*

B.   Oaths are of two sorts, which yield four subdivisions [on account
of each of which one may be liable on one count].

C.   [2B] Awareness of [having sinned through] uncleanness is of two
sorts, which yield four subdivisions.

D.   Transportation [of objects from one domain to the other] on the
Sabbath is of two sorts, which yield four subdivisions.

E.   The symptoms of the presence of the skin disease [of Lev. 13-14,
Heb.: *negaim*] are of two sorts, which yield four subdivisions [M.
Shebu. 1:1A-D].

F.   *Now what differentiates the present passage, in which the formulation
proceeds,* are (1) two, which [indeed] are four [for one who is]
inside, and (2) two which are four [for one who is] outside, *from
the counterpart passage, in which it is taught only,* which yield four
subdivisions, *without further elaboration?*

G. *Here, a passage in which the principal interest concerns the Sabbath, we deal both with generative categories and also their secondary amplifications, while in the parallel, in which the principal interest does not concern the Sabbath, the Tannaite formulation encompasses the generative classification but not the secondary amplification thereof.*

H. *But as to the generative categories, what are they? They are only carrying out from one domain to another. And these are only two [and not four]!* [The poor man takes an article out, the householder puts an article into the poor man's hand, so where are the "two that are four"? (Freedman).] *And should you say, two of them involve liability and two others [are forbidden but] don't involve liability, lo, there is the comparable matter of the symptoms of the presence of the skin disease, so, just as in that classification, all reference pertains to liability [in that case, to uncleanness and the purification rites], so here, too, all classifications involve liability!*

I. *Rather, said R. Pappa, "Here, where the principal interest concerns the Sabbath, the Tannaite formulation covers both liability and the absence of liability, but there, where the principal interest is not in the Sabbath, what is subject to liability is covered, what is not subject to liability is not covered in the Tannaite formulation."*

What is fascinating in that observation is the explicit recognition that there are ways in which the data of a particular subject govern the articulation of that subject – and there are ways in which they do not. So we know at the outset that our framers recognize what is abstract and general, what concrete and restricted to the case at hand.

J. *Now what are the instances of liability? They are only carrying out from one domain to another. And these are only two [and not four]!*

K. *There are two subdivisions of carrying out and two of carrying in.*

L. *But the language at hand refers explicitly only to carrying out!*

M. *Said R. Ashi, "The Tannaite formulation treats bringing in as carrying out. On what basis [do I think so]? Since we learn in the Mishnah:* He who carries an object out from one domain to another is liable. *Doesn't this mean, if he carries it in from public domain to private domain, and yet it is classified as 'carrying out'? And how come? Because any act of removing an object from its original place is classified by the Tannaite authority as 'carrying out.'"*

N. *Said Rabina, "A close reading of our Mishnah paragraph also yields the same result, with its use of* [acts of] **transporting objects out from one domain to another,** *forthwith spelled out in terms of* bringing in an object *from public to private domain* [**the beggar stuck his hand inside and put [a beggar's bowl] into the hand of the householder].**"

O. *That is decisive proof.*

II.1 A. [**Two which are four:**] *Raba said, "The formulation of the Tannaite rule focuses upon domains,* and domains for the purposes of the Sabbath are two."

Now at stake is our topic in particular: How many classifications are in the initial grid?

B.   Said R. Mattenah to Abbayye, "Are there eight [two, which [indeed] are four [for one who is] inside, and (2) two which are four [for one who is] outside]? *There really are twelve.*" [Freedman: In addition to the four acts that involve liability, there are eight that do not, two acts of removal by the poor man without putting the object down, and reversing these, two acts of depositing by the poor man without removing the object; these four are to be viewed from the standpoint of the householder, yielding eight in all.]

C.   *But according to your reasoning, there really are sixteen* [Freedman: for the two actions that involve liability for the poor man are likewise to be regarded from the standpoint of the householder and vice versa, which yield another four].

D.   *He said to him, "But that's no problem. As to the* [3A] *first clause, an action that not only involves no liability but also is permitted is not addressed at all in the Tannaite formulation* [Freedman: if the man without extends his hand and places an article into the hand of the man within, the latter commits no action at all, being passive throughout, and therefore he has done nothing forbidden on the Sabbath]. *But as to the latter clause, in which the action is not culpable but is in any event forbidden, that is a problem"* [to explain why these are not counted as separate actions (Freedman)].

E.   *But with reference to the entirety of laws that pertain to the Sabbath, is there any action that on the one side is specified as not culpable and on the other side is permitted? [The laws deal only with what is not permitted, but may or may not be punishable.] For hasn't Samuel said, "Every reference to 'exempt' in the matter of the Sabbath bears the meaning, 'exempt but forbidden,' except for these three, in which the action is both exempt and permitted: trapping a deer, capturing a snake, and manipulating an abscess"?*

F.   *What Samuel finds it necessary to point out concerns only exemptions involving an affirmative action, but as for exemptions in which there is no positive action at all, there are a great many.*

G.   *[Reverting to the question at hand:] In any event, do we really have twelve [and not sixteen]?*

H.   *Actions that are not culpable, but that can lead to liability for a sin-offering, are taken into account; actions through which one cannot become liable for a sin-offering are not included.* [Freedman: Stretching out one's hand with an article from private to public domain or vice versa may involve a sin-offering, if one deposits the article in the other domain; but acceptance can never lead to this.]

III.1 A.   [If the beggar stuck his hand inside, and the householder took [something] from it, or if the householder put something in it and he [the beggar] removed it – both of them are exempt. If the householder put his hand outside and the beggar took something from it, or if the beggar put something into it and the householder brought it back inside,] both of them are exempt:

B.   *But lo, between the two, a complete act of labor has been carried out!*

What is now introduced is our first intersecting grid: the distinction between a partial and a complete act of labor. That is, one is liable for a whole act of labor, but not for only part of one (we have already seen a parallel to this distinction in the preceding chapter). Then how does that grid – partial action vs. completed one – relate to the present one – the domains of activity? Here is a wonderful example of how two distinct grids are brought into relationship with one another.

C. *It has been taught on Tannaite authority:*

D. Rabbi says, "'And if anyone of the common people sin unwittingly in doing any of the things...' (Lev. 4:27) – he who does the entirety of an action, and not he who does only part of it [is liable]. A single individual who performs a forbidden action is liable; two people who carry it out are exempt."

E. *So, too, it has been stated:*

F. Said R. Hiyya bar Gameda, "This has been set forth on the authority of the collegium, who has said, 'A single individual who performs a forbidden action is liable; two people who carry it out are exempt.'"

III.2 A. [Building on this distinction,] *Rab raised this question of Rabbi:* "If a third party loaded a person with food and drink, and he then carried them outside, what is the law? *Is the removal of one's body considered equivalent to the removal of the object from its place, in which case he is liable? Or perhaps that is not the case?"*

B. He said to him, "He is liable, and it is not parallel to the case of his hand [to which the Mishnah refers, where the article is placed in one's hand and he withdraws it, and he is exempt, in line with this instance: **If on the Sabbath the beggar stands outside and the householder inside, and the beggar stuck his hand inside and put a beggar's bowl into the hand of the householder, or if he took something from inside it and brought it out, the beggar is liable, the householder is exempt**]. *How come? His body is at rest, but his hand is not at rest.*" [Freedman: The body is at rest, so the article on his body is also at rest; he then effects its removal; his hand is not at rest on the ground, so he does not actually remove the article from its place.]

C. [3B] *Said R. Hiyya to Rab, "Son of aristocrats! Haven't I told you that when Rabbi is concentrating on one tractate, don't ask him questions concerning some other tractate, since it may not be in his mind? For if Rabbi weren't an eminent authority, you would have embarrassed him, since he might have given you an answer that is no answer at all. But, in any event, he has given you a perfectly fine answer. For it has been taught on Tannaite authority:* If someone was carrying food and drink while it was still day, and he brought them outside once darkness had fallen, he is liable, and it is not parallel to the case of his hand."

Here comes another distinction, part of its own grid. The division of grids proves too simple. We have made room for one interstitial situation: whole vs. incomplete action. But are all domains only two that are four? What about the domain that is neither public nor private. The first interstitial case, complicating our initial grid, involves a man's hand. We could readily predict the next: it will deal with part of the public domain that is not really public at all, but also is not subject to private ownership, namely, neglected public domain. So we have two kinds of interstitial categories to be brought into relationship with the original spatial one(s): what is neither private nor public, and what is public but not so public as what is really public domain.

III.3   A.   *Said Abbayye, "It is perfectly obvious to me that* a man's hand is not classified as either private domain or public domain. It is not classified as public domain *as shown by the rules governing the poor man's hand* [**If the beggar stuck his hand inside, and the householder took something from it, or if [the householder] put something in it and he [the beggar] removed it – both of them are exempt**]. It is not classified as private domain *as shown by the case of the hand of the householder* [**If the householder stuck his hand outside and put something into the hand of the beggar, or if he took something from it and brought it inside, the householder is liable**]."

        B.   Abbayye raised this question: "As to the hand of a human being, what is the rule as to treating it as equivalent to a neglected part of public domain" [Karmelit: part of public domain that is not much used, therefore regarded as neither public nor private; rabbinical law prohibits carrying from a neglected part of public domain to either public or private domain (Freedman)]. [Freedman: When one stretches out his hand into another domain, it does not enjoy the status of his body; does it occupy the intermediate status of a neglected part of public domain; since it holds an object, its owner should be forbidden to withdraw the hand until the end of the Sabbath, or is that not the case?] *Did rabbis impose the penalty on him, that he not draw the hand back to himself, or did they not do so?"*

        C.   *Come and take note:* If one's hand was full of fruit and he stretched it out – *one Tannaite formulation:* It is forbidden to bring it back inside [until after the Sabbath]; *the other Tannaite formulation:* It is permitted to bring it back in. *Now isn't this what is at stake in the conflict: The one authority maintains that the hand is equivalent to a neglected part of the public domain, the other that it is not?*

        D   *Not at all. All parties concur that it is equivalent to a neglected part of the public domain, but there is no problem, for the one refers to a case in which the hand is below ten handbreadths above the ground, the other, where it is above that height* [below, it is in public domain, and the hand has to be left there; above, it is in an area in which no liability is incurred, so he can bring it back in (Freedman)]. *And if you prefer, I shall say: Both statements pertain to a case in which the hand is less than ten handbreadths off the ground; the hand, moreover, is not equivalent to a neglected part of the public domain; but there still is no problem. The one speaks of a case in which it is still day, the other, a case in which darkness has fallen. If it is still day, rabbis have not penalized the man, if darkness has fallen, they have.*

        E.   *To the contrary, it is more reasonable to state matters contrariwise: If it is still day, so that if he had thrown the article away, he would not have become liable to a sin-offering, rabbis may very well impose a penalty; if it*

		is after nightfall, in which case if he throws the fruit away, he will incur liability to a sin-offering, rabbis oughtn't to penalize him.
III.4	A.	But since this is not the way we respond to the proposal, we may solve the problem raised by R. Bibi bar Abbayye. For R. Bibi bar Abbayye raised this question: "If one stuck a loaf of bread into an oven, have rabbis permitted him to remove it before he incurs a liability to a sin-offering, or have they not done so?" [Freedman: If it remains in the oven until baked, he will incur a sin-offering for having baked on the Sabbath; but rabbis forbid removing bread from the oven on the Sabbath.] *On the strength of the silence before us, you may settle the question that they have not permitted him to do so!* [Since that is not the case, we reject the contrary reading of matters just now proposed.]

III.4 A. But since this is not the way we respond to the proposal, we may solve the problem raised by R. Bibi bar Abbayye. For R. Bibi bar Abbayye raised this question: "If one stuck a loaf of bread into an oven, have rabbis permitted him to remove it before he incurs a liability to a sin-offering, or have they not done so?" [Freedman: If it remains in the oven until baked, he will incur a sin-offering for having baked on the Sabbath; but rabbis forbid removing bread from the oven on the Sabbath.] *On the strength of the silence before us, you may settle the question that they have not permitted him to do so!* [Since that is not the case, we reject the contrary reading of matters just now proposed.]

B. *No, that's no problem. Go ahead and resolve matters just as you propose!*

C. *Or, if you prefer, so you can't resolve the question, but there still is no problem, and this is the resolution of the conflict between the two Tannaite formulations:* The one speaks of a case in which the action is done inadvertently, the other, deliberately. *Where the action is done inadvertently, the rabbis did not penalize the man for what he has done; if the action is deliberate, they did.*

D. *Or, if you prefer, both formulations deal with a case in which the action was done inadvertently, but here what is subject to conflict is whether an action that is done inadvertently is penalized because of the penalty imposed on an action done deliberately. The one authority takes the view that an action that is done inadvertently is penalized because of the penalty imposed on an action done deliberately. The other authority maintains that an action that is done inadvertently is not penalized because of the penalty imposed on an action done deliberately.*

E. *Or, if you prefer, I shall say that an action that is done inadvertently is not penalized because of the penalty imposed on an action done deliberately. But there still is no contradiction: The one speaks of* movement in and out of that same courtyard, [4A] *the other,* movement in and out of a different courtyard.

F. *That is in line with the question that Raba presented to R. Nahman:* "If one's hand was full of produce and he stuck it outside, what is the law as to his bringing it back into that same courtyard?"

G. He said to him, "It is permitted to do so."

H. "...into another courtyard, what is the law?"

I. He said to him, "It is forbidden to do so."

J. *"What's the difference?"*

K. *"After you've measured some salt for it [I'll tell you the difference]! In the one case, his initial intention has not been accomplished, but here, his initial intention has been accomplished."* [Freedman: If he stretches out his hand into the street, he wants to remove the produce from the courtyard, so he may bring the hand back into the courtyard if his intention is unfulfilled, but as to a neighboring courtyard, his intention would be carried out, so we don't permit him to accomplish it.]

III.5 A. *Reverting to the body of the foregoing:*

B. *R. Bibi bar Abbayye raised this question:* "If one stuck a loaf of bread into an oven, have rabbis permitted him to remove it before he incurs a liability to a sin-offering, or have they not done so?"

C.   *Said R. Aha bar Abbayye to Rabina, "Now how can we imagine the case at hand? If he did it inadvertently and did not realize* [before the bread was completely baked that it was the Sabbath, or if he didn't recall that baking on the Sabbath is forbidden (Freedman)], *then whom are rabbis supposed to permit [since the man won't ever know to ask]? But if it is a case in which he afterward did become aware of what had happened, then would he be liable at all? And haven't we learned in the Mishnah:* **All those who may be liable to sin-offerings in fact are not liable unless at the beginning and the end, their [sin] is done inadvertently. [But] if the beginning of their [sin] is inadvertent and the end is deliberate, [or] the beginning deliberate and the end inadvertent, they are exempt – unless at the beginning and at the end their [sin] is inadvertent [M. 11:6J-K]?** *And, on the other hand, if it is a case of deliberate action, then he should have formulated the question in terms of before he incurs a liability to being stoned to death!"*

D.   *Said R. Shila, "In point of fact the reference is to a case of inadvertent action. And as to the question, whom are rabbis supposed to permit [since the man won't ever know to ask]?, it is, third parties."*

E.   Objected R. Sheshet, "So do they say to someone, 'Sin, so that your fellow will gain an advantage'?" [Will someone be told to violate the rule against removing bread from an oven so as to save a third party from the greater violation involved in baking on the Sabbath (Freedman).]

F.   *Rather, said R. Ashi, "In point of fact, it is a case of deliberate action. And formulate it as follows:* before he violates a prohibition by which he would incur a liability to being stoned to death!"

G.   *R. Aha b. Raba repeated the matter in so many words:* "Said R. Bibi bar Abbayye, 'If one stuck a loaf of bread into an oven, rabbis have permitted him to remove it before he should come into a situation in which he would violate a prohibition that is penalized by stoning."

IV.1 A.   **[If on the Sabbath the beggar stands outside and the householder inside, and] the beggar stuck his hand inside [and put a beggar's bowl] into the hand of the householder, or if he took something from inside it and brought it out, the beggar is liable, the householder is exempt]:**

The Mishnah's classification scheme is stable and one dimensional: inside/outside. But there is yet another grid to be considered. It is between taking up an object in one domain, and putting it down in the other domain. In both cases, we demand that the spaces out of which and into which the object is moved be comparable: in both cases a clearly defined area, designated for said object. That forthwith introduces yet another consideration: the space through which an object that is thrown is going to pass. Does the object move inch by inch, coming to rest (in our imagination) at each point in its journey? Or do we take account only of its take-off and its landing? How do we classify the space through which an object moves en route from private to public domain?

That forms an unanticipated grid of distinctions: (1) space in the two established domains, which must be comparable; (2) space through which an object passes, which must be classified in relationship to the existing domains.

B. *But why should he be liable, for lo, we require that the removing of the object and the depositing of the object must involve a space four by four handbreadths square, and that condition has not been met here?*

C. *Said Rabbah, "But who is the authority behind this rule? It must be R. Aqiba, who maintains that we do not require that the removing of the object and the depositing of the object must involve a space four by four handbreadths square, for we have learned in the Mishnah:* He who throws [an object] from private domain to public domain, [or] from public domain to private domain, is liable. [He who throws an object] from private domain to private domain, and public domain intervenes – R. Aqiba declares [him] liable [to a sin-offering]. And sages exempt [him] [M. 11:1]. *R. Aqiba maintains the theory that an object that is intercepted by the air through which it passes is as though it has come to rest there [so when it crosses the public domain, it is as though it had come to rest there, and liability is incurred], and sages take the view that an object that is intercepted by the air through which it passes is not as though it has come to rest there."*

IV.2 A. *But is that to say that it is self-evident to Rabbah that an object that is intercepted by the air through which it passes is as though it has come to rest there? [4B] And that is so when it is within ten handbreadths of the ground? [Freedman: The space above ten handbreadths is not classified as public domain.] But surely Rabbah raised a question on that very matter! For Rabbah raised the question: "If the object passes through the space below ten handbreadths off the ground, do they really disagree? It is in this matter that they disagree: R. Aqiba maintains that in that area, an object that is intercepted by the air through which it passes is as though it has come to rest there [so when it crosses the public domain, it is as though it had come to rest there, and liability is incurred], and sages take the view that an object that is intercepted by the air through which it passes is not as though it has come to rest there. But as to the space above ten handbreadths, all concur that he is not liable. They hold in common – so this theory goes – that we do not treat as comparable the act of throwing and the act of reaching an object across a space. [Freedman: If one* reaches over an object from private domain to private domain across public domain, even if it is above ten handbreadths, he is liable.] *Or perhaps they differ as to the space above ten handbreadths, and what is at issue is this: R. Aqiba maintains that we do treat as comparable the act of throwing and the act of reaching an object across a space. Sages, by contrast, take the view that we do not treat as comparable the act of throwing and the act of reaching an object across a space. But as to the situation prevailing for the space lower than ten handbreadths, all would concur that he is liable. How come? We concur in the principle that an object that is intercepted is treated as though it has come to rest. [Since Rabbah has phrased the question in that way, it is not so clear that Rabbah treats as self-evident the proposition that an object that is intercepted by the air through which it passes is as though it has come to rest there.]"*

B.   No, that's no serious problem. After raising the question, he resolved it: R. Aqiba indeed does maintain that an object that is intercepted by the air through which it passes is as though it has come to rest there.

IV.3 A.   *But maybe – responding to Rabbah's theory that R. Aqiba maintains that we do not require that the removing of the object and the depositing of the object must involve a space four by four handbreadths square – while [Aqiba] doesn't require the deposition of the object in a space four handbreadths square [for liability to be incurred], he does require removal from such a confined space?*

B.   *Rather, said R. Joseph, "Who is the authority behind the cited passage? It is Rabbi."*

C.   *So which ruling of Rabbi is supposed to be invoked here? Should we say it is the following ruling of Rabbi:* If one tossed an object and it came to rest on a projection, if it is a small projection, Rabbi declares him liable, and sages declare him exempt? *But surely in that case – as we shall place it in context – it is in accord with what Abbayye said, for said Abbayye, "Here, with what situation do we deal? It is a tree that stands in private domain, with its foliage extending into public domain, and one tossed the object, and it landed in the foliage. In that case, Rabbi takes the view that we do invoke the conception, of assigning the foliage to the status of the trunk of the tree, and rabbis hold the position that we don't invoke the conception of assigning the foliage to the status of the stock of the tree." [So it cannot be that case at all.] Rather, it has to be the following ruling of Rabbi, which has been taught on Tannaite authority:* If one tossed an object from public domain to public domain, with private domain intervening – Rabbi declares the act liable. And sages declare it exempt. [In that context] said R. Judah said Samuel, "Rabbi would impose liability on two counts, one on the count of removing the object from the one domain, the other on the count of bringing it in to the other domain." *Therefore, it follows, a place four by four is not required either for removal of the object nor for the deposit of the object.*

D.   *But lo, in that same matter, it has been said: Both Rab and Samuel say,* [5A] "Rabbi imposed liability only in the case of a private domain that was roofed over, *in which instance we invoke the principle, the house is as though it were full of objects [and so had no air space at all, thus as soon as the object enters the space, it is as though it has come to rest].* But that rule would not apply to a space that is not roofed over." *And should you say, here, too, it is a case in which it is roofed over, then that poses no problem in the case of private domain that is roofed over, but in the case of public domain that is roofed over, does one incur liability in that same way? And hasn't R. Samuel bar Judah said R. Abba said R. Huna said Rab said,* "If someone transfers an object through four cubits of public domain that is roofed over, he is exempt for liability, since that area is not comparable to the case of the flags of the wilderness." [Freedman: The definition of what constitutes forbidden work on the Sabbath depends on the work that was done in connection with the tabernacle in the wilderness; carrying was necessary, so carrying an object four cubits is work. But there it was done under the open sky, hence Rab's statement;

the same applies here. By 'flags of the wilderness' is meant the whole disposition and encampment of the Israelites; they didn't have any cover in public ground.]

E.   *Rather, said R Zira, "Lo, who is the authority behind our rule? It is 'others.'* For it has been taught on Tannaite authority: Others say, 'If someone stood still in place and caught a tossed object, the one who threw the object is liable; if he moved from his place to catch the tossed object, the one who threw it is exempt.' [If the catcher didn't move, the one who threw is liable, being regarded as having both removed the object and also deposited it; but if the catcher moved and caught the object, the thrower didn't deposit the object, since it doesn't come to rest where it would have solely on the strength of his having tossed the object.] If someone stood still in place and caught a tossed object, the one who threw the object is liable: *Lo, we require that the object come to rest in a space of four cubits, and that condition has not been met. So it must follow that we do not require that the object come to rest in a space of four cubits."*

F.   *But maybe it is coming to rest in such a space that we don't require, but removal from a space of four cubits we do require [for liability to be incurred on the part of the one who tossed the object]? And even in regard to depositing the object, maybe the sense is that he spread out his cloak and caught the object, in which case, the depositing also has taken place in a space of four cubits?*

G.   *Said R. Abba, "Our Mishnah paragraph likewise means that he removes the object from a basket and puts it into a basket, so that there is depositing in a place four cubits square."*

H.   *But the language that is used in our Mishnah paragraph is* **his hand!**

I.   *Repeat it as: a basket in his hand.*

We move to yet another complicating factor. Public domain is itself to be differentiated. Specifically, if within public domain an area is clearly demarcated, then that constitutes private domain within public domain. That distinction, within public domain, will make possible an entirely fresh set of problems. We have shaded into the cubic chess that I promised: three (and then more) dimensions of analysis, each to be kept in clear relationship to the others. The two domains with which we began prove themselves differentiated but also sustain points of differentiation entirely external to themselves.

IV.4   A.   *Well, o.k., forget about a basket in private domain, but a basket located in public domain is classified itself as private domain [so why should one be liable in regard to carrying the basket out of private domain]?*

B.   *Then don't we have to say that the Mishnah paragraph is not in accord with the view of R. Yosé b. R. Judah? For it has been taught on Tannaite authority: R. Yosé b. R. Judah says, "If one stuck a reed in public domain, with a basket on the top of it, and one tossed an object, which landed on it, he is liable [for the object is regarded as private domain]. But if the passage concurred with R. Yosé b. R. Judah, how could the rule be that he is liable [if]* **the householder stuck his hand outside and put [something] into the hand of the beggar [the** householder is liable]? *What he is doing is moving an object from private domain to private domain!*

C.   *You take the view that the passage accords even with R. Yosé b. R. Judah, for in that case, the basket is above ten handbreadths, here it is lower than that [and so is classified as public domain].*

IV.5 A.   *This presented a problem to R. Abbahu: Is the language that is used in our Mishnah paragraph a basket in his hand? The language that is used is,* his hand!

B.   Rather, said R. Abbahu, "It is a case in which he lowered his hand to within three handbreadths of the ground and received the object" [Freedman: everything within three handbreadths of the ground is regarded as part of the ground itself, so the hand becomes a place four cubits square].

The foregoing willy-nilly has given us another point of distinction, which is, distance from the ground itself; the space within three handbreadths of the ground is classified as part of the ground; above ten is classified as a domain unto itself.

C.   *But the language that is persistently used in the Mishnah is* standing!

D.   *It refers to his bending over; or, if you prefer, he is standing, but in a pit; or, if you prefer, it is a very short person.*

E.   *Said Raba, "Oh come on, is a Tannaite authority going to go to the trouble of telling us about all these weird cases?"*

F.   Rather, said Raba, "A person's hand is reckoned as though it were a space of four by four cubits."

G.   *And so when Rabin came,* he said R. Yohanan [said], "A person's hand is reckoned as though it were a space of four by four cubits."

IV.6 A.   Said R. Abin said R. Ilai said R. Yohanan, "If someone threw an object and it landed in the hand of a second party, he is liable."

B.   *Well, then, what is he telling us? That a person's hand is reckoned as though it were a space of four by four cubits? Lo, R. Yohanan said that once!*

C.   *What might you otherwise have maintained? That is the case where the man himself reckons his hand in such a way, but where he doesn't reckon his hand in such a way, I might say that is not so; thus we are informed that that is not the case.*

IV.7 A.   Said R. Abin said R. Ilai said R. Yohanan, "If someone stood in place and caught an object, he is liable. If he moved from his place and caught it, he is exempt."

B.   *So, too, it has been taught on Tannaite authority:* Others say, "If someone stood still in place and caught a tossed object, the one who threw the object is liable; if he moved from his place to catch the tossed object, the one who threw it is exempt." [If the catcher didn't move, the one who threw is liable, being regarded as having both removed the object and also deposited it; but if the catcher moved and caught the object, the thrower didn't deposit the object, since it doesn't come to rest where it would have solely on the strength of his having tossed the object.]

IV.8 A. *R. Yohanan raised this question:* "If he himself tossed the object and moved from the spot and then came back and caught it on the same spot, what is the law?"

B. So what's he asking?

The next item introduces a grid we had not anticipated, in which we distinguish two acts of force done by two individuals from two done by one and the same person. This will mark the end of the line of thought here.

C. *Said R. Adda bar Ahbah, "What he's asking about is* the effect of two acts of force exerted by one and the same man. Are two acts of force in one and the same man reckoned as the action of one man, in which case he is liable for both sides of the transaction, or perhaps they are reckoned as the actions of two separate persons, in which case he is exempt."

D. *The question stands.*

Now we turn to another set of distinctions, one that, we recall, we have already noted in the prior chapter. It is between one's own activity and one's situation as a passive recipient of the actions of another. If one has loaded himself up, that forms one taxon; if others have done so, that forms a different one. That will then allow the interplay between passive and active action, on the one side, and the movement from (or to) a place four cubits square, on the other. When I refer to a mixed grid, here is a fine example of how that works.

IV.9 A. Said R. Abin said R. Yohanan, "If one poked his hand into a courtyard of another party and received rainwater and took it out, he is liable."

B. Objected R. Zira, "So what difference does it make to me whether another person loaded him up or Heaven loaded him up? *The man himself in any event is not the one who has done the uprooting [of the object from its place]?"*

C. *Don't use the language "received" but rather "caught" it with an action that is affirmative.*

D. *Still, we require that the taking up of the object be from a place four cubits square, and that condition has not been met!*

E. Said R. Hiyya b. R. Huna, "It would be a case in which he caught the rain as it rebounded from the well."

F. *But even if it is on the wall, lo, it has not come to rest there!*

G. *It is in line with what* Raba said, "It is a sloping wall," *and here, too, it is a sloping wall.*

IV.10 A. *Now where was that statement Raba made?*

B. *It was in the context of that which we have learned in the Mishnah:*

C. [5B] [If] he was reading in a scroll on the threshold, [and] it rolled out of his hand, he may roll it back to himself. [If] he was reading on the top of the roof, and the scroll rolled out of his hand, before it falls to within ten handbreadths [of the ground], he may roll it back to himself. Once it has fallen to within ten handbreadths [of

the ground], he turns it over onto the written side [to protect it].
[R. Judah says, "Even if it is distant from the ground by only so
much as a hair's breadth, he may roll it back to himself." R.
Simeon says, "Even if it has touched the ground itself, he may roll
it back to himself. For nothing which is prohibited by reason of
Sabbath rest stands against the honor due to the sacred
Scriptures"] [M. Erub. 10:3]. *In which context [he turns it over onto
the written side] we reflected: How come he may turn it over onto the
written side? Surely it has not come to rest [so he should be able to roll it
back], and Raba responded, "It refers to a sloping wall."*

D. *Well, I might well say that Raba made such a statement with reference to a
    scroll, which can very well come to rest, but does water naturally come to
    rest by nature?*

E. Rather, said Raba, "[Yohanan addressed a case in which] he got the
    rain from the top of a water hole."

F. *Well, if it was in a hole, that's pretty obvious! [Who ever doubted it had
    come to rest?]*

G. *What might you otherwise have supposed? Water that falls on water is
    not regarded as having come to rest? He thus informs us that that
    conception is not entertained.*

IV.11 A. *Raba is consistent with opinions expressed elsewhere, for* said Raba,
          "Water that is lying on water – lo, that is a situation in which it has
          come to rest. A nut that is lying upon water – lo, that is not a
          situation in which it has come to rest."

B. *Raba raised this question: "A nut that is lying in a utensil, and a utensil is
    floating on water – do we invoke the criterion of the situation of the nut, in
    which case it has come to rest, or do we go by the criterion of the utensil,
    which, being unstable, has not come to rest?"*

C. *The question stands.*

IV.12 A. As to oil floating on wine there is a dispute between R.
          Yohanan b. Nuri and rabbis, *for we have learned in the Mishnah:*
          Oil which is floating on the surface of wine, and one who has
          immersed on that day and awaits sunset for the completion of
          his rite of purification [a tebul-yom] touched the oil – he has
          rendered unfit only the oil. R. Yohanan b. Nuri says, "Both
          of them are deemed connected to one another" [M. T.Y. 2:5H-
          K].

The next issue takes up our interest in distinguishing whole from
partial actions. But it is framed in a different way. When is an action
completed, and when is it not completed? Here we have someone
moving about all day long, as distinct from his standing still and moving
again. That permits a fresh analysis of the interplay between the two
domains and the distinction between partial and completed action.

IV.13 A. Said R. Abin said R. Ilai said R. Yohanan, "If someone [on the
          Sabbath day] was carrying food and drink, going in and coming out
          all day long [from one domain to the other] – he is liable only when
          he stands still." [Freedman: He was laden in the first place to carry
          the stuff from one part of private domain to another, and if he goes

out instead, it is not removal, since when the food was moved at first there was no intention of carrying from private to public domain.]

B. Said Abbayye, "And that is the case if he stood still to catch his breath." [Freedman: But if he stops merely to rearrange the burden, it is all part of his walking.]

C. *On what basis is such a qualification introduced?*

D. Because a master has said, "If within four cubits one stops to rest, he is exempt; if it is to shoulder the burden, he is liable; beyond four cubits of the starting point, if he stopped to catch his breath, he is liable; if it was to shoulder the burden, he is exempt." [Freedman: One is liable for carrying an object four cubits over public ground – if he himself removed it from the first spot and put it down in the other, in an intentional, single action. Stopping to rest constitutes an act of deposit; when he restarts, there is a new removal; so if he stops to rest within four cubits of the starting point, he is not liable, since he hasn't carried the object four cubits. But stopping to rearrange the burden doesn't constitute an act of deposit; hence when he does eventually stop after four cubits, he has effected removal and depositing in a single action, and is liable; so in Abin's case, he would not be liable when stopping to rest the first time, for the food he carried in and out was not carried in a single act of removal and deposit; but he would be liable if he went in and out after his rest.]

E. *So what does R. Yohanan tell us?* Merely that the original act of removing the stuff was not for this purpose? *Lo, hasn't R. Yohanan already said that once, for* said R. Safra said R. Ammi said R. Yohanan, "One who is transferring goods from one corner to another and changed his mind in regard to them and takes them out [from private to public domain] is exempt [from liability for violating the Sabbath] because to begin with lifting them up was not for that purpose"?

F. *It is a duplication of Amoraic formulations; one has it in the one version, the other, in the other version.*

Once more we turn to the distinction between the two domains, on the one side, and distinctions within the two primary domains, on the other. That rather familiar distinction is reintroduced because of the mixed grid just now composed. Once we distinguish moving from standing still, we forthwith introduce the further, and discrete, distinction among public, private, and neglected public domain. Here is yet another instance in which placing into relationship two or more grids of distinctions generates a whole fresh range of problems awaiting solution.

IV.14 A. *Our rabbis have taught on Tannaite authority:*

B. He who carries articles from a shop into the open space via a colonnade [the shop is private domain, the open space public, while the colonnade is classified as a neglected portion of public domain, not equivalent to public or private domain] is liable.

C.   And Ben Azzai declares him exempt.

D.   *Well, there is no problem understanding Ben Azzai's position, since he takes the view that walking along is equivalent to standing* [so when the man walked through the colonnade, it is as though he merely stood there; we have then two distinct actions, carrying the object from private domain to the neglected part of the public domain, then carrying the object from that to public domain; neither act by itself imposes liability (Freedman)]. *But from the viewpoint of rabbis, granting that they take the view that walking is not equivalent to standing, then under circumstances such as these, how in the world would we find a case in which someone would be liable?*

E.   *Said R. Safra said R. Ammi said R. Yohanan,* [6A] *"It is comparable to carrying an object in the public domain. In that case, even though, so long as he is going along holding the object, he is exempt; when he puts it down he is going to be liable. Here, too, there is no difference."*

F.   *But how are the cases parallel? In that case, wherever the man puts the object down, the location itself is one that is subject to liability; but in this case, if he puts the object down in the colonnade, it is a place that is not subject to liability.*

G.   *Rather, the correct analogy is to someone who is carrying an object in public domain for precisely four cubits. In such a case, even though he is exempt if he puts it down within the four cubits, if he puts it down at the end of the four cubits, he is liable; here, too, the case is no different.*

H.   *But how comparable are the cases? In that case the place is exempt for liability only relative to this man, but for all others it is a place that is subject to liability. Here, by contrast, it is a place that is exempt from liability for all persons.*

I.   *Rather, the correct analogy is to one who carries an object from private to public domain through the neglected sides of the public domain; when he puts the object down in public domain, he is liable. Here the case runs parallel.*

J.   *Objected R. Pappa, "Well, that proposed analogy poses no problems to rabbis, who have said, 'The sides of the public domain are not classified as public domain,' but from the perspective of R. Eliezer, who maintains, 'The sides of the public domain are classified as public domain,' what is to be said?"*

K.   *Said to him R. Aha b. R. Iqa, "Well, while I can well concede that you have heard that in a case in which there is no fencing, R. Eliezer said, 'The sides of the public domain are classified as public domain,' do you have evidence that he takes the same position where there is fencing [as with the colonnade]? Therefore there is a valid analogy for the case at hand."*

IV.15 A. Said R. Yohanan, "But Ben Azzai concedes in the case of one who throws [an object from a shop to public domain through a colonnade, that he is liable]."

B.   *So, too, it has been taught on Tannaite authority:*

C.   He who carries articles from a shop into the open space via a colonnade is liable. That is so whether he carries the object out or carries it in, reaches it across, or throws it.

D.   Ben Azzai says, "He who carries it out or brings it in is exempt; he who reaches it across or throws it is liable.

We move back to our starting point: the two domains. But we wish now to reframe that matter altogether, now producing two domains that are four. In fact, as we rapidly see, we can do just that because we recognize distinctions of other sorts and draw these back into our original grid: delineated space (for example, trenches in public domain or in private domain); roads and piazzas; alleys and courtyards; the sea, a valley, a colonnade; and the like. If we did not already know that these areas bore their own traits and distinctions, we also should have no interest in how they are to be classified in the context of our initial grid.

IV.16 A.   *Our rabbis have taught on Tannaite authority:*

B.   There are four distinct domains for purposes of carrying objects on the Sabbath: private domain, public domain, neglected parts of public domain, and a place totally exempt from all liability.

C.   What is the definition of private domain?

D.   The space of a trench ten handbreadths deep and four broad, and so, too, of a fence ten handbreadths high and four broad – that is private domain without qualification.

E.   What is the definition of public domain? A main road, a large piazza, and alleys open at both ends – that is public domain without qualification.

F.   People are not to carry objects from private domain of that character to public domain of that character, and they are not to bring objects from public domain of that character to private domain of that character.

G.   And if someone took out or brought in an object under such conditions, he is liable for a sin-offering if the act was done inadvertently, and to the penalty of extirpation if the act was done deliberately, or he may even be stoned to death [if there was a formal admonition not to do so on pain of death and a consequent act of rebellion].

H.   The sea, a plain, colonnade, or neglected area of public domain is classified as neither public domain nor private domain. People are not to carry or hand around objects in that area, but if one does so in such an area, he is exempt from penalty. And they are not to carry objects out from domain of that classification to public domain, or from public domain to domain of that interstitial character, nor are they to carry in objects from private domain to domain of that character, or from that domain to private domain, but if one brought out or brought in objects in such wise, he is exempt.

I.   As to courtyards that are publicly owned or blind alleys, if one prepared a symbolic meal of joining for them, they are permitted as to carrying objects about, but if one did not prepare such a symbolic meal of fusion, they are forbidden.

J.   Someone standing on a threshold [less than four handbreadths square, which is a place in which no liability is incurred, not constituting a distinct domain at all but joined to either public or private domain, as the case may be (Abraham)] may take something from the householder or give it to him, may take something from a poor man or give it to him, on condition that he does not take something from the householder and give it to the poor man or take something from the poor man and give it to the householder [so appearing to carry directly from domain to domain], but if one did so in just that way, all three of them are exempt.

K. Others say, "The threshold serves both domains. When the door is open, it is classified as part of the inside of the house; when the door is locked, it is classified along with the outside of the house.

L. "But if the threshold itself was ten handbreadths high and four broad, lo, it constitutes a domain unto itself" [T. Shab. 1:1-6].

IV.17 A. The master has said, [What is the definition of private domain? The space of a trench ten handbreadths deep and four broad, and so, too, of a fence ten handbreadths high and four broad] – that is private domain without qualification: *Excluding what [by the emphatic definition, that is...]?*

B. *It is meant to exclude what R. Judah said in that which has been taught on Tannaite authority:*

C. Still further did R. Judah state, "He who owns two houses on two sides of public domain may put [6B] a board on this side and a board on that side, or a beam on this side and a beam on that side, and carry things around in the middle.

D. They said to him, "A symbolic fusion of space in the public domain may not be undertaken in such a way."

IV.18 A. *And why do they call this,* private domain without qualification?

B. *What might you otherwise have supposed? That where rabbis differ from R. Judah, it is to maintain that so far as carrying alone this is not private domain, but as to throwing objects from side to side, they might concur with R. Judah that it is private domain. So we are informed to the contrary.*

IV.19 A. The master has said, What is the definition of public domain? A main road, a large piazza, and alleys open at both ends – that is public domain without qualification: *Excluding what [by the emphatic definition, that is...]?*

B. *It is meant to exclude what R. Judah said in addition, for we have learned in the Mishnah:*

C. R. Judah says, "If a public path went through them [the boards], one should divert it to the side."

D. And sages say, "It is not necessary [to do so]" [M. Erub. 2:4A-B].

IV.20 A. *And what is the meaning of* without qualification?

B. *Since the opening Tannaite formulation has used the language,* without qualification, *the complementary one also uses the language,* without qualification.

IV.21 A. *But why not also take account of the wilderness? For it has been taught on Tannaite authority:* What is the definition of public domain? A main road, a large piazza, and alleys open at both ends and the wilderness.

B. Said Abbayye, "No problem, the one speaks of a situation in which the Israelites were ensconced in the wilderness, the other speaks of our own time [when the wilderness is just empty space].

IV.22 A. The master has said, And if someone took out or brought in an object under such conditions, he is liable for a sin-offering if the act was done inadvertently, and to the penalty of extirpation if the act was done deliberately, or he may even be stoned to death:

B. He is liable for a sin-offering if the act was done inadvertently – *so what else is new!*

C. *The whole composition, including this needless detail, was required by the Tannaite framer with reference to the other matters, namely,* and to the penalty of extirpation if the act was done deliberately, or he may even be stoned to death.

D. *Big deal – so what else is new!*

E. *In framing matters in this way, we are informed of Rab's view, for* said Rab, "I found a suppressed scroll of the household of R. Hiyya in which was written: 'Issi b. Judah says, "The generative classifications of labor are forty less one, but one bears liability on only a single count [in any one action].""*

F. *But is that so? And haven't we learned in the Mishnah:* The generative categories of acts of labor prohibited on the Sabbath are forty less one [M. Shab. 7:2A], *in connection with which we reflected: What need do we have for the specific number associated with that statement?* And said R. Yohanan, "So that if someone did all of these actions in a single spell of inadvertence, he is liable for each classification of labor"?

G. *Rather, say it this way:* He is liable on only a single count, *in which case we are now informed that such an act of carrying is one of the actions about which there is no doubt whatsoever.*

IV.23 A. The master has said, The sea, a plain, colonnade, or neglected area of public domain is classified as neither public domain nor private domain:

B. *Is it the fact that* a plain...is classified as neither public domain nor private domain? *And lo, we have learned in the Mishnah:* A plain in the dry season is private domain in respect to the Sabbath, and public domain in respect to uncleanness. And in the rainy season it is private domain for both [M. Toh. 6:7]!

C. *Said Ulla, "In point of fact it is classified as neglected public domain. So why is it classified as private domain? Because it is not public domain."*

D. *R. Ashi said, [7A] "For instance, when it has partitions."*

E. *That is in line with what* Ulla said R. Yohanan said, "An enclosure that covers an area more than two seahs which is not enclosed for living purposes, even if it is a kor or two in area – if one throws something from public domain into such an area, he is liable. How come? Because there is a partition, even though the area lacks inhabitants" [so it is classified as private domain].

F. *Well, there is no problem with R. Ashi's statement; he doesn't explain that the Mishnah passage at hand is neglected public domain, since he prefers to invoke Ulla's other statement. But how come Ulla did not explain the passage at hand in accord with that other statement of his?*

G. *He can say to you, "If there are partitions, is it called 'a plain' at all? Surely what it is is simply an enclosed area."*

H. And R. Ashi.

I.   The language that is used in the Tannaite formulation is simply private
      domain!

IV.24 A.   Neglected area of public domain [is classified as neither public
           domain nor private domain]:

      B.   So aren't all these other classifications of space also simply in the category
           of a neglected area of public domain?

      C.   When R. Dimi came, he said R. Yohanan [said], "This was required only
           to cover the case of a corner located near the public domain. Even though
           on occasion masses of people crowd and overflow in that area, still, it is not
           all that convenient for everyday use, so it is treated as equivalent to
           neglected public domain."

IV.25 A.   When R. Dimi came, he said R. Yohanan [said], "The space between
           the pillars of a colonnade is classified as neglected public space.
           How come? Even though sometimes the general public walks there, since
           they can't just stride along there, it's classified as neglected public space."

      B.   Said R. Zira said R. Judah, "The balcony in front of the pillars of a
           colonnade is classified as neglected public space."

      C.   He who holds that the ground between the pillars is so classified will all the
           more so take that view of the balcony. But he who holds that that is so of
           the balcony may take that view only of the balcony, because it is not
           accessible for ordinary use, but not of the ground between the pillars,
           which is entirely accessible for ordinary use.

      D.   Another version: But as to the space between the pillars, through which on
           occasion people amble, that is classified as public domain.

The complete exposition now shades over onto some secondary
issues, all of them fully cogent with the foregoing.

IV.26 A.   Said Rabbah bar Shila said R. Hisda, "With a brick standing upright
           in the public domain, if one threw an object and it stuck to its side,
           he is liable; if it landed on top, he is exempt." [Freedman: When an
           article lies in the street, less than ten handbreadths high and four
           square, it is a place to which liability does not pertain; but that is in
           respect to what can be put to a well-defined, natural use, for
           example, the top of a low wall or of a brick, on which articles may
           be placed; but as to the side of a wall or a brick, that can only give
           accidental service, and in that case, everything less than ten
           handbreadths in height is as the street itself, so when one throws an
           article, and, after it has gone four cubits, it cleaves to the side of the
           brick, it is as though it fell in the street, and he is liable.]

      B.   Both Abbayye and Raba say, "But that is the case with one that is three
           handbreadths high, in which case people won't walk on it; but as to thorns
           or shrubs, even if they are not three handbreadths high" [these rank as a
           distinct domain, because people won't step on them (Freedman)].

      C.   But Hiyya bar Rab said, "Even in the case of thorns and shrubs [that is the
           rule]. But that is not the rule for horse shit" [on which people will avoid
           stepping].

      D.   And R. Ashi said, "Even horse shit."

IV.27 A.   Said Rabbah of the household of R. Shila, "When R. Dimi came, he said R.
           Yohanan [said], 'The dimensions of neglected public space cannot
           be less than four cubits square.'"

B.   And said R. Sheshet, "And it affects an area up to ten cubits square."

C.   *What can possibly be the meaning of the language,* And it affects an area up to ten cubits square? *Should I say that it means, if there is a partition ten handbreadths high, then it is classified as neglected public domain, and if not, it is not classified as neglected public domain? But isn't it, then? And didn't* R. Giddal say R. Hiyya bar Joseph said Rab [said], "In the instance of a house the inner space of which is not ten handbreadths high, but the covering of which brings it up to ten handbreadths high, it is permitted to carry on the roof over the entire area, but within the house, one may carry only in a space of four cubits"? [Freedman: Since it is unfit for a dwelling, its walls are disregarded and it ranks not as private domain but as neglected public domain, and that is the reverse of our hypothesis.] *So what can possibly be the meaning of the language,* And it affects an area up to ten cubits square?

D.   *It means, only up to ten handbreadths is the space classified as neglected public domain, but no higher than that [so that if the top is more than ten handbreadths above the ground, it is not classified as neglected public domain].*

E.   *That is in line with what Samuel said to R. Judah, "Sharp wit! In matters that pertain to the Sabbath don't take account of any space above ten handbreadths." Now for what legal purpose is that statement made? Should we propose that the meaning is,* private domain does not extend beyond ten handbreadths above the ground? But didn't R. Hisda say, "If someone stuck into private domain a pole, on top of which was a basket, and he threw up something into the basket and it came to rest on it, even if it is a hundred cubits high, he is liable, since private domain extends upward without limit"?

F.   *[7B] But if the meaning is, public domain does not extend above ten handbreadths from ground level, well, that is in point of fact our Mishnah paragraph's statement, for we have learned in the Mishnah:* He who throws [something from a distance of] four cubits toward a wall – [if he throws it] above ten handbreadths, it is as if he throws it into the air [which is public domain]. [If it is] less than ten handbreadths, it is as if he throws an object onto the ground [which is private domain] [M. Shab. 11:3A-C]. *So the statement must speak of neglected public domain, bearing the message that the category of neglected public domain does not exist above the height of ten handbreadths. [Then Dimi and Sheshet bear the message that] rabbis accorded to it the leniencies of private and public domain, namely: As to the leniences of private domain, only if it measures four handbreadths square is the area classified as neglected public domain; otherwise it is classified as a place to which liability simply does not attach. And as to the leniences of public domain, only up to ten cubits is it classified as neglected public domain; above that height, it is not classified as neglected public domain at all.*

IV.28 A. *Reverting to the body of the text at hand:* R. Giddal say R. Hiyya bar Joseph said Rab [said], "In the instance of a house the inner space of which is not ten handbreadths high, but the covering of which brings it up to ten handbreadths high, it is permitted to carry on the roof over the entire area, but within the house, one may carry only in a space of four cubits" –

B.   said Abbayye, "But if someone dug out a space four by four cubits and that makes up the measure of the inside of the house to ten cubits, then carrying over the entire space is permitted. *How come? The rest of the area would be classified as holes in private domain,* and holes in private domain are classified as private domain. *For it has been stated:* Holes in private domain are classified as private domain."

IV.29 A.   As to holes in public domain –

B.   Abbayye says, "They are classified as public domain."

C.   Raba says, "They are not classified as public domain."

D.   *Said Raba to Abbayye, "From your perspective, in maintaining holes in public domain are classified as public domain, how does this differ from what R. Dimi, when he came, said R. Yohanan said, 'This was required only to cover the case of a corner located near the public domain. [Even though on occasion masses of people crowd and overflow in that area, still, it is not all that convenient for everyday use, so it is treated as equivalent to neglected public domain.]' But why not classify that space [by your reasoning] as holes in the public domain?"*

E.   *There, it is not convenient to use that space; here, it is convenient to use that space.*

F.   *We have learned in the Mishnah:* He who throws [something from a distance of] four cubits toward a wall – [if he throws it] above ten handbreadths, it is as if he throws it into the air [which is public domain]. [If it is] less than ten handbreadths, it is as if he throws an object onto the ground [which is private domain] [M. Shab. 11:3A-C]. *Now, when we reflected on this statement, we asked: Why is it merely* it is as if he throws an object onto the ground [which is private domain]? *Surely it doesn't come to rest there [but bounces]! And said R. Yohanan, "This rule was repeated in regard to a cake of juicy figs [which stick]." Now, if you take the position that the holes in public domain are equivalent to public domain, why invoke the image of a cake of juicy figs? You can invoke the case of a splinter or anything else, but suppose it is a case in which it landed in a hole!*

G.   *Well, as a matter of fact, sometimes this was taught in the language, the case of a splinter or other object is different, because they come back, and sometimes he used the language, it refers to a wall that doesn't have a hole. And how do you know it? Because the first clause uses the language,* [if he throws it] above ten handbreadths, it is as if he throws it into the air [which is public domain]. *But if you suppose that it is a wall that has a hole, then why is it as though he threw it into the air? Lo, it comes to rest in the hole. And if you should say, the Mishnah statement pertains to a hole that is not four cubits square, didn't* R. Judah say R. Hiyya said, "If one threw an object above ten handbreadths and it went and came to rest in a hole of any size at all, that brings us to the dispute of R. Meir and rabbis, *for R. Meir takes the view that in our imagination we hollow the hole to complete it to the requisite dimensions, so liability is incurred, and rabbis take the view that we do not do so." So it follows that the reference is to a wall without a hole.*

H.   *That proves the point.*

IV.30 A. *Reverting to the body of the foregoing:* "If someone stuck into private domain a pole, on top of which was a basket, and he threw up something into the basket and it came to rest on it, even if it is a hundred cubits high, he is liable, since private domain extends upward without limit" –

B. *may we say that R. Hisda does not accord with Rabbi, for it has been taught on Tannaite authority:* If one tossed an object and it came to rest on a projection, if it is a small projection, Rabbi declares him liable, and sages declare him exempt?

C. [8A] *Said Abbayye, "In the case of private domain, all parties concur with R. Hisda. But here, with what situation do we deal? It is a tree that stands in private domain, with its foliage extending into public domain, and one tossed the object, and it landed in the foliage. In that case, Rabbi takes the view that we do invoke the conception of assigning the foliage to the status of the trunk of the tree, and rabbis hold the position that we don't invoke the conception of assigning the foliage to the status of the stock of the tree."*

The hive that is now introduced in certain dimensions forms a domain unto itself – a movable domain, but a domain. So the issue becomes, when is a hive a domain, when is it a mere object? And that, in turn, stands in relationship with the refinements of the definition of public domain that we have now mastered. Along these same lines at No. 32 comes another such object that may or may not form a domain unto itself.

IV.31 A. Said Abbayye, "If one threw a hive into the public domain, ten handbreadths high but not six broad, he is liable; if it is six broad, he is exempt." [A round object with a diameter of six contains enough space for a square of four to be inscribed; since an object four square is a distinct domain, no liability is incurred for throwing one domain into another (Freedman).]

B. Raba said, "Even if it is not six broad, he is exempt. How come? It is not possible for a piece of cane not to project ten handbreadths above the earth." [Abraham: In order to incur liability, the whole of the article thrown must rest in public domain. Since it is ten handbreadths high, it is not possible that the top and bottom canes of the circumference shall be absolutely even and straight, so something must project above ten from ground level, which is a place of non-liability, not public domain.]

C. If he overturned the mouth [where the hive was not six handbreadths broad] [and threw the hive], then, if it is a bit more than seven in height, he is liable; if it is seven and a half high, he is exempt. [Freedman: The walls of an object are regarded as extending beyond its opening down to the ground itself as soon as the opening comes within a shade less than three handbreadths from the ground; when this overturned hive, which is a shade more than seven in height, enters within just under three handbreadths from the ground and is regarded as already resting on the ground, the whole is within ten from the ground and therefore he is liable;

but if it is slightly taller than this, it is partly above ten, hence there is no liability.]

D. R. Ashi said, "Even if it is seven and a half, he is liable. How come? The partitions are made for the contents [to make it a receptacle, not to form an imaginary extension]."

IV.32 A. Said Ulla, "A column nine handbreadths high located in the public domain, on which the public rearrange their burdens, and someone threw an object and it came to rest on it – he is liable. *How come? If such a column were less than three handbreadths high, the public would step on it [so it's public domain pure and simple]; if it is from three to nine high, they don't step on it but they also don't rearrange their burdens on it [since it's too low]; if it is nine high, they certainly do rearrange their burdens on it."* [Abraham: It's put to public use and is part of public domain.]

IV.33 A. *Said Abbayye to R. Joseph, "And what about a pit nine cubits deep?"*

B. *He said to him, "So, too, is the rule with a pit."*

C. *Raba said, "But that is not the rule with a pit. How come? What can be used only with unusual effort is not classified as a public utility."*

D. R. Adda bar Mattena objected to Raba, "If someone's basket was lying in public domain, and it was ten cubits high and four cubits broad, then people may not move objects from inside it to public domain, or from public domain to the space inside it. If it is less than this, they may do so. And so with a hole. *Now doesn't this refer to the second clause [one nine handbreadths high or deep]?"*

E. *No, it refers to the first clause.*

F. *An objection was raised:* [8B] If someone intended to take up his abode for the purpose of the Sabbath in public domain, and he placed his symbolic fusion meal in a pit above ten handbreadths, it is an effective fusion meal; if it was below ten handbreadths, it is not a valid fusion meal. *Now what is the situation to which reference is made here? Should I say that he put it in a pit ten handbreadths deep, so that "above" means that he raised the bottom a bit and put the fusion meal there, and "below" means he lowered it and put it there, then what's the difference between above and below?* He's in one place, his fusion meal is in another, distinct place. [Abraham: The whole of the pit is ten deep, so it's private domain, and no object in it, even if raised to the edge, may be taken out into public domain; so the meal is inaccessible and invalid; thus he is in one place, public domain, the meal in another, private domain.] *So isn't it a hole that is not ten handbreadths deep? And it is stated explicitly, it is an effective fusion meal! So that proves that what can be used only with unusual effort is classified as a public utility.*

G. *On some occasions he replied to them, "But both he and his fusion meal are located in neglected public domain, and why is it called public domain at all? Because it's not private domain." And on some occasions he replied to them in this way: "He is in public domain, and his fusion meal is in neglected public domain, and the formulation is that of Rabbi, who has said, 'Whatever is forbidden by reason of Sabbath rest is not subject to a prohibition at twilight'* [so he had access to the food at twilight, which is just the moment at which the fusion meal serves to effect acquisition for the man of that spot as his resting place for the

Sabbath (Abraham)]. *And don't dare say that I'm merely putting you off, but I am making a precise and exact statement to you, in line with what we have learned in the Mishnah:* **If it was shallow water and a public path passed through it, he who throws [an object for a distance of] four cubits is liable. And what is the measure of shallow water? Less than ten handbreadths in depth. [If there was] shallow water, and a public path goes through it, he who throws into it to a distance of four cubits is liable [M. Shab. 11:4B-E].** *Now there is no problem explaining why there are two references to this shallow water; one refers to summer, the other, winter, and it was required to do so for both seasons. For if we knew the rule only about the summer, we might have supposed that it is then customary for people to cool themselves in the pool [which is then public domain], but I might have thought that that is not so in winter And if we had the rule for winter, I might have thought that he used the water because he was stained with mud so he would go into it, but in summer I might suppose that that is not the rule; so both references are necessary. But why in the world refer twice to the fact that* **a public path passed through it?** *It must then follow that passage through an area only with difficulty is classified as a valid passage, but utilization only with difficulty is not classified as utilization."*

H.   *A done deal.*

IV.34 A.   *Said R. Judah, "In the case of a bundle of canes, if one threw it down and raised it up [so moving it, but didn't lift it entirely from the ground] and repeatedly did so, he is not liable – until he actually lifted it up."*

Yet another interstitial domain is constituted by a threshold, which may be assigned to private or to public domain. What we see is how a given grid is itself subdivided, while being brought into relationship with other, free-standing grids.

IV.35 A.   **The master has said: Someone standing on a threshold may take something from the householder or give it to him, may take something from a poor man or give it to him:**

B.   *As to this threshold, how is it to be defined? Should I say, it is a threshold leading out of the public domain [into an alley]? Then how can the language serve,* **may take something from the householder?** *Lo, it is a question of carrying the object out from public to private domain. But then, how can the language serve,* **may take something from a poor man,** *when he is carrying it from private to public domain? And if it is a threshold of neglected public domain, then how can you use the language,* **may take something from the householder or give it to him?** *That bears the implication that the same rule applies even to begin with! But, after all, there is an operating prohibition in play [that forbids carrying between neglected public domain and public or private domain, even though, if one does so, the act is not penalized]!*

C.   *So it must mean, a threshold that serves a place that to begin with is not subject to liability, for instance, an area not four handbreadths square. And that is in accord with what, when he came, R. Dimi said R. Yohanan [said], "An area that is not four cubits by four cubits – it is permitted for those located in private domain and those located in public domain to put down and shoulder their goods therein, on* condition that they not exchange [items from persons in the framework of the one to those in the framework of the other]."

IV.36 A.   The master has said: [Someone standing on a threshold may take something from the householder or give it to him, may take something from a poor man or give it to him,] on condition that he does not take something from the householder and give it to the poor man or take something from the poor man and give it to the householder [so appearing to carry directly from domain to domain], but if one did so in just that way, all three of them are exempt:

B.   *May we then say that this refutes the position of Raba?* For said Raba, "He who moves an object from the beginning to the end of four full cubits in public domain, even though he [9A] carries it over himself [through space that is more than ten handbreadths above the ground (Abraham)] is liable."

C.   *Not at all, for in that case, the object has not come to rest, while here, it has come to rest.* [In the position posited by Raba, we disregard the method of its passage and take account of carrying an object for four cubits in the street, that alone (Abraham).]

IV.37 A.   Others say, "The threshold serves both domains. When the door is open, it is classified as part of the inside of the house; when the door is locked, it is classified along with the outside of the house [lying at the opening of a blind alley between the alley and the public domain (Abraham)]:

B.   *Is that the case even though it has no stake?* [Abraham: A stake is put at the side of the opening, which is treated as though it formed a complete partition stretching right across; the threshold is excluded from the partitioning influence of a stake, which was fixed at the inner side of the threshold.] And didn't R. Hama bar Guria say Rab said, "That which lies within the opening of the gate has to have another stake to render the area permitted"? *And if you say it is a case in which there is not an area of four by four cubits,* hasn't R. Hama bar Guria said Rab said, "What lies within the opening, even though it is not an area of four by four cubits, has to have another stake in order to render carrying in the area permitted"?

C.   *Said R. Judah said Rab, "Here we deal with a threshold of an alley, half of the threshold being covered, half uncovered, with the covering being on the inner side; so when the door is open, it is classified as part of the inside of the house; when the door is locked, it is classified along with the outside of the house."*

D.   *R. Ashi said, "In point of fact we are dealing with a threshold of a house, it is one that is covered over with two beams, neither of them four handbreadths in width, with less than three handbreadths between them, with the door in the middle. When the door is open, it is classified as part of the inside of the house; when the door is locked, it is classified along with the outside of the house."*

IV.38 A.   But if the threshold itself was ten handbreadths high and four broad, lo, it constitutes a domain unto itself:

B.   *That sustains the position of R. Isaac bar Abdimi, for said R. Isaac bar Abdimi, "R. Meir would say, 'In any situation in which you find* two domains, which form a single domain, for instance, a pillar in private domain that is ten handbreadths high and four broad, it is forbidden to adjust one's load on it, as a precautionary decree on account of the possibility of one's doing so on a hill of those dimensions that is located in public domain.'" [That is private domain, so one may not move an article from it into public domain; when such a comparable locus is in private domain, it is forbidden, too, lest people draw the conclusion from the one case that it is permitted to do the same in the other.]

I.1 begins with a comparison of the parallel beginnings of two Mishnah tractates. II.1 addresses an equivalent issue of accounting for the formulation of the Mishnah statement. Moving on from form to substance, III.1 raises a question of exegesis of the rule of the Mishnah. No. 2 then builds on the foregoing in raising a theoretical problem at the interstices of the prior rule, drawing us back to the deeper grasp of what is at stake in the Mishnah's law. Continuing the analysis of the implications of the Mishnah's rule, Nos. 3-4+5 ask yet another interstitial question, building on the foregoing. IV.1-5, with an appendix at Nos. 6-12+13 (not to mention a footnote at No. 2), raise yet another exegetical question for the Mishnah's rule, by which intersecting principles are brought to bear on the simple allegation of that rule. Then No. 14 is tacked on because the same authorities cited at No. 13 recur in the analysis of No. 14's Tannaite complement. No. 15 then continues the foregoing. No. 16 introduces a Tannaite complement, which defines domains in a more refined way than those introduced in the Mishnah statement. In many ways, what we have here is the definitive statement of the theoretical system adumbrated by our Mishnah paragraph. No wonder it is given a talmud of considerable weight, Nos. 17-24+25, 26-30. The issues introduced in that talmud are worked out through Nos. 31-33, 34. No. 35 then reverts once more to the original Tannaite passage and commences yet another talmud. The exposition goes on to Nos. 36-38. The whole then forms a superb composite on a single theme, beautifully worked out in all of its principles and their applications.

So much for a successful formation of a huge talmud out of a single problematic. Do I then maintain that we can account for the character of the document as a whole by appeal to that single trait of intellect? In the following, we see that the generative problematic serves where it serves, while the framers of the document addressed a distinct program alongside. And that other program, as I have explained at length (in *The Principal Parts of the Bavli's Discourse: A Final Taxonomy. Mishnah Commentary, Sources, Traditions, and Agglutinative Miscellanies*), takes up the task of Mishnah exegesis, pure and simple. To highlight the distinction, I now repeat the process of indenting passages that do not spin out the program of the generative problematic I have set forth.

1:2

A.   [9B] A man should not sit down before the barber close to the afternoon [prayer],

B.   unless he has already prayed.

C.   Nor [at that time] should a man go into a bathhouse or into a tannery,

D.   nor to eat, nor to enter into judgment.

E.   But if they began, they do not break off [what they were doing].

F.   They do break off [what they were doing] to pronounce the recitation of the Shema.

G.   But they do not break off [what they were doing] to say the prayer.

I.1   A.   *What is the meaning of* close to the afternoon [prayer]? *Should we say that it is* near the principal afternoon prayer? *But why not, since there will be ample time left in the day? But if it means, near the minor afternoon prayer, then what is the meaning of,* But if they began, they do not break off [what they were doing]? [Abraham: There were two times for the afternoon, the principal time, or first one, at 12:30 p.m., and the minor time, which was from 3:30 to sunset.] *Shall we then have to say that this is a refutation of the position of R. Joshua b. Levi? For* said R. Joshua b. Levi, "Once the time has come for reciting the afternoon prayer, it is forbidden for someone to taste a thing prior to saying the prayer of the afternoon worship."

       B.   No, it refers to near the principal afternoon prayer, but at issue is a fancy haircut, such as Ben Elasah would get [which took a long time, and might finish even before the principal afternoon prayer].

II.1   A.   Nor [at that time] should a man go into a bathhouse:

        B.   *that is, for the entire schvitz, beginning to end.*

III.1   A.   Or into a tannery:

         B.   *that means, tanning on a large scale.*

IV.1   A.   Nor to eat:

         B.   *that means, a long meal.*

V.1   A.   Nor to enter into judgment:

        B.   *that means, the beginning of a trial.*

V.2   A.   *R. Aha bar Jacob said, "In point of fact, it refers to a perfectly normal haircut, and why shouldn't one sit down for such a haircut to begin with? It is a precautionary decree, lest the scissors break. Likewise, the rule,* nor [at that time] should a man go into a bathhouse, *means, merely to sweat, and to begin with why not? Lest he faint. So, too, the rule,* or into a tannery, *means, to begin with to inspect it, and why not? Lest he see his goods being ruined, and that will upset him [and he'll forget about the worship]. So, too,* nor to eat, *means even a short meal, and to begin with why not? It may end up lasting longer than expected. And along these same lines,* nor to enter into judgment, *means, even to the giving of the verdict, and to begin with why not? There may be further argument and the original judgment may be upset.*

V.3 A. At what point is the beginning of the haircut [after which one doesn't have to break off for the prayer]?

B. Said R. Abin, "Once the barber puts his sheet on the customer's lap."

V.4 A. At what point is the beginning of the bathing process [after which one doesn't have to break off for the prayer]?

B. Said R. Abin, "Once one takes off his coat."

V.5 A. At what point is the beginning of the tanning process [after which one doesn't have to break off for the prayer]?

B. Said R. Abin, "Once one ties an apron around his shoulders."

V.6 A. At what point is the beginning of the eating [after which one doesn't have to break off for the prayer]?

B. Said Rab, "When one has washed his hands."

C. And R. Hanina said, "When he has loosened his belt."

D. *But there is no conflict, the one refers to us, the other to them [in the Land of Israel]. [The former wore a tight belt, the latter didn't.]*

V.7 A. *Said Abbayye, "As to our colleagues in Babylonia, from the perspective of him who has said, 'The recitation of the evening prayer is optional,' once they have loosened their belt, we don't bother them again [to stop the meal prior to saying the prayer]; from the perspective of him who has said that it is obligatory, do we trouble them to do so? Lo, the recitation of the afternoon prayer in the opinion of all parties is obligatory, and yet we have learned,* **But if they began, they do not break off** *[what they were doing], in connection with which said R. Hanina, 'That is after he has loosened his belt.'"*

B. *[10A] At that time, drunkenness is uncommon, but here, at the evening meal, it is common [so one must refrain from the meal, even if he has loosened his belt, until prayers are said, if these prayers are deemed obligatory]. Or also, in the case of the afternoon prayer, since a set time is assigned to it, one will be concerned and not come to transgress; but as to the evening prayer, since no set time is assigned to it but it can be recited all night long, he will not be preoccupied about it and may end up transgressing.*

C. *Objected R. Sheshet, "So is it such a big deal to loosen one's belt? Anyhow, let him get up as is and say the prayer."*

D. It is on account of, "Prepare to meet your God, O Israel" (Amos 4:12).

V.8 A. *Rabbah bar R. Huna put on stockings and said his prayer, citing the verse, "Prepare to meet your God, O Israel" (Amos 4:12).*

B. *Raba took off his cloak, clasped his hands, and said his prayer, saying, "I am like a slave before his master."*

C. *Said R. Ashi, "I saw R. Kahana, when there was anguish in the world, removing his cloak, clasping his hands, and saying his prayers, with the words, 'I am like a slave before his master.' But when there was tranquillity in the world, he would put on and wrap himself in his cloak and pray, saying the verse, 'Prepare to meet your God, O Israel' (Amos 4:12)."*

V.9 A. *Raba saw R. Hamnuna prolonging his prayer. He said, "They relinquish an everlasting life in order to occupy themselves with immediate gratification."*

	B.	*For he maintained the theory that the time of prayer and the time of Torah study are separate from one another.*
V.10	A.	R. Jeremiah was in session before R. Zira, and they were engaged in the study of a tradition. The time came for praying, so R. Jeremiah hastened to adjourn. R. Zira cited in his regard the verse, "He who turns away from hearing the Torah – even his prayer is an abomination" (Prov. 28:9).
V.11	A.	At what point is the beginning of a lawsuit?
	B.	R. Jeremiah and R. Jonah –
	C.	one said, "From the moment that the judges cloak themselves."
	D.	And the other said, "From the time that the litigants commence laying out their cases."
	E.	*But they don't really differ. The one speaks of a situation in which they have already entered upon the judgment of the case, the other in which they have not already entered upon the judgment of the case.*
V.12	A.	*Between the pillars, R. Ammi and R. Assi were in session and studying. Every few minutes they knocked at the side of the door and announced, "If anybody has a suit, let him come on in."*
V.13	A.	R. Hisda and Rabbah bar R. Huna were in session in court all day long. They felt weak. R. Hiyya bar Rab of Difti repeated for them the following Tannaite statement: "'And the people stood about Moses from the morning unto the evening' (Ex. 18:13) – now can it enter your mind that Moses was sitting and judging cases all day long? When would his study of Torah be carried out? But it is to tell you: Any judge who judges a case in truth and fidelity even for a single moment is regarded by Scripture as though he were turned into a partner of the Holy One, blessed be He, in the works of creation. For here it is written, 'And the people stood about Moses from the morning unto the evening' (Ex. 18:13), and elsewhere, 'And there was evening, and there was morning, one day.'"
V.14	A.	How long are judges to sit in judgment?
	B.	Said R. Sheshet, "To meal time."
	C.	*Said R. Hama, "What verse of Scripture makes that point? 'Woe is you, land, when your king is a child and your princes eat in the morning! Happy are you, land, when your king is the son of aristocrats and your princes eat at the right time, for strength and not to get drunk' (Qoh. 10:16-17) – for the strength of the Torah, and not for drunk with wine."*
V.15	A.	*Our rabbis have taught on Tannaite authority:*
	B.	The first hour is the meal time for gladiators; the second, for robbers, the third, for heirs, the fourth, for laborers, the fifth, for everybody else.
	C.	Now is that so? And didn't R. Pappa say, "The fourth hour is the time for the main meal of everybody"?
	D.	Rather: The fourth is the time for everyone, the fifth, the meal time for workers, the sixth, the meal time for disciples of sages. From that point onward in the day, it is like throwing a stone into a barrel [and no benefit will come of the meal].

	E.	*Said Abbayye, "But we have made that statement only of one who has tasted nothing in the morning, but if someone has eaten something in the morning, there is no problem."*
V.16	A.	Said R. Adda bar Ahbah, "One may recite the prayer in the bathhouse."
	B.	*An objection was raised:* When one enters a bathhouse – if it is a place where people stand dressed, he may recite Scripture or the prayer there [T.: the Shema or say the prayer there], and he obviously may greet his fellows there; he may don his phylacteries and obviously he need not remove them if he came in wearing them. If it is a place where people stand naked, he may not greet his fellows there, and obviously he may not recite Scripture or the Shema or the prayer there, and he must remove his phylacteries, and obviously he may not put them on. If it is a place where people stand both naked and dressed, he may greet his fellows there, but he may not recite Scripture or the Shema or the prayer there, and he need not remove his phylacteries, but he may not put them on there to begin with [T. Ber. 2:20]!
	C.	*When R. Adda bar Ahbah made that statement, it concerned* a bathhouse in which there was no one located at all.
	D.	But lo, said R. Yosé bar Hanina, "The bathhouse of which they have spoken is even one in which there is no other person present; the toilet of which they have spoken is even one in which there is no shit."
	E.	*Rather, when R. Adda bar Ahbah made that statement, it concerned a new one.*
	F.	*But this is precisely what Rabina asked as a question:* "What if a locale is designated for use as a toilet? What is the law? Does that designation apply or not?" *And, we recall, he did not solve that problem. Now isn't the same rule pertinent to the bathhouse?*
	G.	*Not at all, perhaps* [10B] *a bathhouse is exceptional, because it stinks.*
V.17	A.	He may not greet his fellows there:
	B.	*That supports what R. Hamnuna said in the name of Ulla:* "It is forbidden for someone to greet his fellow in the bathhouse, on the strength of the verse, 'And he called it, The Lord is peace' (Judg. 6:24)."
	C.	*Well, if that's so, then it also should be forbidden to say, "By faith," in the toilet, since it's written, "The faithful God" (Deut. 7:9). And should you say, well, that's so – didn't Raba bar Mehasayya say R. Hama bar Guria said Rab said, "It is permitted to say, 'By faith,' in the toilet"?*
	D.	*In that case, the name itself is not stated, as we translate it, "God is faithful," but here the name itself is designated "peace," as it is written, "And he called it, the Lord is peace.'"*
V.18	A.	And said Raba bar Mehasayya said R. Hama bar Guria said Rab, "He who gives a gift to his fellow has to inform him: 'That you may know that I the Lord sanctify you' (Ex. 31:13)."
	B.	*So, too, it has been taught on Tannaite authority:*
	C.	"That you may know that I the Lord sanctify you" (Ex. 31:13):

D.   The holy one, blessed be He, said to Moses, "Moses, I have a fine gift [for you] in my treasury, and it is called Sabbath, and I desire to present it to [the people of] Israel. Go and inform them."

E.   On this basis, said Rabban Simeon b. Gamaliel, "One who gives bread to a child must inform its mother."

F.   *What does he do to him?*

G.   *Said Abbayye, "He smears him with oil or puts eyeshadow on him."*

H.   *But these days, when we are afraid of witchcraft, [what should the individual who gives the child bread do]?*

I.   Said R. Pappa, "He smears on him some of the same thing [that was on the bread he gave him to eat]."

J.   Is that so? But didn't R. Hama bar Hanina say, "He who gives a gift to his fellow doesn't have to inform him, as it is said, 'And Moses didn't know that the skin of his face shone by reason of his speaking with him' (Ex. 34:29)"?

K.   *No problem, the one refers to something that is apt to come out, the other, to something that is not apt to come out.*

L.   *Well, the Sabbath is surely something that was apt to come out [yet God made sure Israel knew about the gift]?*

M.   *The reward for it was not apt to come out [and Moses was told to inform the people about it].*

V.19   A.   *[Himself a priest,] R. Hisda was holding in hand two gifts of oxen [assigned to the priesthood]. He said, "To whoever will come and tell me a new tradition in Rab's name shall I give these!"*

B.   *Said to him Raba bar Mehasayya, "This is what Rab said, 'He who gives a gift to his fellow has to inform him, as it is said, "That you may know that I the Lord sanctify you" (Ex. 31:13).'"*

C.   *He gave them to him.*

D.   *[The other] said to him, "Do you so prize the traditions of Rab?"*

E.   *He said to him, "Yes, I do."*

F.   *He said to him, "This is what Rab said: 'A piece of clothing is valued by the one who wears it.' [As Rab's disciple, you value what he said.]"*

G.   *He said to him, "Did Rab really say that?! Well, I value the second higher than the first, and if I had another ox, I'd hand it over to you for that one."*

V.20   A.   And said Raba bar Mehasayya said R. Hama bar Guria said Rab, "One should never single out one of his children from the others, since for the sake of two selas' weight of silver that Jacob gave to Joseph more than to the other children, his brothers were jealous of him, and matters unfolded so that our ancestors had to descend to Egypt."

V.21   A.   And said Raba bar Mehasayya said R. Hama bar Guria said Rab, "One should always try to take up residence in a town that was only recently settled, for, since it was only recently settled, its sins are few: 'Behold, now, this city is recently near to flee to, and it is little' (Gen. 19:20). *What can be the meaning of 'near'? Should we say that it really was near and small? But obviously they could see that on their own. Rather, it must mean, since it was only recently settled, its sins are few.*"

B.   Said R. Abin, "What verse of Scripture sustains that reading? 'Oh, please let me escape thither' (Gen. 19:20), and the numerical value of the word for 'please' is fifty-one. But Sodom had been in existence for fifty-two years, while its prosperity lasted for [11A] twenty-six: 'Twelve years they served Chedorlaomer and thirteen years they rebelled, and in the fourteenth year' (Gen. 14:4)." [That leaves twenty-six years not at peace, plus twenty-six of peace prior to the destruction.]

V.22 A.   And said Raba bar Mehasayya said R. Hama bar Guria said Rab, "Any town the roofs of which are higher than that of the synagogue in the end will be destroyed: 'To exalt the house of our God and to repair the ruins thereof' (Ezra 9:9)."

B.   *Now that judgment pertains only to the houses, but as to towers or turrets, there is no problem.*

C.   *Said R. Ashi, "I made sure that Mata Mehassayya would not be destroyed."*

D.   *Yeah, sure – but it was destroyed.*

E.   *But it wasn't destroyed because of that particular sin.*

V.23 A.   And said Raba bar Mehasayya said R. Hama bar Guria said Rab, "[Let me live] under Ishmael but not under a Roman, under a Roman but not under a Magus, under a Magus but not under a disciple of a sage, under a disciple of a sage but never under a widow and orphan."

V.24 A.   And said Raba bar Mehasayya said R. Hama bar Guria said Rab, "Any illness but a bellyache, any pain but a heartache, any torment but not migraine, any evil but not a bad wife."

V.25 A.   And said Raba bar Mehasayya said R. Hama bar Guria said Rab, "If all the seas were ink and all the reeds pens and all the heavens parchment and all men scribes, they would not suffice to write down all the intricacies of dominion."

B.   *What is the pertinent verse of Scripture that makes that point?*

C.   Said R. Mesharshayya, "'The heaven for height, the earth for depth, and the heart of kings is unsearchable' (Prov. 25:3)."

V.26 A.   And said Raba bar Mehasayya said R. Hama bar Guria said Rab, "Fasting is as good for dreams as fire for tow."

B.   Said Hisda, "But that is for that very day."

C.   And said R. Joseph, "Even on the Sabbath."

V.27 A.   *R. Joshua b. R. Idi visited the household of R. Ashi. They prepared for him a third-grown calf and said to him, "Will the master taste something?"*

B.   *He said to them, "I am observing a fast."*

C.   *They said to him, "But doesn't the master concur with what R. Judah said, for said R. Judah, 'A person may borrow against his fast and pay it back'?"*

D.   *He said to him, "It is a fast on account of a dream, and said Raba bar Mehasayya said R. Hama bar Guria said Rab, 'Fasting is as good for dreams as fire for tow.' And said Hisda, 'But that is for that very day.' And said R. Joseph, 'Even on the Sabbath.'"*

VI.1 A.   **But if they began, they do not break off [what they were doing]. They do break off [what they were doing] to** pronounce the recitation of the Shema. But they do not break off [what they were doing] to say the prayer:

B.   *But the opening clause is explicit:* They do not break off [what they were doing]*!*

C.   *The latter reference pertains to study of Torah, as has been taught on Tannaite authority:* Colleagues who were engaged in the Torah interrupt their studies for the recitation of the Shema but they don't do so for the prayer.

VI.2 A.   Said R. Yohanan, "That was said only of such as R. Simeon b. Yohai and his colleagues, whose Torah study was their profession, but such as we must break off for both reciting the Shema and saying the prayer."

B.   *But hasn't it been taught on Tannaite authority:* Just as they do not interrupt for the prayer, so they don't interrupt for the recitation of the Shema?

C.   *When that Tannaite statement was set forth, it had to do with intercalating the year. For said R. Adda bar Ahbah, and so, too, the elders of Hagronayya repeated,* "Said R. Eleazar bar Sadoq, 'When in Yavneh we were engaged in the intercalation of the year, we would not interrupt our work either to recite the Shema or to say the prayer.'"

Any notion that the Bavli concerns itself mainly with the abstract exploration of thought problems expressed in concrete data is challenged by this perfectly characteristic and routine exegetical composite. I.1-V.1 clarify details of the language of the Mishnah paragraph. V.2 continues that same process. The same goes forward at Nos. 3-6+7. We have an appendix on the theme of a detail of No. 7 running through Nos. 8-10. No. 11, with its appendix at Nos. 12-15, then reverts to the clarification of the Mishnah sentence. A further secondary composition follows at No. 16, bearing its own appendix at No. 17. An enormous appendix, Nos. 18+19, 20-26+27, shaped around a common attributive formula, is tacked on because an item of that appendix is used at No. 17. VI.1, with secondary expansion at No. 2, analyzes the language of the Mishnah statement and glosses the matter.

1:3

A.   A tailor should not go out carrying his needle near nightfall,
B.   lest he forget and cross [a boundary];
C.   nor a scribe with his pen.
D.   And [on the Sabbath] one should not search his clothes [for fleas], or read by the light of a lamp.
E.   Nonetheless they state:
F.   [On the Sabbath] a teacher sees [by the light of a lamp] where the children are reading, but he does not read.
G.   Similarly:
H.   A male Zab should not eat a meal with a female Zab, because it leads to transgression.

We shall now see that there is no predicting (at least for the current case) where the generative problematic will govern the exposition of a Mishnah paragraph, and where that exposition will be guided by thin and routine exegetical concerns. We could not have predicted that the foregoing would attract attention to its implications for the interplay of distinct grids. But that is what happens. We dredge up an interstitial case: the two domains clearly differentiated, but the situation of a human being between the one and the other. This situation we are able to portray through the medium of a single individual's standing in one domain and drinking water in the other. The water passes from one domain to the other – but through that person's innards. Do we subdivide the person or not? That is a question that is possible only within a system of taxonomic inquiry: how two grids intersect, the spatial, the personal (in this case). And what makes the matter still more interesting is we forthwith introduce the interstitial classification of neglected public domain! That surely attests to the decision to think in one way – the one dictated by the hermeneutic I have identified – rather than in some other.

I.1   A.   *We have learned in the Mishnah:* **A man should not stand in private domain and drink in public domain, in public domain and drink in private domain, unless he has poked his head and the greater part of his body into the same domain as that in which he drinks. [11B] And so in the case of a wine press. A man scoops up water out of a gutter less than ten handbreadths from the ground. And from a waterspout in any manner he may drink [M. Er. 10:6].**

B.   *The question was raised: What is the rule in regard to neglected public domain?*

C.   *Said Abbayye, "It is the same."*

D.   *Raba said, "[The prohibition of moving an object between neglected public domain and public domain or private domain] itself is only a precautionary decree, so should we now go and issue a precautionary decree tacked on to another such decree?"*

E.   *Said Abbayye, "On what basis do I make my statement? Because it is said in the Mishnah,* **And so in the case of a wine press.** *Now what is this wine press? If it is private domain, that is covered in the Mishnah, and if it is public domain, that, too, is covered in the Mishnah, so isn't it neglected public domain?"*

F.   *And Raba said,* "**And so in the case of a wine press** *refers to tithes."*

G.   *And so, too, said R. Sheshet,* "**And so in the case of a wine press** *refers to tithes."*

H.   *For we have learned in the Mishnah:* "**One drinks [wine] at the press – whether [it is mixed] with hot water or cold water – he is exempt [from removing the tithes]"** *– the words of R. Meir. R. Eleazar bar Sadoq declares [him] liable [to removing the tithes]. But sages say, "Concerning [the wine mixed with] hot water, he is liable [to removing the tithes], but concerning [the wine mixed with] cold*

water, he is exempt [from removing the tithes]" [M. Ma. 4:4]. That
is because he puts back the rest. [Abraham: The vat is the utensil
into which the juice of the grapes runs; it descends into the pit
underneath. Once it is in the pit its processing as wine is complete
and it is liable to tithes; before they are given, nothing may be
drunk. While it is yet in the vat its processing is not complete, so a
little wine may be drunk even before the tithes are designated. That
is so only if it is drunk directly over the vat. If it is taken out, that
action itself confers upon it the status of finished wine, and the
tithes are then owing. When it is taught, "And the same applies to a
wine vat," it means, if one drinks wine from the vat, he is regarded
as taking it away, unless he has his head and greater part of his
body in the vat, and must render the tithes before he drinks. Wine
was not drunk neat but diluted with water; if with cold, the rest can
be poured back into the vat, if with hot, it can't; the hot mixture will
ruin the rest. Meir holds that in both cases, since he doesn't take the
wine away from the vat, he can drink a little without tithing;
Eleazar differs; sages agree with Meir if cold water is used for
diluting.]

I.   *We have learned in the Mishnah:* A tailor should not go out carrying
        his needle near nightfall, lest he forget and cross [a boundary].
        Now surely this must mean that it is stuck in his garment! [Abraham:
        Then even carrying it out on the Sabbath is only rabbinically
        forbidden as a precautionary measure, lest he carry it in some more
        ordinary way, and yet he must also not go out before the Sabbath as
        a preventive measure lest he do so on the Sabbath; we therefore
        have a preventive measure made to safeguard another such
        measure.]

J.   *Not at all, he can't do so holding it in the ordinary way, in his hand.*

K.   *Come and take note:* A tailor should not go out carrying his needle
        stuck in his garment. *Doesn't this mean, on the eve of the Sabbath?*

L.   *Not at all. That was taught with respect to the Sabbath itself.*

M.   *But hasn't it been taught on Tannaite authority:* On the eve of the
        Sabbath toward dark a tailor should not go out carrying his needle
        stuck in his garment?

N.   *Lo, who is the authority behind that formulation? It is R. Judah, who has
        said,* "A craftsman is liable for carrying out an object as he
        ordinarily would in his trade." *For it has been taught on Tannaite
        authority:* A tailor must not go out carrying his needle stuck in his
        garment, nor a carpenter with the beam on his shoulder, nor a
        weaver with the button in his ear, nor a dyer with the color
        sample around his neck, nor a moneychanger with a denar in his
        ear, but if he does do so, he is not liable, though the act is
        forbidden," the words of R. Meir. R. Judah says, "A craftsman is
        liable for carrying out an object as he ordinarily would in his
        trade, but everyone else is exempt from liability to punishment"
        [T. Shab. 1:8B-H].

The foregoing has introduced another grid, this one formed by two
distinct lines: doing a deed in the ordinary way, doing it in an
extraordinary way; the doing of a deed by a craftsman, the doing of a

deed by a common person. How do we hold these grids together, on the basis of the initial distinction between and among domains? This is, again, an instance of a well-constructed cubic chessboard.

I.2   A.   *One Tannaite formulation states:* A person afflicted with flux should not go out with his pus-bag, but if he goes out, he is not liable, though the act is forbidden. *Another Tannaite formulation states:* A person afflicted with flux should not go out with his pus-bag, but if he goes out, he is liable to a sin-offering.

       B.   *Said R. Joseph, "No problem, the one represents the position of R. Meir, the other of R. Judah."*

       C.   *Said to him Abbayye, "Well, I can concede that you have heard from R. Meir that that is the rule for something that is not ordinarily carried in such a way, but have you heard him take that position in connection with something that has to be carried in such a way? And if you don't concede my point, then what about the following: In the case of* an unskilled person who hollowed out a measure from a log on the Sabbath, *would he be exempt on R. Meir's view?"* [Abraham: Surely not, for if so, only a skilled worker will be liable for carrying out something of his own trade; it must be that a person is liable for doing any labor in the manner that would be routine for that person, the same is so for the person afflicted with flux and his pus-bag.]

       D.   *Rather, said R. Hamnuna, "No problem, the one refers to a person afflicted with flux who has produced two attested flows of pus, the other, one afflicted with flux who has produced three."* [After three, he owes a sacrifice, so he needs the pouch to know whether or not he produces a third; since he needs it, it is in the ordinary way that he carries it so he must be liable (Abraham).]

       E.   *And what's the difference in respect to one who has suffered two such appearances, so that he should be liable? It is because he needs it for an examination? Then one who has suffered three appearances also needs it for counting!*

       F.   *But is it needed for that very day?* [He doesn't need the pouch on the Sabbath, since he would not be liable should the third attack come on the Sabbath; he commences counting only on the next day (Abraham).]

       G.   *But it's needed to protect his clothing from the pus.*

       H.   *Said R. Zira, "The Tannaite authority at hand takes the view that anything done only to keep things clean is not taken into account.* [Abraham: When something is done not for its own sake but to prevent something from getting dirty, it is not regarded as a positive act and involves no liability.] *For we have learned in the Mishnah:* **He who puts a dish on end against the wall so that it will rinse off, lo, this is under the law, if water be put. If [he did so] [12A] so that it [rain] should not harm the wall, it [the water] is not under the law, if water be put [M. Makh. 4:3]."** [The latter action is simply to keep the wall clean and is not taken into account in assessing whether dealing with the water flow involves utilizing the water in a purposeful manner, in which case the water has the power to impart susceptibility to uncleanness to dry produce that comes into contact with it.]

I.   *But are the cases truly parallel? In that case he doesn't want the flow at
         all, but here he really needs the pus-pouch to catch the pus. The valid
         comparison is only with the latter clause of the same composite:* A trough
         into which the rain dripping from the roof flowed – the drops [of
         water] that splashed out and those that overflowed are not under
         the law, if water be put. *But the water that is in it falls under the
         rubric, "And if water be put" [since that water is wanted]* [M.
         Makh. 4:5A-B]. [Abraham: This shows that when a man's
         intentions are fulfilled, the action is taken into account; here, too, he
         carries the pouch with a definite intention, which is fulfilled, so he
         should be liable.]

To solve the problem of conflicting grids, we can invoke yet another
set of intersecting lines. Now the distinction is between an action the
cause of which one approves and one the cause of which one does not
approve. When we introduce that distinction, of course, we stand at the
edge of a whole new realm of distinctions, those of psychology or
attitude. Then there are three enormous, and distinct, grids that have to
be placed into relationship and sorted out: domains, actions, attitudes.

J.   *Rather, both Abbayye and Raba say, "No problem, the one represents the
         view of R. Judah, the other, R. Simeon."* [Judah holds one is culpable
         for an act even if the cause of the act is unwanted; Simeon denies
         liability; here the cause of carrying the pouch is the pus, which isn't
         wanted (Abraham).]

I.3   A.   A Tannaite statement of the household of R. Ishmael: "A man
             may go out on the eve of the Sabbath at dusk wearing his
             phylacteries."
      B.   *How come?*
      C.   Since Rabbah bar R. Huna said, "A man is liable to touch his
             phylacteries occasionally, a view based on an argument a
             fortiori from the headplate of the high priest: If the headplate,
             which contains only one reference to the Divine Name, is
             subject to the statement of the Torah, 'And it shall always be on
             his forehead' (Ex. 28:38), so that he will not neglect it,
             phylacteries, which contain numerous mentions of the Divine
             Name, all the more so," *therefore he will keep them in mind that
             way.*

I.4   A.   *It has been taught on Tannaite authority:*
      B.   Hanania says, "A person is obligated to examine his clothing
             on the eve of the Sabbath at dusk."
      C.   *Said R. Joseph, "That is one of the great laws concerning the
             Sabbath."*

II.1 A.   And [on the Sabbath] one should not search his clothes [for
             fleas]:
      B.   *The question was raised: "Does this mean that on the Sabbath day
             one should not search his clothes [for fleas]? Then it would
             stand for the position of R. Eliezer, for it has been taught on Tannaite
             authority: Said R. Eliezer, 'He who kills a louse on the Sabbath is as
             though he killed a camel.' And then the phrase,* or read by the light

		of a lamp, *would refer to the consideration that one may end up tilting the lamp? Or perhaps both actions are forbidden lest he tilt the lamp?"*

     C.   Come and take note: They may not search garments nor read by the light of a lamp.

     D.   *But is that formulation any more formidable than that of our Mishnah [for the same question arises in that case as much as in ours]!*

     E.   Come and take note: They may not search garments by the light of a lamp, nor read by the light of a lamp. These represent some of the laws that they stated in the upper room of Hananiah b. Hezekiah b. Garon. That proves that both actions are prohibited lest he tilt the light of the lamp.

     F.   *Sure does.*

II.2   A.   Said R. Judah said Samuel, "It is forbidden even to distinguish by lamp light between one's own clothing and one's wife's."

     B.   *Said Raba, "We have made that statement only in connection with townsfolk, but as to country people, the clothing is readily distinguished. And even in the case of townsfolk, that statement concerns the clothing only of old ladies, but as to those of young women, they are easy to tell apart."*

II.3   A.   *Our rabbis have taught on Tannaite authority:*

     B.   In the public domain they do not search garments for lice, because of considerations of self-respect.

     C.   Along these same lines said R. Judah, and there are those who say it in the name of R. Nehemiah, "In the public domain they try to vomit, because of considerations of self-respect."

II.4   A.   *Our rabbis have taught on Tannaite authority:*

     B.   He who examines his clothing on the Sabbath may crush the louse and toss it away, so long as he doesn't actually kill it.

     C.   Abba Saul says, "He may take it and toss it away, so long as he doesn't squeeze it."

     D.   Said R. Huna, "The decided law is: He may press it and throw it away, and that is fitting, even on a weekday."

II.5   A.   *Rabbah would kill them; R. Sheshet would kill them.*

     B.   *Raba tossed them into a pan of water.*

     C.   *R. Nahman said to his daughters, "Kill them and let me hear the sound of those despicable things."*

II.6   A.   *It has been taught on Tannaite authority:*

     B.   R. Simeon b. Eleazar says, "'They don't kill vermin on the Sabbath,' the words of the House of Shammai. And the House of Hillel permit."

     C.   And so did R. Simeon b. Eleazar say in the name of Rabban Simeon b. Gamaliel, "'On the Sabbath they don't negotiate terms for a daughter's betrothal, nor for teaching reading to a child, nor for teaching him a trade, nor do they comfort mourners, nor do they visit the sick,' the words of the House of Shammai. And the House of Hillel permit."

II.7   A.   *Our rabbis have taught on Tannaite authority:*

B.   He who on the Sabbath comes to visit a sick person says, "Today it's the Sabbath, so one can't cry out, but recovery will come soon."

C.   And R. Meir says, "One may say, 'May [the Sabbath] show compassion.'"

D.   [12B] R. Judah says, "'May the Omnipresent have compassion on you and on all Israelite sick.'"

E.   R. Yosé says, "'May the Omnipresent have compassion on you in the midst of all Israelite sick.'"

F.   Shebna of Jerusalem, when he would come in, would say, "Peace," and when he would leave, he would say, "Today it's the Sabbath, so one can't cry out, but recovery will come soon. And his compassion is abundant, so enjoy the Sabbath rest in peace."

G.   *And with which authority does the following statement of R. Hanina concur:* "He who has a sick person in his house has to include him in a blessing for all of the sick of Israel"?

H.   *In accord with whom? It is in accord with R. Yosé.*

II.8   A.   And said R. Hanina, "It was with difficulty that sages permitted comforting the mourners and visiting the sick on the Sabbath."

II.9   A.   *Said Rabbah bar bar Hannah, "When we would go after R. Eleazar to pay a call on a sick person, [we heard that] sometimes he would say to him, 'The Omnipresent remember you in peace,' and sometimes he would say, 'The Omnipresent remember you in peace.'"*

B.   *But how could he have acted in such a way? Didn't R. Judah say,* "A person should always ask what he needs in the Aramaic language"? *[How could he use Hebrew or Aramaic, without distinction?]* And R. Yohanan said, "Whoever asks for what he needs in Aramaic – the ministering angels don't accede to him, for the ministering angels don't understand Aramaic"!

C.   *A sick person is an exceptional situation, for* the Presence of God is with him. For said R. Anan said Rab, "How on the basis of Scripture do we know that the Holy One, blessed be He, nourishes the sick? 'The Lord will strengthen him upon the bed of languishing' (Ps. 41:4)."

D.   *So, too, it has been taught on Tannaite authority:*

E.   He who goes in to visit the sick should not sit on the bed or on the stool or chair but must cloak himself and sit on the ground, for that the Presence of God hovers above the bed of the sick, as it is said, "The Lord sets himself upon the bed of languishing" (Ps. 41:4).

F.   Further said Rabin said Rab, "How on the basis of Scripture do we know that the Presence of God hovers above the bed of the sick? 'The Lord sets himself upon the bed of languishing' (Ps. 41:4)."

III.1 A.   **Or read by the light of a lamp:**

B.   Said Raba, "That is the rule even if the lamp is located at a height twice a man's stature or two ox goads up, even ten rooms on top of one another."

III.2 A.   *The rule pertains to one, who should not read by himself, but it's o.k. for two to do so.*

B.   *But hasn't it been taught on Tannaite authority:* neither one nor two?

C.   *Said R. Eleazar, "No problem,* the former refers to two persons together studying a single subject, the other, two."

D.   Said R. Huna, "But if it is by the light of a bonfire, even ten people are forbidden to do so" [each sitting far from another, anyone of them may forget and stir up the flame (Abraham)].

III.3 A.   Said Raba, "But if it is an eminent authority, it is permitted."

B.   **An objection was raised: A man should not read by the light of a lamp, lest he tilt it. Said R. Ishmael b. Elisha, "I shall read by lamplight, I won't tilt it." Once he was studying and he wanted to tilt the lamp. He said, "How great are the teachings of sages, who have said, 'A man should not read by the light of a lamp, lest he tilt it.'" R. Nathan says, "He studied and he did tilt it, but he wrote in his notebook, 'I, Ishmael b. Elisha, studied on the Sabbath and tilted the lamp. When the house of the sanctuary is rebuilt, I shall bring a mighty fat sin-offering'" [T. Shab. 1:13].**

C.   *Said R. Abba, "R. Ishmael b. Elisha is an exception,* since so far as teachings of the Torah were concerned, he treated himself as a common person." [But he didn't have to do so.]

III.4 A.   *One Tannaite statement:* On the Sabbath a waiter may examine cups and plates by the light of a lamp, *and another Tannaite statement:* On the Sabbath a waiter may not examine cups and plates by the light of a lamp.

B.   *No problem – the one speaks of a permanent waiter, the other a temporary. Or, if you prefer, I shall say, both refer to a permanent waiter, but there still is no problem, the one speaks of a lamp that burns oil, the other, one that burns naphtha [which has a bad smell, so one won't tilt it].*

III.5 A.   *The question was raised: As to a temporary waiter and a lamp fed with oil, what is the rule?*

B.   Said Rab, "There is a law [permitting it], but they do not give public instructions along those lines."

C.   But R. Jeremiah bar Abbah said, "There is a law [permitting it], and they do give public instructions along those lines."

III.6 A.   *R. Jeremiah bar Abba visited the household of R. Assi. The waiter got up and examined the dishes by the light of a candle. R. Assi's wife said to him, "But you don't do it that way."*

B.   *He said to her, "Let him be. He concurs with the theory of his master."*

IV.1 A.   **Nonetheless they state: [On the Sabbath] a teacher sees [by the light of a lamp] where the children are reading, but he does not read:**

B.   *But didn't you say in the first clause, a teacher sees? Isn't that so as to read? [What can the phrase, but he does not read, possibly mean?]*

C.   No, it is to supervise the beginnings of the sections.

	D.	And so said Rabbah bar Samuel, "But he may arrange the beginnings of the sections."

D. And so said Rabbah bar Samuel, "But he may arrange the beginnings of the sections."

E. But may he not arrange the entirety of the section? [13A] *Then it has been objected:* Rabban Simeon b. Gamaliel says, "School children would arrange the sections and would recite them by the light of a lamp" [T. Shab. 1:12]!

F. *If you wish, I shall say, this refers to the heads of the sections, and if you wish, I shall say, children are in an exceptional situation, because, with the fear of the master upon them, they won't end up tilting the lamp.*

V.1 A. Similarly: A male Zab should not eat a meal with a female Zab, because it leads to transgression.

B. *It has been taught on Tannaite authority:*

C. R. Simeon b. Eleazar says, "Come and see the extent to which observance of purity has spread through Israel. For we have not learned in the Mishnah: One who is clean should not eat with an unclean woman, but only, a male afflicted with flux should not eat with a female afflicted with flux, because of the possibility of its leading to transgression.

D. "Along these same lines, a person afflicted with flux uncleanness who keeps the cultic cleanness rules at home should not eat with a similar person who does not, lest he lead the latter to associate with him" [T. Shab. 1:14].

V.2 A. *So if he does associate with him, what difference does it make? But rather, read it as follows:* lest he feed him unclean things.

B. *So can't a person afflicted with flux who observes cultic cleanness eat unclean food?*

C. Said Abbayye, "It is a precautionary decree, lest he give him food that is not properly tithed."

D. Raba said, "Most common folk do give tithes, but it is a precautionary decree, lest he visit him regularly and feed him unclean things when he is in a state of cleanness."

V.3 A. *The question was raised:* What is the law concerning a menstruating woman's sleeping with her husband, she in her garment, he in his?

B. Said R. Joseph, "*Come and take note:* 'Fowl may be served up on the table together with cheese, but it may not be eaten with it,' according to the House of Shammai. And the House of Hillel say, 'It may neither be served up with it nor eaten with it' [M. Ed. 5:2B-C]." [The answer here, too, is no.]

C. *But that case is exceptional, since there is no counterindication of what to do, but here, the couple will restrain one another. And it stands to reason that a case in which there is contrary opinion is exceptional, for there is the further clause of the same:* Rabban Simeon b. Gamaliel says, "Two guests eat on one table, this one meat, and that one cheese, and they do not scruple" [M. Hul. 8:2C].

D. *Now hasn't it been said in that connection:* Said R. Hanin bar Ammi said Samuel, "That rule has been repeated only in a case in which they don't know one another, but if they know one another, they are forbidden to do so." *Here, too, it is a case in which they know one another.*

E. *But how are the cases comparable? There we may have separate viewpoints but no distinguishing object on the table to keep them from sharing one another's food, but here there are both distinct viewpoints but also a distinguishing feature [the requirement that they not touch one another].*

F. *There are those who say, "Come and take note:* **Rabban Simeon b. Gamaliel says, 'Two guests eat on one table, this one meat, and that one cheese, and they do not scruple [M. Hul. 8:2C].'"** *And it has been said in that connection:* Said R. Hanin bar Ammi said Samuel, "That rule has been repeated only in a case in which they don't know one another, but if they know one another, they are forbidden to do so." *Here, too, it is a case in which they know one another.*

G. *There we may have separate viewpoints but no distinguishing object on the table to keep them from sharing one another's food, but here there are both distinct viewpoints but also a distinguishing feature [the requirement that they not touch one another].*

H. *Come and take note:* **Similarly: A male Zab should not eat a meal with a female Zab, because it leads to transgression.**

I. *Here, too, there may be separate viewpoints but no distinguishing object on the table to keep them from sharing one another's food.*

J. *Come and take note:* "And has not eaten upon the mountains, neither has lifted up his eyes to the idols of the house of Israel, neither has defiled his neighbor's wife, neither has come near to a woman who is menstruating" (Ezek. 18:6) – the verse thus treats as comparable one's wife who is menstruating and the wife of his neighbor. Just as in the case of the wife of his neighbor, even if he is wearing his garment and she hers, it is forbidden to sleep together, so in the case of his wife when she is menstruating, even if he is wearing his garment and she hers, it is forbidden to sleep together.

K. *That's decisive proof.*

V.4 A. *Now this differs from what R. Pedat said, for* said R. Pedat, "The Torah has declared forbidden close approach only in the case of incest: 'None of you shall approach to any that is near of kin to him to uncover their nakedness' (Lev. 18:6)."

V.5 A. *When Ulla would come home from the household of the master, he would kiss his sisters on their hand.*

B. *Some say, "On their breast."*

C. *He then contradicts what he himself has said, for* said Ulla, "Even merely coming near is forbidden, as we say to the Nazirite, 'Go, go around about, but do not even come near the vineyard.'"

V.6 A. *It was set forth as a Tannaite statement by the household of Elijah:*

B. **There is the case of a man who studied much Scripture, repeated much Mishnah, extensively served as a disciple of sages, but died when his years were only half done, and his wife took his** *tefillin* **and made the circuit of synagogues and schoolhouses, crying and weeping, saying to them, "My** lords, it is written in the Torah, *For it is your life and the length of your days* (Deut. 30:20).

C.   "On what account did my husband, who studied much Scripture, repeated much Mishnah, [13B] extensively served as a disciple of sages, die when his years were only half done?"

D.   No one knew what to answer her. But one time Elijah, of blessed memory, was appointed to deal with her, saying to her, "My daughter, on what account are you crying and weeping?"

E.   She said to him, "My lord, my husband studied much Scripture, repeated much Mishnah, extensively served as a disciple of sages, but died when his years were only half done."

F.   He said to her, "When you were in your period, on the first three days of your period, what was your practice?"

G.   She said to him, "My lord, God forbid, he never touched me, even with his little finger. But this is what he said to me, 'Do not touch a thing, perhaps you may come into doubt about something.'"

H.   "As to the last days of your period, what was your practice?"

I.   She said to him, "My lord, I ate with him, drank with him, and in my clothing slept with him in the same bed, and, while his flesh touched mine, he never had the intention of any inappropriate action [such as sexual relations before the period had fully ended]."

J.   He said to her, "Blessed be the Omnipresent, who killed him. For so is it written in the Torah: *To a woman during the unclean time of her menstrual period you shall not draw near* (Lev. 18:17)" [The Fathers According to R. Nathan II:I.2].

K.   *When R. Dimi came, he said, "It was a wide bed."*

L.   In the West they said, "Said R. Isaac bar Joseph, 'There was an apron interposed between them.'"

I see no way in which the indented compositions and composites do more than present inert facts: propositions, or attitudes, or exegesis of words or phrases or rules, that lead nowhere beyond themselves. I.1+2 introduce an intersecting Mishnah paragraph and then draw on our Mishnah paragraph for facts toward the solution of the problem at hand. Nos. 3, 4 then supply a further item pertinent to the Mishnah rule. II.1 examines the correct reading of the Mishnah rule. Nos. 2-9 complement the Mishnah statement with further relevant rules. III.1, 2-3 define the enforcement of the Mishnah rule. No. 4 adds a further rule, and Nos. 5-6 invent a secondary question based on No. 4. IV.1 examines the language of the Mishnah statement. V.1, with a talmud at No. 2 and a secondary expansion at Nos. 3+4, adds a Tannaite complement to the Mishnah statement.

1:4

A. These are some of the laws which they stated in the upper room of Hananiah b. Hezekiah b. Gurion when they went up to visit him.

B. They took a vote, and the House of Shammai outnumbered the House of Hillel.

C. And eighteen rules did they decree on that very day.

What follows is a massive encyclopaedia of information required to understand the brief allegations of the Mishnah. I do not identify in the exposition of that Mishnah a single sustained analytical argument. It is important to consider the entirety of the treatment of M. 1:4C, because what we have here is an alternative to the kind of talmud I have highlighted up to this point. What follows is a massive collection of information. It is not analyzed, but simply laid out. But here is no massive miscellany, an aimless agglutination of free-standing compositions into a composite made up of one thing and another, joined together because of a common theme, name of authority, passage of Scripture, or some other essentially extrinsic trait. What follows is not only not a massive miscellany, but is a fine talmud – but a different talmud from the one I claim defines the Bavli's intellectual character. And, I should add, I found translating these pages enormously interesting, no less engaging than translating the prior ones. But it was different labor altogether, demanding a measure of patience, lacking a compelling interest in a problem of theory, such as makes the Talmud such an interesting writing.

II.1 A. And eighteen rules did they decree on that very day:

B. *What are the eighteen rules?*

C. *It is in line with what we have learned in the Mishnah:* These render heave-offering unfit: he who eats food unclean in the first remove; and he who eats food unclean in the second remove; and he who drinks unclean liquid; he whose head and the greater part of whose body enters drawn water; and one who was clean on whose head and the greater part of whose body three logs of drawn water fall; and a scroll, and hands, and a person who has completed his rites of purification and awaits sunset to be completely clean [a tebul-yom]; and food and utensils which have been made unclean by [unclean] liquids [M. Zab. 5:12].

II.2 A. *Who is the Tannaite authority who stands behind the rule:* He who eats food unclean in the first remove and he who eats food unclean in the second remove *renders the heave-offering unfit* [14A] *but doesn't impart to it uncleanness?*

B. Said Rabbah bar bar Hannah, "It is R. Joshua, *for we have learned in the Mishnah:* R. Eliezer says, '(1) He who eats food unclean in the first remove is unclean in the first remove; (2) [he who eats] food unclean in the second remove is unclean in the second remove; (3)

[he who eats) food unclean in the third remove is unclean in the third remove.' R. Joshua says, '(1) He who eats food unclean in the first remove and food unclean in the second remove is unclean in the second remove. (2) [He who eats food] unclean in the third remove is unclean in the second remove so far as Holy Things are concerned, (3) and is not unclean in the second remove so far as heave-offering is concerned – in the case of unconsecrated food which is prepared in conditions of cleanness appropriate to heave-offering [M. Toh. 2:2].'"

II.3   A.   As to one who eats food in the first or second remove from uncleanness, *how come rabbis decreed uncleanness in that case? Because sometimes one may eat unclean unconsecrated food, but then take a drink of liquid in the status of heave-offering and put it in his mouth and so render the liquid unfit.*

       B.   As to one who drinks unclean liquids, *how come rabbis have decreed uncleanness in that case? Because sometimes one may be drinking unclean liquid and may take food in the status of heave-offering and put it in his mouth, and so invalidate the other.*

       C.   *Big deal – that's the same thing as before!*

       D.   *What might you otherwise have supposed? The one is common, the other not [so rabbis would not make a decree for the second matter]? So we are informed that that is not the case.*

II.4   A.   He whose head and the greater part of whose body enters drawn water: *How come rabbis decreed uncleanness in that case?*

       B.   Said R. Bibi said R. Assi, "For to begin with they would immerse in cave water that was collected together and [while valid for purification purposes,] fetid, and they would then pour over themselves drawn water. But when they began to treat this as a fixed requirement, rabbis made a decree that such water is unclean."

II.5   A.   *What is the meaning of* a fixed requirement?

       B.   Said Abbayye, "It is that they would say, 'These are not what effect purification, but these and those together effect purification.'"

       C.   *Said to him Raba, "So what difference does it make? One way or the other they were immersing in the valid water!"*

       D.   Rather, said Raba, "They would say, 'These are not what effect purification, but only those waters are what effect purification.'"

II.6   A.   And one who was clean on whose head and the greater part of whose body three logs of drawn water fall: *How come rabbis decreed uncleanness in that case?*

       B.   *If it weren't for this, the other decree wouldn't stand up.*

II.7   A.   And the holy scroll: *How come rabbis decreed uncleanness in that case?*

       B.   Said R. Mesharshayya, "Because to begin with they would put away food in the status of heave-offering along with a scroll of the Torah, saying, 'This is holy and that's holy.' But when they say that it brought about a waste of food, rabbis decreed uncleanness for the scrolls."

II.8   A.   And hands: [Supply: *How come rabbis decreed uncleanness in that case?*]

       B.   Because hands fidget [Abraham: they are apt to touch things; hence unless the owner takes care that they not touch an unclean object after he washed them, they are treated as unclean].

C.   *A Tannaite statement:* Also hands that have touched a holy scroll invalidate heave-offering, *in line with what R. Parnakh said.* For said R. Parnakh said R. Yohanan, "He who when naked holds a scroll of the Torah will be buried naked, too."

D.   Naked?! *Do you imagine,* naked?!

E.   Rather, said R. Zira, "Naked, meaning, without religious duties to his credit."

F.   *Do you imagine* without religious duties to his credit!?

G.   *Rather, say,* "Naked: without credit for that particular religious duty."

II.9   A.   *Which of them did rabbis decree to begin with? Should I say that it was that one* [that hands are unclean in general] *that they decreed first of all?* [14B] *Then once they enacted that one, why did they need the other one, too?*

      B.   *So it must have been the latter that was decreed to begin with, then the other was decreed in regard to the hands as well.*

II.10 A.   **And the tebul-yom:**

      B.   *But the uncleanness of the one who has immersed on the selfsame day derives from the Torah, for it is written,* "And when the sun is down, he shall be clean, and afterwards he shall eat Holy Things" (Lev. 22:7)!

      C.   *Remove from the list:* and the tebul-yom.

II.11 A.   **And food which have been made unclean by [unclean] liquids:**

      B.   *What kind of unclean liquid? Should we say it was liquid made unclean by a dead creeping thing? Then the law derives from the Torah and not from rabbinical decree, since it is written,* "And all drink that may be drunk in every such utensil shall be unclean" (Lev. 11:34).

      C.   Rather, it is through water that is made unclean by reason of the hands, and it is a decree on account of liquid that derives from unclean by reason of a dead creeping thing.

II.12 A.   **And utensils which have been made unclean by [unclean] liquids:**

      B.   *What kind of unclean liquid? Should we say it was liquid deriving from a person afflicted by flux? But that derives from the Torah, as it is written,* "And if the person unclean with flux spit upon a clean person, he shall wash his clothes and bathe himself in water" (Lev. 15:8) – what is in the hand of a clean person I have declared unclean for you.

      C.   Rather, it refers to liquid that is unclean by reason of contact with a dead creeping thing, and it is a decree on account of the liquid that exudes from a person afflicted with flux.

II.13 A.   **And hands:**

      B.   *Well, then, did the disciples of Shammai and Hillel make that decree? Shammai and Hillel themselves made that decree, for it has been taught on Tannaite authority:* Yosé b. Yoezer of Seridah and Yosé b. Yohanan of Jerusalem decreed uncleanness on the land of the gentiles and on glassware. Simeon b. Shatah ordained the requirement of a marriage settlement for a wife and made a decree concerning uncleanness for metal utensils. Shammai and Hillel decreed uncleanness on the hands. *And should you say that the meaning is,* Shammai and his party and Hillel and his party, didn't R. Judah say Samuel said, "Eighteen matters did they issue as decrees, and concerning eighteen matters they differed," but Hillel and Shammai differed in only three passages. *For* said R. Huna, "In three passages they differed, *and no more.*" *And should you propose, on account of their rule, they made a decree to suspend the status of things touched by the hands, and on account of the decree of their disciples, they made the decree to burn such food, hasn't Ilfa said, "To begin with, the decree involving hands meant that food touched by them was to be burned"?*

C.   *Rather, Hillel and Shammai came along and made the decree, but people didn't accept it from them, and then their disciples came along and made the decree, and people accepted it from them.*

D.   *Still, in point of fact, it was Solomon who made that decree, for* said R. Judah said Samuel, "At the moment that Solomon issued the decree concerning the making of the symbolic fusion meal and the washing of the hands, an echo came forth and said, '"My son, if your heart be wise, my heart shall be glad, even mine" (Prov. 23:15), and "My son, be wise and make my heart glad, that I may answer him who reproaches me" (Prov. 27:11).'"

E.   *Solomon came along* [15A] *and made the decree in regard to Holy Things, and they [Hillel and Shammai] came along and made the decree also in respect to heave-offering.*

II.14   A.   *Reverting to the body of the text:* R. Judah said Samuel said, "Eighteen matters did they issue as decrees, and concerning eighteen matters they differed" –

B.   *But hasn't it been taught on Tannaite authority:* They came to an agreement?

C.   That day they differed, the next day they came to an agreement.

II.15   A.   *Reverting to the body of the text:* Said R. Huna, "In three passages they differed" –

B.   Shammai says, "[Dough which is made] from a qab [of flour is liable] to a dough-offering [Num. 15:20]." And Hillel says, "[Dough made] from two qabs." And sages say, "It is not in accord with the opinion of this party nor in accord with the opinion of that party, but: [Dough made] from a qab and a half of flour is liable to the dough-offering." After the measures were expanded in size [so six Jerusalem logs were now deemed five new logs], they ruled: Dough made from five fourths of a qab is liable. R. Yosé says, "[If it is made from exactly] five, it is exempt. [If it is made from] five and a bit more, it is liable" [M. Ed. 1:2].

C.   *And further?*

D.   Hillel says, "A full hin [three qabs] of drawn water [poured into a pool lacking forty seahs of suitable water] invalidates an immersion pool." (But a person is liable to say a teaching in the language of his master –) and Shammai says, "Nine qabs." And sages say, "It is not in accord with the opinion of this party or in accord with the opinion of that party." But: Two weavers came from the dung gate in Jerusalem and gave testimony in the name of Shemaiah and Abtalion: "Three logs [= 36 qabs] of drawn water invalidate an immersion pool." And sages confirmed their report [M. Ed. 1:3].

E.   *And further?*

F.   Shammai says, "For all women it is sufficient [to be regarded as unclean by reason of menstruation] from the time [of their first having a flow]." Hillel says, "[It is retroactive] from the examination [at which the blood was found] to the examination [last made, before the blood was found], and even for a number of days." And sages say, "[The rule is] not in accord with the opinion of this party nor in accord with the opinion of that party, but [a woman is regarded as having been unclean only] during the preceding twenty-four hours [when] this lessens the period from the present examination to the last examination, [and she is held to have been unclean only] during the period from examination to examination [when] this lessens the period of twenty-four hours" [M. Ed. 1:1]

G.   *And aren't there any more? Lo, there is this one:*

H.   Shammai says not to lay on hands. Hillel says to lay on hands [M. Hag. 2:2G].

I.   *When R. Huna made his statement, it was with reference to a case in which there is no dispute on the part of their masters over and above theirs [but here they are part of a chain of disputes].*

J.   *Well, there's this one:* He who gleans grapes for the wine press – Shammai says, "The grapes have been rendered susceptible to uncleanness." Hillel says, "The grapes have not been rendered susceptible to uncleanness." But Hillel concurred with Shammai.

K.   *That's an exception, because there Hillel was shut up by Shammai.*

II.16   A.   [Supply: *Reverting to the body of the text:*] Yosé b. Yoezer of Seridah and Yosé b. Yohanan of Jerusalem decreed uncleanness on the land of the gentiles and on glassware –

B.   *Lo, it was the rabbis of "the eighty years" who made that decree. For* said R. Kahana, "When R. Ishmael b. R. Yosé fell ill, Rabbi sent word to him, 'Tell us two or three of the things that you said to us in your father's name.'

C.   "He said word to them, 'This is what father said: "One hundred and eighty years before the house of the Temple was destroyed, the wicked kingdom took over the dominion over Israel; eighty years prior to the destruction of the Temple the decree was made that the lands of the peoples around the Land of Israel and utensils made out of glass were subject to uncleanness, forty years prior to the destruction of the Temple the sanhedrin went out into exile from the Temple and held its sessions in a stall [on the Temple mount]."'"

D.   *For what practical law does such information serve?*

E.   Said R. Isaac bar Abdimi, "It is to indicate that they did not judge cases involving extrajudicial penalties."

F.   *Extrajudicial penalties do you say? But did not R. Judah say in the name of Rab, "Now may that man be remembered for good, and R. Judah b. Baba was his name, for if it were not for him the laws involving extrajudicial penalties would have been forgotten in Israel"?*

G.   *Now should you say that [the two Yosés] also lived during those eighty years, hasn't it been taught on Tannaite authority:* Hillel, Simeon [his son], Gamaliel, and Simeon [his son] ruled as patriarchs for one hundred years prior to the Temple's destruction? *And Yosé b. Yoezer of Seridah and Yosé b. Yosé of Jerusalem were many years prior to them!*

H. [15B] *Rather, they came and made the decree in regard to a clod of earth of gentile lands, that heave-offering that had touched it was to be burned as unclean without doubt, but they made no decree at all in regard to the contained air space of that territory, while the rabbis of the eighty years came and decreed that the status of heave-offering affected by the contained air space of gentile territory was to be kept in suspense.*

I. *Does that bear the implication that the original decree concerned burning [the heave-offering so affected]? But didn't Ilfa say, "To begin with, the decree involving hands meant that food touched by them was to be burned"? So it follows that the original decree made reference to burning only by reason of the uncleanness of hands, but it made no reference to burning heave-offering on account of contamination on any other count!*

J. *Rather, they came along and made a decree to suspend the status of what had been in touch with a clod of dirt of gentile land, and they decreed nothing at all in regards to the contained air space of gentile land; then the rabbis of the eighty years came along and decreed that what was affected by the clod of dirt should be burned, and the status of heave-offering affected by the contained air space was to be kept in suspense.*

K. *Nonetheless, as a matter of simple fact, that was decreed in Usha [centuries later], for we have learned in the Mishnah:* On account of six matters of doubt do they burn heave-offering: concerning a doubt in regard to a grave area; and concerning a doubt in regard to dirt which comes from abroad; because of a doubt concerning the clothing of an am haares [who does not observe cultic cleanness in eating everyday food]; and because of a doubt concerning utensils which were found; because of a doubt concerning drops of spit which were found; because of a doubt concerning human urine that was nearby the urine of a beast – because of certainly touching them, which is a matter of doubt in respect to their [imparting] uncleanness, they burn the heave-offering. R. Yosé says, "Even because of a doubt about having touched them in the private domain." And sages say, "[Because of a doubt about having touched them] in the private domain, they leave it in suspense. And [if the matter of doubt took place] in the public domain, it is clean" [M. Toh. 4:5]. *And said Ulla, "The disposition of these six matters of doubt was ordained in Usha."*

L. *Rather: They came along and made a decree to suspend the status of heave-offering affected by a clod of gentile dirt, but made no decree at all as regards that which has been affected by the contained air space of gentile land, and the rabbis of the eighty years came and decreed that in both instances the status of the produce was to be held in suspense; then they came along at Usha and made a decree to burn what was affected by a clod of dirt, but, as to what was affected by the air space, they left the matter as is.*

II.17 A. *As to glassware, how come rabbis made a decree that glassware is subject to uncleanness?*

B. Said R. Yohanan said R. Simeon b. Laqish, "Since the beginning of the process of making them is with sand, rabbis assigned it to the status of earthenware."

C.   *But by that reasoning,* like earthenware, they should not be subject to the purification process of an immersion pool, *but then how come we have learned in the Mishnah:* **These interpose in utensils: (1) pitch, (2) and the gum of myrrh. On glass utensils – whether inside or outside [M. Miq. 9:5A-C]?** [It follows that a purification process in an immersion pool takes effect for glass utensils.]

D.   *Here with what case do we deal?* It was a glass utensil that had a hole, filled by molten lead, *in line with the theory of R. Meir, who maintained,* "The status of an object entirely depends upon what holds it together" [and so the status of the glass utensil in this case is the same as that of a metal one, which is purified in an immersion pool]. *For it has been taught on Tannaite authority:* As to the status of glassware that was perforated and mended with molten lead – said Rabban Simeon b. Gamaliel, "R. Meir declares it susceptible to uncleanness, and sages declare it insusceptible."

E.   *Well, then, by the same reasoning* [that they are classified as earthenware utensils] **[16A]** they should not be subject to uncleanness through what touches their outer parts, *but, in that case, how come we have learned in the Mishnah:* **Vessels of wood, and vessels of leather, and vessels of bone, and vessels of glass: When they are flat, they are clean, and when they form receptacles, they are [susceptible of becoming] unclean. [If] they are broken, they are clean. [If] one went and made [new] vessels, they receive uncleanness from now and henceforth. [As to] vessels of clay and vessels of alum crystal, their [capacity to receive] uncleanness is alike. (1) They [both] become unclean and convey uncleanness by [their] contained air space, and they impart uncleanness from their outer sides. (2) But they do not contract uncleanness from their outer parts. And breaking them is purifying them [M. Kel. 2:1]?** *So it is only earthenware utensils and alum utensils that are alike in respect to how they contract uncleanness, but nothing else [but glassware should share the same trait, if Simeon b. Laqish is correct]!*

F.   *Say:* Since, if they are broken, they can be repaired, rabbis treated them in the category of metal utensils.

G.   Well, then, if they are comparable to metal utensils, when repaired they should revert to the original uncleanness as do metal utensils, *for we have learned in the Mishnah:* **Metal utensils: Their flat [parts] and their receptacles are unclean. [If] they have been broken, they have been purified. [If] one went and made of them [new] vessels, they have returned to their former uncleanness. Rabban Simeon b. Gamaliel says, "[They return] not to every uncleanness but [only] to the uncleanness of the soul [corpse uncleanness]"** [M. Kel. 11:1]! *By contrast, in respect to glassware, we have learned in the Mishnah:* **Vessels of wood, and vessels of leather, and vessels of bone, and vessels of glass: When they are flat, they are clean, and when they form receptacles, they are [susceptible of becoming] unclean. [If] they are broken, they are clean. [If] one went and made [new] vessels, they receive uncleanness from now and henceforth** [M. Kel. 2:1]! *That is to say,* from now and henceforth, *but retroactively, not at all.*

H.   *The uncleanness affecting glassware derives from the decree of rabbis, and the reversion to a prior uncleanness likewise derives from the ruling of rabbis. In respect to uncleanness deriving from the authority of the Torah, rabbis were prepared to impose retrospective uncleanness upon an existing, Torah-based, uncleanness, but in regards to an uncleanness that to begin with is defined only on rabbinical authority, rabbis were not prepared to impose retrospective uncleanness.*

I.   *Well, one way or the other, in flat form, glassware should be unclean, since flat metal utensils are declared by the law of the Torah to be susceptible to uncleanness!*

J.   *Rabbis made a distinction in that case, so as not to burn on account of such utensils heave-offering and Holy Things.* [Such things should be burned when made by an uncleanness defined by rabbis only in the six cases of doubt listed above (Freedman).]

K.   [16B] *R. Ashi said, "In point of fact they are in the same category as earthenware utensils, and as to your challenge, that, in that case, they should not be affected by uncleanness that touches their outer parts, since in this case the inside is visible as the outside, [that leniency does not apply]."*

II.18   A.   "Simeon b. Shatah ordained the requirement of a marriage settlement for a wife and made a decree concerning uncleanness for metal utensils":

B.   *But the fact that metal utensils are subject to uncleanness derives from the Torah, for it is written,* "Howbeit the gold and silver– anything that can stand in fire – you shall pass through fire and it shall be clean..." (Num. 31:22). *It was necessary to make such a decree with respect to the prior uncleanness [indicating that when repaired they revert to that prior status], for said R. Judah said Rab,* "There was the incident involving Shalsion, the queen, who made a banquet for her son, but all her utensils were made unclean, so she had them broken and gave them to the goldsmith; he melted them down and made new utensils of them. Then sages said, 'They revert to their prior status of uncleanness.'" *How come? They wanted to establish a protective fence to make sure that the rite of purification through the water of separation [the purification rite for corpse uncleanness described in Num. 19] would not fall into desuetude.*

C.   *Well, that poses no problem from the perspective of him who has said that sages ruled in this regard not for all forms of uncleanness but only for the uncleanness that comes from corpse contamination [only corpse uncleanness would be revived, since the cited verse speaks of uncleanness deriving from the dead]. But from the perspective of him who has said that uncleanness reverts when the metal utensil is repaired, no matter its source, what is to be said in explanation of the ruling?*

D.   Said Abbayye, "It was a precautionary decree, lest the hole that damages the utensil and so removes it from uncleanness might not be so large as to meet the standard that renders the object useless and therefore no longer susceptible to uncleanness."

E.   Raba said, "It was a precautionary decree, lest people say that immersion on that very day will serve to purify the object" [while immersion serves only to ready the object for cleanness, which takes place only when the sun sets; making a hole and repairing the object would permit reuse immediately; people might then see such a process and suppose that it had been immersed, and so immersion would purify the object on the selfsame day and not only after sunset completed the process].

F. *What's at issue between them?*

G. *At issue between them is a case in which the smith recast the object.* [Abbayye's consideration applies; maybe a small hole would have been enough; Raba's reason is not pertinent, since it is obvious that the object is a new one (Freedman).]

II.19 A. *Any more enactments [among the eighteen]?*

B. *The following, which we have learned in the Mishnah:* He who leaves utensils under the waterspout – all the same are large utensils and small utensils – and even utensils made of dung, of stone, and of dirt – it [the water] renders the immersion pool unfit. All the same is the one who leaves and the one who forgets, in accord with the words of the House of Shammai. And the House of Hillel declare clean in the case of the one who forgets. Said R. Meir, "They took a vote and the House of Shammai outnumbered the House of Hillel. And they [the Shammaites] agree in the case of the one who forgets [not under the spout but] in the courtyard, that it is clean." Said R. Yosé, "Still the dispute stands in its place" [M. Miq. 4:1].

C. *Said R. Mesharshayya, "Said a member of the household of a master, '*All concur that if one left them there when it was clouding over – the utensils purified in the immersion pool are unclean; if he put them there when the clouds were dispersing, all concur that they are clean. Where there is a difference is a case in which he put them there when it was clouding over, but then the clouds dispersed, and then the clouds gathered again. One authority holds that the initial intentionality is nullified, the other, that it wasn't.'"

D. *Now, from the perspective of R. Yosé, who has maintained,* Still the dispute stands in its place, *there are fewer than eighteen.*

E. Said R. Nahman bar Isaac, "Also on that day they made the rule that Samaritan women are classified as unclean with menstrual uncleanness from their cradles."

II.20 A. *Any more enactments [among the eighteen]?*

B. *The following, which we have learned in the Mishnah:* All movables bring the uncleanness [as tents] when they are as thick as an ox goad. Said R. Tarfon, [17A] "May I ruin my sons, that this is a ruined law, which the hearer heard and erred, that: The farmer passes [by the tomb] and the ox goad is on his shoulder, and one side of it overshadowed the tomb, and they declared him unclean, because [of the rule governing] utensils which overshadow the corpse." Said R. Aqiba, "I shall repair it so that the words of sages may endure. Thus: All movables bring the uncleanness on the man who carries them if they are thick as an ox goad, and on themselves if they are of any measure at all, and on another man and utensils if they are a square handbreadth" [M. Oh. 16:1]. And said R. Yannai, "The goad of which they have spoken is a handbreadth not in thickness but in circumference, and they made this law in regards to its circumference on account of its thickness."

[Freedman: If its thickness is a handbreadth, it induces uncleanness of seven days by the law of the Torah; sages extended this to the former case to prevent confusion, and this is one of the eighteen enactments.]

C.   *But from the perspective of R. Tarfon, who said, "May I ruin my sons, that this is a ruined law, which the hearer heard and erred," there are less than eighteen enactments!*

D.   Said R. Nahman bar Isaac, "Also on that day they made the rule that Samaritan women are classified as unclean with menstrual uncleanness from their cradles." *And in the other question [putting utensils under a spout] he concurs with R. Meir.*

II.21 A.   *Any more enactments [among the eighteen]?*

B.   He who gleans grapes for the wine press – Shammai says, "The grapes have been rendered susceptible to uncleanness." Hillel says, "The grapes have not been rendered susceptible to uncleanness." But Hillel concurred with Shammai.

C.   Said Hillel to Shammai, "How come grapes have to be vintaged in a state of cultic cleanness but olives don't have to be gathered in a state of cultic cleanness?"

D.   He said to him, "So if you get me really mad, I'll make a decree of uncleanness also in the matter of gathering olives, too."

E.   They plunged a sword into the schoolhouse, saying, "Let anyone come in who wants to, but no one is going to get out of here," and on that day, Hillel sat humble before Shammai like just another disciple. **And that day was as hard for Israel as the day on which the golden calf was made [T. Shab. 1:16B].**

F.   *Well, Shammai and Hillel made this decree, but they wouldn't take it from them, and then their disciples came along and made the same decree, and they took it from them [so it's one of the eighteen decrees now].*

G.   *Anyhow, what's the operative consideration?*

H.   Said Zeiri said R. Hanina, "It was a decree against the possibility of vintaging the grapes in unclean baskets."

I.   *Well, that poses no problem to him who holds that a unclean utensil brings the exuding liquid under consideration [and so renders it able to impart susceptibility to uncleanness]. But from the perspective of him who has said that an unclean utensil does not bring exuding liquid under consideration, [for the grape juice that exudes in the basket is not wanted, the owner would prefer it not go to waste, and if the owner doesn't want a fluid, the fluid does not impart susceptibility to uncleanness,] what is to be said?*

J.   Rather, said Zeiri said R. Hanina, "It is a precautionary decree, lest he vintage the grapes in baskets lined with pitch [which prevents loss of the fluid, so the owner doesn't care about its exuding, and consequently, it is wanted, and therefore imparts susceptibility to uncleanness]."

K.   Raba said, "It is a decree on account of the clusters that cleave tightly." [Freedman: These have to be separated by force, causing juice to spurt out; the farmer does that himself, so the juice makes the grapes susceptible to uncleanness; there is then a preventing measure, extending this consideration to all exuding juice.]

L.   For said R. Nahman said Rabbah bar Abbuha, "Sometimes someone
       goes to his vineyard to find out whether the grapes are ready for
       vintaging, and he takes a bunch of grapes to squeeze it, and
       sprinkles juice on the grapes, and at the time of vintaging the
       grapes, the moisture is still dripping on them."

II.22 A.   *Any more enactments [among the eighteen]?*

       B.   Said [17B] Rabi the hunter said Samuel, "Also that the produce of
              food in the status of heave-offering is itself in the status of heave-
              offering was enacted on that day, too."

       C.   *How come?*

       D.   Said R. Hanina, "It is a precautionary decree, on account of clean
              heave-offering in the possession of an Israelite" [so that he won't
              hold on to produce in that status but will hand it over to a priest,
              since it can produce nothing he can keep anyhow].

       E.   *Said Raba, "If people are suspect on that account, then to begin with they
              won't designate heave-offering anyhow, he can assign a single grain of
              wheat to serve as heave-offering for the whole, in Samuel's view, and since
              he doesn't do it in such a niggardly way, he is certainly regarded as
              reliable."*

       F.   Rather, said Raba, "It is a precautionary decree on account of
              unclean heave-offering in the priest's domain, to make sure he
              doesn't hold on to it and be led to sin."

II.23 A.   *Any more enactments [among the eighteen]?*

       B.   *Said R. Hiyya bar Abba in the name of Ulla, "Also: The rule, **He who
              was overtaken by darkness on the road gives his purse to a gentile**
              [M. Shab. 24:1A], was enacted on that day as well."*

II.24 A.   *Any more enactments [among the eighteen]?*

       B.   Said Bali said Abimi of Sanvatah, "The decrees against gentile
              bread, oil, wine, and women all are among the eighteen decrees."

II.25 A.   *That poses no problem from the perspective of R. Meir, but from the view
              of R. Yosé, there are only seventeen.*

       B.   *There is the one of R. Aha bar Adda, for* said R. Aha bar Adda said R.
              Isaac, "They made the decree concerning their bread because of
              their oil, their oil because of their wine."

       C.   *What's the sense of the statement, concerning their bread because of
              their oil? How is the prohibition of oil weightier than the prohibition of
              their bread? [Was there reason to prohibit their oil more than to prohibit
              their bread?]*

       D.   *Say:* They made the decree concerning their bread and their oil,
              their oil because of their wine, and against their wine on account of
              their daughters, and against their daughters on account of
              something else, and they decreed against something else on account
              of the other thing.

       E.   *What's the something else?*

       F.   Said R. Nahman bar Isaac, "They decreed that a gentile child
              imparts uncleanness that is in the status of flux uncleanness, so that
              Israelite children won't get into the habit of playing with him by
              reason of sodomy."

       G.   *If so, from R. Meir's perspective, now there are nineteen!*

       H.   *Food and drink made unclean by liquid he treats as a single item.*

5

The Bavli's Intellectual Character

By the Bavli's intellectual character, in particular, I mean, what gives the Bavli traits of abstraction, such that it tells us more than this and that about many things, but some one thing about everything. That is, by asking about the intellectual character of the writing – how it defines problems, how it solves problems – I presuppose that the writing in fact exhibits a character of an intellectual sort. This monograph and the others that go with it begin with that premise and test it. I begin by asking how and whether the document comprises more than a mass of interesting information about the Mishnah, on the one side, and stories and sayings, on the other. I have shown that, at important points, the Bavli indeed comprises much more than a compilation of facts, that is sets forth an argument, a proposition, a method that transcends data and governs the formation of thought. I also have shown that at important points, the Bavli sets forth information and that alone or mainly, having none of that intellectual character that, at other points, makes the writing remarkably engaging and challenging.

In the two chapters we have addressed, I have identified an exceedingly important aspect of the character of the document as a whole, so far as the Bavli commands respect for its intellectual vigor, not merely for its religious interest. I should invoke the story of the Bavli once it reached closure as the best evidence for the character of the whole as an intellectually engaging writing, not merely a valuable compilation of information. I should claim that the many, many centuries, into the twenty-first of the Common Era, in which the best intellects of eternal Israel has engaged with the Bavli, provide probative evidence of the definition, and character, of this writing: a work of intellect, imparting to facts importance beyond themselves; a work of applied reason and practical logic, capable of turning concrete things into exemplifications of abstractions of remarkably universal pertinence. So while the result of the repertoire of Chapters Three and Four proves mixed, the upshot is unambiguous.

By this point, I fear, readers will suppose that I have chosen to set forth some rather obvious propositions about the character of the Bavli, since the evidence I have laid out is so one-sided a demonstration of my proposition. But a measure of thought about the title of the book, therefore the program, will suggest otherwise. I promise to describe "the Bavli's intellectual character." That represents a definition of the problem of description of the document that stands in opposition to other definitions of how to frame and solve the same problem. By speaking of "character," thus focusing upon the traits of the writing itself, I reject other ways of describing the document and its fundamental sort of intellection, its "intellect" or its "mind." Indeed, it was only in response to someone else's formulation of the issue, which is altogether different from mine, that I began to think along the lines that brought me to this project in particular.

Specifically, the idea for this book came to me in a monograph of someone who describes himself as my student, but who has learned nothing from me and whom, in fact, I have never met. He is David Kraemer, who did everything wrong in his *The Mind of the Talmud: An Intellectual History of the Bavli*[1] and so drew my interest to the problem he attempted to solve, which is how to characterize the Bavli's intellectual character, that is, its "mind." What he did wrong was to propose a historical solution to a problem that is not historical in any terms; he then trapped himself in a morass of argument on the historicity of attributions of statements to named authorities, since, after all, history requires sequence, first came this, then came that. Imagining that a problem of "mind" can be reduced to a problem of history (a perfectly stupid error!), Kraemer then lost sight of the document he wished to describe.

The reason, I think, is a methodological error that I have corrected here. Kraemer imagines that we write "an intellectual history" of a document. So he asks historical questions. I think that when we describe a document, we describe the traits of that document, viewed (for the purpose of description) not in any historical context but only as a phenomenon in its own terms: what do I see here, in what the writers choose to tell me, what do I learn from the ways in which these writers wish to communicate with me? For intellect is intellect, it is thought process, category formation, identification of problematic and instantiation thereof. If we say "intellect," we mean what is intellectual, and to me, that means, what is a matter of how the mind works, in the deepest sense, we mean philosophy. Documents may have histories, but

---

[1] (New York, 1990: Oxford University Press) xv + 217.

so far as they cohere and form a writing of integrity, what is important about documents is not their histories but their character: hence the character of the Bavli, as against "an intellectual history of the Bavli." And, in point of fact, Kraemer does not even know what it would take to characterize what we both would call "the mind of the Talmud."

That is a strong judgment, and it bears amplification and demonstration in detail. So let me now focus on Kraemer's book, and we shall see what a miserable failure he has put forth in the name of telling us about "the mind of the Talmud." For his account succeeds neither as history nor as phenomenology; and in fact, he wrote his book without even reading other books that address the same question, his work showing alarming ignorance of how others have tried to formulate and solve the problem he purports to address. But it is not enough just to point out that Kraemer didn't bother to do his homework; that marks him as a poor scholar, but it does not condemn his results. Let me spell out what he has done wrong, so that the choices I explore in this monograph will become clearer; by showing other people's errors, I explain why I have done what I have, and why what I have done is the right and necessary way.

Claiming to "trace the development of the literary forms and conventions of the Babylonian Talmud and analyze those forms as expressions of emergent rabbinic ideology," which expresses the conviction of "the inaccessibility of perfect truth," and concluding that [not the determination, but the mere] "pursuit of truth...becomes the ultimate act of rabbinic piety," Kraemer spells out his program in these terms: "[The book is]...a literary history. It traces the development of literary forms and conventions by which rabbinic sages...recorded their opinions and rulings. What motivates this examination is the assumption...that literary conventions are reflections of ideological choices and that by tracing the history of literary developments we can say something of the history of ideas. This is also, therefore, intended as an intellectual history of the Jews who produced the Bavli."

While Kraemer claims not to rely for his history upon the attributions of sayings to given authorities, he alleges, "We can...know, at the very least, that certain forms of expression were typical in certain generations, and, given additional data, we can even say that it is likely that the essence of a certain opinion was held in the circle of disciples of a particular sage. Since this work is a history of literary forms as ideological expressions, we do have access to the sort of information needed to write such a history." Upon that formulation, the historical half of this book rests. But the formulation evokes the notion that, even though I cannot prove A, the accumulation of evidence of the same kind as A – "typical in certain generations," "circle of disciples of a particular sage" – provides proof that A on its own cannot. I doubt that many will find persuasive this rather facile and blatantly circular solution to the problem of the historicity of attributions; to his credit Kraemer himself calls it circular (p. 24). But then for several chapters he walks around in circles, supposedly proving we can rely on attributions as a whole, if not one by one. The whole of his elaborate proof resting not on individual names but on groups of names ("generations of sages, but not individuals...are so distinguished") and alleging that "verification...will extend only to the level of the generation, not to particular individuals" therefore is hardly compelling. Since Kraemer's "history of Amoraic literary expression" does not command assent, the claim that he has described "an intellectual history of the Bavli" rests on infirm foundations.

But we cannot dismiss the book as another exercise in pseudorthodoxy and pietistic gullibility. For in the succeeding chapters Kraemer also claims accurately to characterize the document as a whole, as it existed at the end of its formation. His descriptive proposition therefore is to be addressed entirely distinct from the claim to account for the history of the formation of the document. He alleges that the anonymous and commanding discourse of the document concerns not conclusion but argumentation. While received materials (Kraemer: "for the Amoraim") contain "both brief and discursive" writing, "conclusion and argumentation," for the unattributed and definitive discourse ("for the stam" not italicized, a foreign word meaning, "what is not attributed to a named authority") *"there is only argumentation."* In the words he has italicized is Kraemer's principal descriptive allegation. All else rests upon that characterization.

Now it is certainly the fact that on occasion derivative cases are set forth, sometimes at great length, to put forward theoretical possibilities on sorting out conflicting principles, and these not uncommonly conclude, "the question stands." The argument then is the main thing: conflict of principles, left unresolved. So there is ample anecdotal material in the document – we know not the proportion or place in the composition of the whole – to validate Kraemer's claim in detail. But the passages that present conundrums invariably attend to interstitial issues, and none of them, so far as I have observed, present without resolution the conflict of fundamental principles (for example, contradictions between the premises of two distinct Mishnah paragraphs are never left in conflict but always harmonized). So that phenomenon, which does conform to Kraemer's description, is not primary to the document, its modes of thought and argument.

Kraemer adduces in evidence of his claim that the document concerns itself with argument, not decision, by showing a variety of specific traits characteristic of what he calls the anonymous layer of the writing. He finds, for instance, that the redactor will "extend the range of the original argumentation" (p. 80). "The authors of the gemara also saw fit to create argumentation out of amoraic sources that were originally not argumentational" (p. 84). They created "fictional argumentation" (p. 87), "argumentation for its own sake" (p. 90). He then claims to have illustrated the point that "the Babylonian gemara is, at the level of its anonymous composition, an uncompromisingly deliberative/argumentational text." He properly compares this Talmud to the other one, the Talmud of the Land of Israel (a.k.a., the Yerushalmi) and finds that a principal difference is that the Yerushalmi reaches conclusions, the Bavli does not.

A considerable problem in assessing his evidence, argument, and therefore proposition, has to be specified here. All of these cases are treated as exemplary, but, unfortunately, Kraemer never tells us what proportion of the document as a whole, or of some sizable sample thereof, is comprised by them. So we have argument from anecdote and episode, without any sustained demonstration of the determinate characteristics of the writing as such. Nonetheless, from this point forward, Kraemer regards it as established fact that the Bavli has been given "an argumentational form." The remainder of the book is devoted to "the indeterminability of truth," an issue that the document under discussion on its own terms hardly portrays as urgent. Indeed, I am inclined to suspect the authors of the Bavli would have been amazed to be told that their document was more interested in argument than in "truth," meaning, determinate conclusions. To the contrary, since, as a matter of fact, the Bavli forms a highly systematic representation of a complete, proportionate, and authoritative system, Kraemer seems to wish to answer a question the document itself does not require that we ask.

What apparently has happened is that Kraemer has evidently found compelling a couple of philosophical books on the subject of the indeterminacy of truth and has identified his philosopher's stone. So he finds in the issue (his idiosyncratic reworking of the claims, along these same lines, of the literary critics of the deconstructionist school) a basis on which to explain the traits of the document in terms that are intellectually generally accessible, a worthwhile exercise, if carried out in a somewhat mechanical manner. If, then, the meaning is indeterminate, as deconstructionism wants us to believe, so, too, must be the message, Kraemer wishes us to conclude; all that is left is process. Now no one would reject the notion that process is critical; that is, indeed, the very burden of this book of mine. But Kraemer seriously misrepresents the document by misunderstanding the process, missing the point that the way people think and set forth their ideas itself constitutes a medium for the communication – through the medium itself – of a message that is repeated everywhere and all the time. The entire history of the reception of the Bavli testifies that the document was meant to teach truth, not merely exemplify process. But the implausibility of Kraemer's result does not form an important reason to disbelieve his book.

Rather, let us ask ourselves whether, in his representation of the document, Kraemer has accurately described its paramount traits. It seems to me that, to do so, he would have wanted to answer a variety of fairly basic questions. The first must be, does the document seen in the aggregate repeatedly utilize a few fixed forms and time and again take up a few determinate intellectual initiatives? If it does, then we may speak, as Kraemer does, of "the Talmud," and if not, we may not. Second, if it can be shown that the document is cogent, saying the same thing of many things, then what is the principal focus of the document? I am inclined to wonder whether Kraemer's characterization will stand up to the scrutiny made possible by the answers to these questions. For from Kraemer's description of the Bavli, we should hardly know the simple fact that, while cogent and coherent as he claims, the rhetorical focus of coherence is upon a prior document, the Mishnah. My analysis of eleven tractates, presented in *The Bavli's One Voice: Types and Forms of Analytical Discourse and Their Fixed Order of Appearance* (Atlanta, 1991: Scholars Press for South Florida Studies in the History of Judaism), has shown that the Bavli is set forth in a systematic way as a commentary to the Mishnah, and, depending upon the tractate, from 85 percent to 97 percent (by my admittedly rough and ready reckoning) of the whole serves as Mishnah commentary. Kraemer does not deal with that fact, to which his characterization of the writing is monumentally irrelevant.

Further, from Kraemer's description, we should hardly have realized that the Bavli does set forth a highly propositional program, which it repeats time and again throughout. The allegation that the purpose of the document is to represent argument, not conclusion, contradicts that fact, spelled out both in these pages and in my *The Bavli's One Statement. The Metapropositional Program of Babylonian Talmud Tractate Zebahim Chapters One and Five* (Atlanta, 1991: Scholars Press for South Florida Studies in the History of Judaism). In other words, it is difficult for me to identify, in the terms of Kraemer's description, the paramount literary and propositional program of the Bavli as sustained and not merely episodic as exemplary analysis has shown it to be. So not only is his proposition on the indeterminacy of truth on the face of it implausible, his characterization of the document as a matter of fact simply fails to encompass the document's fundamental and indicative traits, since he has not bothered to tell us what he thinks the Bavli is. I hasten to add, in

Kraemer's defense, that the results to which I have alluded are very recent, so he is not to be blamed for not knowing what, when he was writing his book, no one knew. But my characterization of the Bavli, even before Kraemer produced his book, did not end with my *Judaism: The Classical Statement. The Evidence of the Bavli* (Chicago, 1986: University of Chicago Press), and *The Bavli and Its Sources: The Question of Tradition in the Case of Tractate Sukkah* (Atlanta, 1987: Scholars Press for Brown Judaic Studies), two books of mine that Kraemer does know and utilize (despite his disgraceful review of the former). The results of the second of these monographs is spelled out in the appendix.

But, as a matter of fact, there were two other works (not summarized in the appendix), which take up precisely the same problem of description as the one treated in the second half of Kraemer's book, in print when he was at work. These are *The Making of the Mind of Judaism* (Atlanta, 1987: Scholars Press for Brown Judaic Studies) and *The Formation of the Jewish Intellect. Making Connections and Drawing Conclusions in the Traditional System of Judaism* (Atlanta, 1988: Scholars Press for Brown Judaic Studies). In these two works I formulated precisely the same question that Kraemer's book asks; but I framed it in terms and categories quite different from his. The results were what led me precisely to the results, as to the overall characteristics of the writing, set forth just now: We deal with a sustained and systematic commentary to the Mishnah, and the problem of the intellectual history of the document is to be defined in the framework of a writing in exegetical form, but with a well-framed propositional program. Of all of this Kraemer knows nothing. How might he have framed his research, had he chosen to see the document as a whole from the perspective of the writing at the end of its formation? For one thing, he would have dropped the words "history" and "historical" from the numerous sentences in which they occur, beginning with the title. But that hardly forms a weighty flaw in his work. In my view the intellectual interest of his inquiry would not have greatly suffered, given the rather formidable chasm that separates the first half of the book from the second (for instance, the authorities who take a principal place in the first four chapters play a negligible role in the final three, where philosophers, not Talmudists, predominate in the footnotes). Indeed, I am inclined to think he could have written Chapters Five through Eight without the results of Chapters One through Four.

But the accuracy of the description of the document that Kraemer puts forward would have gained. A brief account of how I have defined the task will explain why I think the flaws in his description are formidable. In the former work I describe the distinctive modes of thought that produced a kind of writing in Judaism quite different in the basic structure of its mentality and interior traits of logic and, especially, the formation of large-scale structures of knowledge from the kind of writing carried out by contemporary Christian theologians – even on the same questions. I then described and analyzed, in the context of the concrete expression of mind provided by principal canonical writings, the four critical processes of thought, which I call logics, as I see them, three being propositional logics, the philosophical, teleological, and metaproposition, and one a non-propositional logic, the logic of fixed association. In this description of the modes of coherent thought and cogent argument, I was able to characterize precisely what Kraemer claims to describe, namely, the intellectual traits of the writing. I cannot point to a single passage in his book in which he tells us about not "truth" (for example, "truth in the classical philosophical tradition" p. 175) but logic in the framework of intelligible thought. Telling about "truth" leads us to attend to mere propositions, for example, this is so, that is not so. But a description of the intellectual processes of a piece of writing should tell us about modes of thought: what is plausible and why, what is found cogent, how are connections made, for instance.

In the latter work, turning to the larger tasks of comparison and contrast of documents, where reliable intellectual history *is* possible (as what I call "the documentary history of ideas"), I claimed to account for how Judaic system builders framed their systems by comparison to the modes of cogent discourse characteristic of prior ones, beginning with the pentateuchal system of Judaism. "The formation of the Jewish intellect" interprets the word "formation" in two senses. The first is "formation" as the ways in which that intellect formed a Judaic system, and the second is "formation" as an account also concerning the structure of that intellect, that is, of what modes of thought that intellect was formed. First I set forth the order, proportion, structure, and composition of a Judaic system, that is, a worldview and way of life addressed to a defined social entity called (an) "Israel." Second, I explained how framers of such a system made connections and drew conclusions in the setting up of their system. The order was deliberate. *For the order of the formation of the intellect is from the whole to the parts.* The reason is that it is the systemic statement that to begin with defines the logic needed to make that statement. The manner of making connections and drawing conclusions – the true life of intellect – does not percolate upward into the framing of the systemic statement.

What Kraemer has said about the traits of the Bavli therefore is not only dubious as a characterization of the writing as a whole. It is also monumentally beside the point, if the issue is the intellectual structure (if not history) of the Bavli. In this rather facile, shallow, and private work, therefore, Kraemer has presented an intellectual history which is neither historical, nor intellectual, since what he describes as the indicative intellectual traits of the document prove in fact to be subordinate and contingent, not systemic, not typical, and not determinative. Would that we could argue only from example, select evidence and ignore whether it is representative, characterize what may not be characteristic at all! But plausible propositions rest upon a thorough and accurate knowledge of the document as a whole and in its parts. Kraemer simply has not done the slow, hard work of adducing literary evidence in behalf of the task of the description, analysis, and interpretation of "the mind of the Talmud." Whether or not the Bavli really favors argument over conclusion because its authors believe that truth is indeterminate simply is not settled in these pages.

True, it can be shown that Kraemer is wrong as to the facts on every point he wishes to make about both the method and the propositional program of the document. But at issue here is not whether he is right or wrong, but only whether he has composed at least what we may judge to be a plausible, if arguable, case for his proposition, and I do not think he has done his homework adequately or set for himself a sufficiently rigorous challenge, involving thorough research. The book misses the mark because the first part – the historical – has evaded the problem of historicity, the second – the literary – has substituted argument by example for systematic research, and the third – the philosophical – fails to present an accurate description of the document's program of logic and its metapropositional consequences. It is not merely that the book lacks its own point (iqqar haser min hassefer). It is that Kraemer really doesn't see the point of the document at all. Here I have said what that point is, through two stunning chapters of what I claim is one of the world's genuinely remarkable intellectual achievements. Readers can then judge for themselves whether my examples persuasively show the intellectual character of the writing – and compare my mode of formulating and solving the problem of description with the one that, in its errors, persuaded me to spell out things I had had in mind but thought a bit routine. Only when I see how someone misses the point that strikes me as obvious am I able to persuade myself that what is self-evident in the writing has still to be spelled out. The character of the Bavli is formed out of distinct components, one of them an exegetical program, another of them an intellectual program. The generative problematic formed out of the formation of mixed grids imparts to the Bavli a principal component of its intellectual program.

Appendix

1. The Bavli: System or Tradition?
A Reprise of the First Seven Monographs

Two premises characterize all prior descriptions and histories of the Talmud of Babylonia or the Bavli, first, attributions of sayings to named authorities are reliable, second, what is attributed is factual. All prior scholarship, including that of such contemporaries as David Weiss Halivni and Adin Steinsaltz, rests on gullibility as to veracity of attributions and historicity of stories and sayings. If we abandon as simply undemonstrated these two uncritical principles, a different approach is called for. It is one that begins with the document as a whole and its indicative traits, working backward and inward into the smaller and finally the smallest whole units of thought. What is to be done when we work from the whole to the parts is shown, in part, in the seven monographs summarized here.

The Talmud of Babylonia, a.k.a. the Bavli, is a vast, anonymous writing, which has served for the community of Judaism as the principal and authoritative statement of canonical theology and law. Reaching closure by the end of the seventh century, on the eve of the birth of Islam, the document together with its commentaries, codes of its laws, and compilations of ad hoc decisions ("responsa") defined Judaism. The importance of the Bavli as the foundation document of a complex and variety set of societies, located in Asia, Europe, Africa, and North and South America, cannot be overstated. Anyone interested in media for the representation, in words, of the entirety of the social order – indeed, of a theory of world order extended from here to eternity – will find in the Talmud of Babylonia an important example of writing for a utopian constitution. The anonymity of the writing, its use of two languages, its form as a commentary to a prior document, and the ubiquity of its never identified "voice" – these paramount traits make analysis of the document exceedingly difficult. And yet, if we want to know how language serves to set forth a vision of the social order, we shall have to find out how such a foundation document is composed. For in investigating the components and the composition of the writing, we may hope to follow the passage of a vision of society from the imagination of intellectuals to the practical and concrete formulation of writers.

One fundamental problem that requires closest attention is whether a document of this kind derives from a long agglutinative process, as the sediment of the ages accumulates into a hard tradition, or whether heirs of diverse materials reshape and restate the whole in a single formulation of their own. What is at stake in solving that problem is knowledge of how foundation documents emerge: over time, through tradition, or all at once, through the intellection of some few persons working together in one specific context? If the former, then in the formative history of the writing, we trace what we may rightly call tradition – a historical study. If the latter, then in the analytical deconstruction and reconstitution of the tradition the framers set before us a single cogent vision, formulated into words at some one moment, a system, whole and complete – a philosophical study. In a series of seven monographs, I have examined the literary traits of the Bavli with decisive results in favor of the hypothesis that the Bavli forms not the outcome of a long sedimentary tradition, but the statement of its own framers (whether we call them compilers, authors, editors, or an authorship does not matter). Since colleagues in other fields, though interested in the methodological issues and substantive results, may find tedious the close reading of these seven books, I briefly summarize in this reprise the principal components of a large-scale and sustained research project that has come to conclusion.

My research differs from that which has gone before in one fundamental way. Prior scholarship has invariably begun its work on this as on all other documents of the canon of Judaism in its formative age by identifying the smallest units of thought, for example, sentences and paragraphs, and analyzing them in relationship to other such atoms. Obscuring the documentary lines of structure and order, earlier studies have therefore composed literary history out from atoms to molecules. But to do so, people have had to take for granted the veracity of attributions to named authorities of these smallest whole units of thought. All literary history therefore has rested upon the fact that to a given authority, a statement is assigned; since he really said it, we know when and where the saying was made, and from that point onward, we proceed. Furthermore, all prior authorities also take for granted that what a sage said was so was really so, and hence, once more, an uncritical agenda guided all research. Lest readers suppose that I overstate the credulity of all prior work, I refer them to the survey conducted by my graduate students of twenty years ago and edited by me under the title *The Formation of the Babylonian Talmud. Studies in the Achievements of Late Nineteenth- and Twentieth-Century Historical and Literary-Critical Research* (Leiden, 1970: E. J. Brill). A more appropriate title would have been *Studies in the Failures...*, since the critical program of modern scholarship was never adopted and always botched by most of those we studied in that book: Graetz, Jaqitz, Weiss, Zuri, Halevy, Lewin, Kaplan, Klein, Epstein, S. Lieberman, H. Albeck, and Halivni. The sole exception to the long and dark history of utter credulity was Abraham Weiss.

I begin with a different premise, which is that we do not know what we cannot show. Since we cannot demonstrate that what is attributed to a named authority was really said by him, we have to find a different, and factual, foundation for our work. In my judgment that foundation is to be located at the outer limits of the documents themselves: how we now have them, the document viewed whole and complete, its indicative traits being those imposed at ultimate redaction. To take a homely metaphor, we study the anonymous writing the way we study an onion, by peeling back the layers, moving from outer to innermost ones. That other approaches than mine persist today goes without saying. Recent works by David Weiss Halivni,[1] David Kraemer,[2] Richard Kalmin,[3] on the Bavli, and Daniel Boyarin for Midrash,[4] persist in relying entirely on attributions as the starting point of all inquiry. Still others write on problems of description and history of the rabbinic literature without addressing the critical program at all. The single most striking instance is the broadly circulated work of the popularizer Adin Steinsaltz, who persists in invincible ignorance in repeating as accurate statements about the character of the Bavli allegations that were demolished a hundred years ago; Steinsaltz simply does not keep up with the scholarly literature, even that produced in kosher, Orthodox yeshivot.[5]

---

[1]Halivni's work is in his *Sources and Traditions*, now in several volumes, in Hebrew. He has yet to respond to the sustained and detailed critique of his method, which I have published in a variety of essays, and the impression is now broadly held that he cannot reply to criticism and therefore ignores it.

[2]*The Mind of the Talmud: An Intellectual History of the Bavli* (New York, 1990: Oxford University Press), xv + 217.

[3]*The Redaction of the Babylonian Talmud: Amoraic or Saboraic?* Monographs of Hebrew Union College 12 (Cincinnati, 1989: Hebrew Union College).

[4]*Intertextuality and the Reading of Midrash* Indiana Studies in Biblical Literature (Bloomington & Indianapolis, 1990: Indiana University Press), xiii + 161.

[5]Let me give one example of the abysmal misrepresentation of the Talmud that he has committed. In his introduction to the Bavli, he states, "The Talmud...deals with an overwhelmingly broad subject – the nature of all things according to the Torah. Therefore its contours are a reflection of life itself. It has no formal external order, but is bound by a strong inner connection between its many

diverse subjects....The authority of the Talmud lies in its use of this rigorous method in its search for truth with regard to the entire Torah – in other words, with regard to all possible subjects in the world, both physical and spiritual." His allegation that the Talmud follows no "formal external order" is simply false, and every student of the Bavli who has simply outlined two or three sustained composites knows that it is false. If he were right, people should imagine that the Talmud is about nothing in particular. But in fact the Bavli is very much about some few things – in all their rich particulars. And that statement pertains to the Bavli's substantive propositions, the things that, through an infinity of details, the framers wish to show time and again. Not only is the Bavli not disorderly, it is both orderly and, in a strict sense, wonderfully repetitious, because it says the same thing about many things. He is wrong not merely because the Talmud's character contradicts his rather airy characterization of it, but because he massively misses the mark in his witless misunderstanding of the document. What he facilely alleges is all-encompassing is a selective piece of writing; what he see as essentially pointless – the document as a whole – proves purposeful and well crafted. That explains why he is wrong, and why vast stretches of the Bavli prove he is wrong. If he studied not merely words and phrases and sentences, but the composition and construction of entire paragraphs and chapters, he would has seen that obvious and blatant fact. He misrepresents a document that he knows only as to its parts but not as a whole. The Talmud speaks in a single voice. It everywhere speaks uniformly, consistently, and predictably. It follows rules that govern language choice, the order of topics to be introduced, the cogency of paragraphs set forth in sequence. And these are external traits of order. The voice is the voice of a book. True, the document seems, in the main, to intend to provide notes, an abbreviated script which anyone may use to reconstruct and reenact formal discussions of problems: about this, one says that. Curt and often arcane, these notes can be translated only with immense bodies of inserted explanation. All of this script of information is public and undifferentiated, not individual and idiosyncratic. We must assume people took for granted that, out of the signs of speech, it would be possible for anyone to reconstruct speech, doing so in accurate and fully conventional ways. So the literary traits of the document presuppose a uniform code of communication: a single voice. The Talmud is not a mere compilation of this and that, the result of centuries of the accumulation, in a haphazard way, of the detritus of various schools or opinions. The Talmud that is exceedingly carefully and well crafted, a sustained and cogent inquiry. Scarely a single line is out of place; not a sentence in the entire passage sustains the view of a document that is an agglutinative compilation. I state very simply how the Talmud analyzes any Mishnah passage. We begin with the clarification of the Mishnah paragraph, turn then to the examination of the principles of law implicit in the Mishnah paragraph, and then broaden the discussion to introduce what I called analogies from case to law and law to case. These are the three stages of most discussions. Within the protracted discussion, we note numerous cross-references. Various propositions are systematically tested and examined. It would be very easy to outline the discussion, beginning to end, and to produce a reasoned account of the position and order of every completed composition and the ordering of the several compositions into a composite. And that composite really does provide a beginning and an end. Steinsaltz's allegation is that the Bavli "has no formal external order." Nothing could be further from the truth.

Before setting forth the main results, I have to make reference to my work of (re)translating the Bavli,[6] which was required before any

---

[6]I refer to *The Talmud of Babylonia. An American Translation* (Chico, then Atlanta, 1984-1993: Scholars Press for Brown Judaic Studies).

I.	*Tractate Berakhot*
II.A.	*Tractate Shabbat*
II.B.	*Tractate Shabbat*
III.A.	*Tractate Erubin. Chapters One through Five*
III.B.	*Tractate Erubin. Chapters Six through Ten*
VI.	*Tractate Sukkah*
XI.	*Tractate Moed Qatan*
XIII.A.	*Tractate Yebamot. Chapters One through Five*
XIII.B.	*Tractate Yebamot. Chapters Six through Ten*
XIII.C.	*Tractate Yebamot. Chapters Eleven through Sixteen*
XIV.A.	*Tractate Ketubot. Chapters One through Six*
XIV.B.	*Tractate Ketubot. Chapters Seven through Thirteen*
XVII.	*Tractate Sotah*
XVIII.A.	*Tractate Gittin. Chapters One through Four*
XVIII.B.	*Tractate Gittin. Chapters Five through Nine*
XIX.A.	*Tractate Qiddushin. Chapters One through Two*
XIX.B.	*Tractate Qiddushin. Chapters Three through Four*
XX.A.	*Tractate Baba Qamma. Chapters One through Three*
XX.B.	*Tractate Baba Qamma. Chapters Four through Six*
XX.C	*Tractate Baba Qamma. Chapters Seven through Ten*
XXI.A.	*Tractate Baba Mesia. Introduction. Chapters One and Two*
XXI.B.	*Tractate Baba Mesia. Chapters Three and Four*
XXI.C.	*Tractate Baba Mesia. Chapters Five and Six*
XXI.D.	*Tractate Bava Mesia. Chapters Seven through Ten*
XXII.A.	*Tractate Baba Batra. Chapters One through Three*
XXII.B.	*Tractate Baba Batra. Chapters Four and Five*
XXIII.A	*Tractate Sanhedrin. Chapters One through Three*
XXIII.B	*Tractate Sanhedrin. Chapters Four through Eight*
XXIII.C	*Tractate Sanhedrin. Chapters Nine through Eleven*
XXIV.	*Tractate Makkot*
XXV.A.	*Tractate Abodah Zarah. Chapters One and Two*
XXV.B.	*Tractate Abodah Zarah. Chapters Three, Four, and Five*
XXVII.A	*Tractate Shebuot. Chapters One through Three*
XXVII.B	*Tractate Shebuot. Chapters Four through Eight*
XXVIII.A.	*Tractate Zebahim. Chapters One through Three*
XXVIII.B.	*Tractate Zebahim. Chapters Four through Eight*
XXVIII.C.	*Tractate Zebahim. Chapters Nine through Fourteen*
XXIX.A.	*Tractate Menahot. Chapters One through Three*
XXIX.B.	*Tractate Menahot. Chapters Four through Seven*
XXIX.C.	*Tractate Menahot. Chapters Eight through Thirteen*
XXXI.A.	*Tractate Bekhorot. Chapters One through Four*
XXXI.B.	*Tractate Bekhorot. Chapters Five through Nine*
XXXII.	*Tractate Arakhin*
XXXIII.	*Tractate Temurah*
XXXIV.	*Tractate Keritot*

analytical inquiry could commence. The reason is that the main problem in analyzing a sample of the Talmud of Babylonia is presented by the run-on character of the writing. Visually, what we see whether in the original languages or in English or German, Spanish or French or Italian, or any of the other languages into which the document has been translated whole or in part, simply are long columns of undifferentiated words, the sole division between a set of sentences drawn from the Mishnah and (ordinarily) much longer and more elaborate discussion of those sentences. Substantively, what we quickly perceive is that a passage of the Bavli moves far beyond the limits of Mishnah commentary, and that movement twists and turns, so that a vast amount of information will be introduced that is only tangentially relevant to the starting point in the Mishnah. Before any picture of the rules of composition of the document can emerge, we have to devise a method of identifying a whole unit of thought – beginning to end – and differentiating among its parts. This is not merely a formal problem, readily solved, as I had solved it two decades ago, by marking off chapters, paragraphs, and sentences (to draw on the metaphor of contemporary division).[7] It is a problem of a very substantial order. The reason is that the Bavli on the surface appears to be run-on, and many have found the writing to be not only confusing but confused, the result of a stream of consciousness, not propositional, not crafted and purposive at all.

The run-on and meandering quality of a Talmudic discussion is difficult to analyze as a single, cogent composition, and therefore impossible to classify as the work of showing how the Bavli's one voice speaks, until we realize a simple fact. The Talmud of Babylonia in contemporary terms would be presented heavy with footnotes and appendices. That is, in our mode of setting forth our ideas and the documentation for them, we include in our text the main points of proposition, evidence, and argument; we relegate to footnotes the

---

XXXVI.A   *Tractate Niddah. Chapters One through Three*
XXXVI.B   *Tractate Niddah. Chapters Four through Ten*

[7]I published my results, in the context of the analysis of the Mishnah's division of purities, in *A History of the Mishnaic Law of Purities* (Leiden, 1977: E.J. Brill), XXI. *The Redaction and Formulation of the Order of Purities in the Mishnah and Tosefta.* There I showed how "chapter, subdivision of a chapter, a paragraph, and a sentence" (marked in my reference system by a capital Roman numeral, a Roman numeral in small letters, an Arabic numeral, and a capital letter) serve as metaphors for how a "completed unit of systematic exposition, subunit of exposition, formation of the smallest whole units of thought into a cogent statement, and the smallest whole unit of thought," respectively, would do its work.

sources upon which we draw; we place in appendices substantial bodies of secondary material, relevant to the main body of our text only tangentially, yet required for a full presentation of what we wish to say. The authorship of the Talmud of Babylonia accomplishes, within the technical limitations that governed its formulation of its proposition, evidence, and argument, what we work out through footnotes and appendices. Much of the materials subordinated to the proposition, evidence, and argument derives from finished pieces of writing, worked out for use in a document we do not now have (and cannot even imagine!), now providing useful, if not essential, documentation for the document that we do have. Accordingly, my retranslation, for analytical purposes, made possible the work that is described here.

The Bavli and Its Sources: The Question of Tradition in the Case of Tractate Sukkah (Atlanta, 1987: Scholars Press for Brown Judaic Studies)

Having worked out [1] the description of texts, read one by one, in such works as my *Judaism: The Evidence of the Mishnah, The Integrity of Leviticus Rabbah,* and parallel studies,[8] and [2] the analysis of those same texts seen in relationship to one another, that is, the comparison and contrast among a set of documents, hence to connection, as in *Judaism: The Classical Statement. The Evidence of the Bavli,* on the relationship of the Yerushalmi and the Bavli, *Comparative Midrash: The Plan and Program of Genesis Rabbah and Leviticus Rabbah* and *From Tradition to Imitation: The Plan and Program of Pesiqta deRab Kahana and Pesiqta Rabbati,*[9] I here proceeded to [3] the interpretation of texts under the aspect of continuity. When we describe the relationships between two documents or among three or more, we know what a given group of editors or authorities has contributed on its own, and also how that authorship restated or reworked what it received from a prior group. The authorship of a

---

[8]*Judaism. The Evidence of the Mishnah* (Chicago, 1981: University of Chicago Press). Paperback edition, 1984. Second printing, 1985. Third printing, 1986. Second edition, augmented (Atlanta, 1987: Scholars Press for Brown Judaic Studies); *The Integrity of Leviticus Rabbah. The Problem of the Autonomy of a Rabbinic Document* (Chico, 1985: Scholars Press for Brown Judaic Studies).

[9]*Judaism: The Classical Statement. The Evidence of the Bavli* (Chicago, 1986: University of Chicago Press); *Comparative Midrash: The Plan and Program of Genesis Rabbah and Leviticus Rabbah* (Atlanta, 1986: Scholars Press for Brown Judaic Studies); *From Tradition to Imitation. The Plan and Program of Pesiqta deRab Kahana and Pesiqta Rabbati* (Atlanta, 1987: Scholars Press for Brown Judaic Studies) [with a fresh translation of Pesiqta Rabbati *Pisqaot* 1-5, 15]; note also *Canon and Connection: Intertextuality in Judaism* (Lanham, 1986: University Press of America), Studies in Judaism Series; and *Midrash as Literature: The Primacy of Documentary Discourse* (Lanham, 1987: University Press of America) Studies in Judaism Series.

document that stands in a relationship of connection to prior writings will make use of their materials essentially in its own way. The authorship of a document that works in essential continuity with prior writings will cite and quote and refine those received writings but will ordinarily not undertake a fundamentally original statement of its own framed in terms of its own and on a set of issues defined separately from the received writings or formulations. In this monograph, for Bavli-tractate Sukkah, I showed that the Bavli proves connected with earlier documents and also with some received sayings not written down in a systematic way in prior compilations. But the connections appear episodic and haphazard, not systematic, except in respect to the Mishnah. The Bavli cannot be shown systematically and generally to continue the program and inquiry of predecessors. The Bavli contains ample selections from available writings. The authorship of the Bavli leaves no doubt that it makes extensive use of extant materials, sayings, and stories. But in the Bavli we deal with an authorship of amazingly independent mind, working independently and in an essentially original way on materials on which others have handed on a quite persuasive and cogent statement. Tosefta on the one side, Scripture and a heritage of conventional reading thereof on the other – neither has defined the program of our document or determined the terms in which it would make its statement, though both, in a subordinated position and in a paltry limited measure, are given some sort of a say. The Bavli is connected to a variety of prior writings but continuous with none of them.

Making the Classics in Judaism: The Three Stages of Literary Formation (Atlanta, 1990: Scholars Press for Brown Judaic Studies)

Two questions in the framing of a theory of the history of the anonymous literature of formative Judaism form the program of this book. The first is, what is the correct starting point of analysis of a document and its formative history? The second is, what are the principal results of starting from that designated point of entry? I test the hypothesis that the discrete sayings (lemmas) form the correct point of entry and show, through the formation and testing of a null hypothesis, that that hypothesis is false. We cannot begin work in the assumption that the building block of documents is the smallest whole unit of thought, the lemma, nor can we proceed in the premise that a lemma traverses the boundaries of various documents and is unaffected by the journey. The opposite premise is that we start our work with the traits of documents as a whole, rather than with the traits of the lemmas of which documents are (supposedly) composed. Since, in a variety of books, I had set forth the documentary hypothesis for the analysis of the rabbinic literature of late antiquity,[10] I turned immediately to the exploration of the second of the two possibilities. How shall we proceed, if we take as our point of entry the character and conditions of the document of integrity, seen whole? Once I have demonstrated beyond any doubt that a rabbinic text is a a well-crafted text and not merely a compilation of this and that, and further specified in acute detail precisely the aesthetic, formal, and logical program followed by each of those texts, I am able to move to the logical next step. That is to show that in the background of the documents that we have is writing of three types: [1] writing that is not shaped by documentary requirements, [2] writing that is not shaped by the documentary requirements of the compilations we now have, and also [3] writing that is entirely formed within the rules of the documents that now present that writing. These then are the three kinds of writing that form, also, the three stages in the formation of the classics of Judaism. Which kind of writing dictates the character of a document? In the work that followed, I demonstrated that it is writing of the third type; authors, compilers, or editors formed a theory of what they wished to do in their particular compilation, and then they picked and chose out of the heritage of prior writings, reproducing verbatim what they had received, revising as they wished, or something in between – the whole a process of selection. This hypothesis, deriving from the present work, derived from *The Bavli and Its Sources* and dictated the problem of *Tradition as Selectivity* and also *The Bavli That Might Have Been.*

Tradition as Selectivity: Scripture, Mishnah, Tosefta, and Midrash in the Talmud of Babylonia. The Case of Tractate Arakhin (Atlanta, 1990: Scholars Press for South Florida Studies in the History of Judaism)

The specific research problem of this book is how the Bavli (the Talmud of Babylonia), as exemplified in one tractate, relates to its sources, by which I mean, materials it shares with other and (by definition) earlier redacted documents. In this instance what I want to know is how Bavli Arakhin deals with the topic and facts set forth at [1] Lev. 27:1-7, 16-25, the prior reading of [2] Sifra to those verses, [3] the received version of those same facts set forth by [3] Mishnah-tractate Arakhin, and the exegesis of Mishnah-tractate Arakhin by [4] Tosefta Arakhin. What is at stake is an account of just how "traditional" the

---

[10]For the Talmud of the Land of Israel, a.k.a. the Yerushalmi, for example, in *The Talmud of the Land of Israel. A Preliminary Translation and Explanation* (Chicago, 1983: University of Chicago Press), XXXV. *Introduction. Taxonomy;* and *Judaism in Society: The Evidence of the Yerushalmi. Toward the Natural History of a Religion* (Chicago, 1983: University of Chicago Press). Second printing, with a new preface (Atlanta, 1991: Scholars Press for South Florida Studies in the History of Judaism).

Bavli is. The question that defines the problem is how the Bavli has formed of available writings (redacted in documents now in hand) a single, cogent, and coherent statement presented by the Bavli's authorship as summary and authoritative: a canonical statement on a given subject. In what ways does a Bavli tractate frame such a (theologically canonical) statement out of what (as attested in extant writings) its authorship has in hand? In the exercise of which the present work is a continuation, *The Bavli and Its Sources*, the prior source was the Talmud of the Land of Israel. The prior sources in this book are the Tosefta and Sifra. In both monographs my question is whether and how – in concrete, literary terms – a document makes its part of such a traditional statement, speaking, for its particular subject, in behalf of the entirety of the antecedent writings of the Judaic system at hand and standing in a relationship of continuity – not merely connection – with other such writings. The answer to that question will tell me how a traditional writing is formulated. If the question has no answer, and in the Bavli it does not, then it must follow that the Bavli is a document that has been framed through a process of not tradition but selection. And that is how I see the Bavli. Here, therefore, we inquire into the standing of a Bavli tractate as testimony on its subject within the larger continuous system of which it is reputed to form a principal part. What we want to know about that testimony therefore is how the Bavli relates to prior documents. The reason is that we want to know whether or not the Bavli constitutes a statement of a set of such antecedent sources, therefore a step in an unfolding tradition, so Judaism constitutes a traditional religion, the result of a long sedimentary process. As is clear, the alternative and complementary issue is whether or not the Bavli makes its own statement and hence inaugurates a "new tradition" altogether. In these pages I drew to a conclusion my work on the relationship between the Bavli and prior writing, both formed into completed documents (Yerushalmi, Sifra) and also not contained in closed compilations now available to us. In *The Bavli and Its Sources* I had shown that earlier authorships – represented by the Talmud of the Land of Israel – wished to investigate in the Mishnah the points they wished to prove by reference to verses of Scripture important in our tractate – these have little or nothing in common with the points of special concern systematically worked out by the authorship of the Bavli. The Bavli's authorship at ca. 600 approaches Mishnah exegesis with a program distinct from that of the Yerushalmi's authorship of ca. 400, and the Bavli's authorship reads a critical verse of Scripture within a set of considerations entirely separate from those of interest to the authorships of Leviticus Rabbah and Pesiqta deRab Kahana of ca. 450 and 500. Any notion that the Bavli's authorship has taken as its principal task the restatement of received ideas on the Mishnah topics and Scripture verses at hand derives no support to speak of from the sample we shall examine. The same result, for Arakhin, emerged in this monograph.

Language as Taxonomy. The Rules for Using Hebrew and Aramaic in the Babylonian Talmud (Atlanta, 1990: Scholars Press for South Florida Studies in the History of Judaism)

Another, and separate, route of inquiry was defined by the linguistic traits of the Bavli, which differ from those of all other writings in the rabbinic canon of late antiquity except for the Yerushalmi. These traits support the claim that the Bavli explicitly recognizes the availability, and authority, of received writings or documents or traditions and the Bavli's authors distinguish their own contribution from what they have received – a case, in contemporary literary critical jargon, of not intertextuality but intratextuality. Not only by routinely and ubiquitously using such language as "as it is said," or "as it is written," did the authorities of the Talmud of Babylonia separate their statements from those of Scripture. Also by their choice of the very language in which they would express what they wished to say on their own account they differentiated themselves from their antecedents. When it came to citations from prior, non-scriptural authorities, they used one formation of the Hebrew language, specifically, Middle, or Mishnaic, Hebrew; when it came to the conduct of their own analytical process, they used one formation of the Aramaic language, Eastern or Talmudic Aramaic. They never alluded to authoritative facts, they always cited them in so many words; but the indication of citation – in a writing in which the modern sigla of quotation marks and footnotes were simply unavailable – came to expression in the choice of language. The Bavli is in one language, not two, and that language is Aramaic. The infrastructure of the document, its entire repertoire of editorial conventions and sigla, are in Aramaic. When a saying is assigned to a named authority, the saying may be in Hebrew or in Aramaic, and the same named authority may be given sayings in both languages – even within the same sentence. But the editorial and conceptual infrastructure of the document comes to expression only in Aramaic, and when no name is attached to a statement, that statement is always in Aramaic, unless it forms part of a larger, autonomous Hebrew composition, cited by, or parachuted down into, "the Talmud." The Talmud speaks in a single voice, forms a unitary discourse, beginning, middle, and end, and constitutes one wholly coherent and cogent document, everywhere asking questions drawn from a single determinate and limited repertoire of intellectual initiatives – and always framing those questions, pursuing those inquiries, in Aramaic. Then where and why do the framers of this writing utilize the

Hebrew language? Specifically, what signal is given, what purpose is served by the bi- or multilingualism of the Talmud, what do we know without further ado, when we are given a composition or a component of a composition in Hebrew, and what is the implicit meaning of making a statement in Aramaic? The answer is that the choice of language signals a taxonomic meaning. If we know which language is used, we also know where we stand in the expression of thought, and the very language in which a statement is made therefore forms part of the method of thought and even the message of discourse of the document. What is said in Hebrew is represented as authoritative and formulates a normative thought or rule. What is said in Aramaic is analytical and commonly signals an argument and formulates a process of inquiry and criticism. That is how language serves a taxonomic purpose: Hebrew is the language of the result, Aramaic, of the way by which the result is achieved; Hebrew is the formulation of the decision, Aramaic, of the work of deliberation. Each language serves to classify what is said in that language, and we always know where we stand, in a given process of thought and the exposition of thought, by reference to the language that is used at that particular place in the sustained discourse to which we are witness.

The Bavli That Might Have Been: The Tosefta's Theory of Mishnah Commentary Compared with That of the Babylonian Talmud (Atlanta, 1990: Scholars Press for South Florida Studies in the History of Judaism)

Yet a third kind of inquiry seemed to me called for, one that compared two or more documents' authorships' approach to the same problem. Since the Bavli is set forth as a commentary to the Mishnah, I decided to compare the Bavli's authorships' definition of their work with the Tosefta's counterparts' framing of the same task. For the Tosefta forms a commentary to the Mishnah, and so, too, does the Talmud of Babylonia or the Bavli. The latter document differs from the former in its conception of what is to be done with the Mishnah. By comparing the Tosefta's with the Bavli's treatment of the Mishnah, I show not only that the Bavli's approach to Mishnah commentary differs from the Tosefta's (which is hardly surprising), *but that the differences in the aggregate are uniform and predictable.* I prove beyond doubt, on the basis of a substantial sample, the fact that the comparison yields a fixed and coherent set of contrasts. So what? It follows, in my way of thinking, that, as I demonstrated to be the case for the Tosefta's authorship in my *The Tosefta: Its Structure and Its Sources,*[11] so, too, the Bavli's authorship

---

[11](Atlanta, 1986: Scholars Press for Brown Judaic Studies).

referred to a coherent and cogent program of exegetical principles when they turned to the Mishnah. That is why I attach such weight to the fact that the differences between the two documents – like those between the Bavli and the prior, and available, Yerushalmi, dealt with in *The Bavli and Its Sources*, are fixed and predictable. When we compare one document's reading of the original source to the other document's reading of that same source, therefore, we are able to show by the persistence of a fixed set of differences that the latter document is a well-crafted and thoughtfully composed statement, not a mere compilation of this and that: a composition, not a compilation. Since the Bavli is commonly represented as a mere conglomeration of whatever people happened to have received – a sedimentary piece of writing, not a planned and considered one, the result of many centuries of accumulation, not the work of a generation or two of thoughtful writers – these results provide a detailed argument against one proposition and in favor of another. What is important therefore is not only difference, but a pattern of difference: the Bavli's framers differ in their theory of Mishnah commentary from the Tosefta's framers, and the differences are consistent throughout. In the contrast between the Tosefta and the Talmud of Babylonia, the Talmud of Babylonia emerges as a well-crafted and highly purposive document, and certainly not a mere compilation of this and that, the result of centuries of the accumulation, in a haphazard way, of the detritus of various schools or opinions. Any sample of the Talmud that we take presents itself as exceedingly carefully and well crafted, a sustained and cogent inquiry. Scarely a single line is out of place; not a sentence in the entire passage sustains the view of a document that is an agglutinative compilation. Ordinarily, for example, at any given passage of the Bavli, we begin with the clarification of the Mishnah paragraph, turn then to the examination of the principles of law implicit in the Mishnah paragraph, and then broaden the discussion to introduce what I called analogies from case to law and law to case. These are the three stages of our discussion. It would be very easy to outline a given Talmudic discussion, beginning to end, and to produce a reasoned account of the position and order of every completed composition and the ordering of the several compositions into a composite.

The Rules of Composition of the Talmud of Babylonia. The Cogency of the Bavli's Composite (Atlanta, 1991: Scholars Press for South Florida Studies in the History of Judaism)

The Bavli's authors of compositions and framers of composites followed not only rules of language, but also laws of composition. These laws told them how to formulate their thought within a limited and determinate repertoire of rhetorical patterns and further dictated what

issues must come first, which ones may be treated later, in the exposition
of their ideas. These rules may be discerned only when we define the
units of complete discourse that were to be composed. In this work I
show that the composite of several distinct compositions formed the unit
of complete discourse, and that, when the framer of a large-scale passage
of the Bavli referred to rules of language and laws of composition that
would govern his work, his goal was to put together in correct form and
sequential order a set of composites. The rules of composition then
governed composing composites. Here I show that all authors found
guidance in the same limited repertoire of rules of composition. Not
only so, but a fixed order of discourse – a composition of one sort, A,
always comes prior to a composite of another type, B. A simple logic
instructed framers of composites, who sometimes also were authors of
compositions, and who sometimes drew upon available compositions in
the making of their cogent composites. When we understand that logic,
which accounts for what for a very long time has impressed students of
the Talmud as the document's run-on, formless, and meandering
character, we see the writing as cogent and well crafted, always
addressing a point that, within the hegemony of this logic, and not some
other, was deemed closely linked to what had gone before and what was
to follow. And on that basis we perceive as entirely of a piece, cogent
and coherent, large-scale constructions, not brief compositions of a few
lines, which therefore become subject to classification whole and
complete. So the work of uncovering the laws of composition involve
our identifying the entirety of a piece of coherent writing and classifying
that writing – not pulling out of context and classifying only the
compositions that, in some measure, form constituents of a larger whole.
Were we to classify only the compositions, we should gain some
knowledge of types of writing accomplished by authors, but none
concerning types of writing that comprise our Talmud. Why insist that a
composite – and not the several compositions that may find their
redactional location within a given composite – forms the basic building
block of thought, and the irreducible minimum of discourse, of the Bavli?
The reason is that only when we grasp how a variety of materials, some
of them already completed compositions, are drawn together into a
single sustained and comprehensive statement shall we understand the
work of the compiler. The Bavli is a work of purposive compilation, and
when we understand the rules of composition in the twin sense – the
writing of compositions, the formation of composites – we shall have a
clear picture of what the framers of the Bavli did. By contrast, if we
knew only the rules that dictated the writing of the distinct compositions
that the framers utilized, we should know only how the parts took shape,
but not how the whole, served by those parts, found its coherence and

cogency. The importance of recognizing that some pieces of writing were composed to serve the purposes of the formation of a particular document in which they occur, others to serve the purposes of some other document than the one we now have, and still others to serve the purposes of a document that we now cannot even imagine in the present context then is clear. The results of this work – demonstrating the cogency of the Bavli's composite – prepared the way for this final chapter in a six-year study.

The Bavli's One Voice: Types and Forms of Analytical Discourse and Their Fixed Order of Appearance (Atlanta, 1991: Scholars Press for South Florida Studies in the History of Judaism)

This monograph provides a final solution to the Bavli problem framed in narrowly literary terms: Who speaks through the Bavli? Is it the voice of the penultimate and ultimate authorship, or does the document resonate with the voices of a variety of authors and authorships? Here I demonstrate through analysis of eleven tractates and classifying more than three thousand composites that the Bavli throughout speaks in a single and singular voice. It is single because it is a voice that expresses the same limited set of notes everywhere. It is singular because these notes are arranged in one and the same way throughout. The Bavli's one voice, sounding through all tractates, is the voice of exegetes of the Mishnah. The document is organized around the Mishnah, and that is not a merely formal, but a substantive, order. At every point, if the framers have chosen a passage of Mishnah exegesis, that passage will stand at the head of all further discussion. Every turning point brings the editors back to the Mishnah, always read in its own order and sequence. So the Bavli speaks in a single way about some few things, and that is the upshot of this sustained inquiry. It follows that well-crafted and orderly rules governed the character of the sustained discourse that the writing in the Bavli sets forth. All framers of composites and editors of sequences of composites found guidance in the same limited repertoire of rules of analytical rhetoric: some few questions or procedures, directed always toward one and the same prior writing. Not only so, but a fixed order of discourse dictated that a composition of one sort, A, always come prior to a composite of another type, B. A simple logic instructed framers of composites, who sometimes also were authors of compositions, and who sometimes drew upon available compositions in the making of their cogent composites. So we have now to see the Bavli as entirely of a piece, cogent and coherent, made up of well-composed, large-scale constructions.

The Bavli's one voice utilizes only a few, well-modulated tones: a scale of not many notes. When we classify more than three thousand composites, spread over eleven tractates, we find that nearly 90 percent of the whole comprises Mishnah commentary of various kinds; not only so, but the variety of the types of Mishnah commentary is limited, as a review of the representation of Temurah in detail, and of the ten tractates of our sample in brief characterization, has shown. Cogent composites are further devoted to Scripture or to topics of a moral or theological character not closely tied to the exegesis of verses of Scripture; these form in the aggregate approximately 10 percent of the whole number of composites, but, of tractates to begin with not concerned with scriptural or theological topics (in our sample these are Sanhedrin and Berakhot), they make up scarcely 3 percent of the whole. So the Bavli has one voice, and it is the voice of a person or persons who propose to speak about one document and to do so in some few ways. Let me spell out precisely what I mean. The results of the survey of eleven tractates and classification of all of the composites of each one of them yield firm and one-sided results. First, we are able to classify all composites in three principal categories: [1] exegesis and amplification of the law of the Mishnah; [2] exegesis and exposition of verses of, or topics in, Scripture; [3] free-standing composites devoted to topics other than those defined by the Mishnah or Scripture. That means that my initial proposal of a taxonomic system left no lacunae. Second, with the classification in place, we see that much more than four-fifths of all composites of the Bavli address the Mishnah and systematically expound that document. These composites are subject to subclassification in two ways: Mishnah exegesis and speculation and abstract theorizing about the implications of the Mishnah's statements. The former type of composite, further, is to be classified in a few and simple taxa, for example, composites organized around [1] clarification of the statements of the Mishnah, [2] identification of the authority behind an anonymous statement in the Mishnah, [3] scriptural foundation for the Mishnah's rules; [4] citation and not seldom systematic exposition of the Tosefta's amplification of the Mishnah. That means that most of the Bavli is a systematic exposition of the Mishnah. Third, the other fifth (or less) of a given tractate will comprise composites that take shape around [1] Scripture or [2] themes or topics of a generally theological or moral character. Distinguishing the latter from the former, of course, is merely formal; very often a scriptural topic will be set forth in a theological or moral framework, and very seldom does a composite on a topic omit all reference to the amplification of a verse or topic of Scripture. The proportion of a given tractate devoted to other than Mishnah exegesis and amplification is generally not more than 10 percent. My figure is distorted by the special problems of tractates Sanhedrin and Berakhot, and, in the former, Chapter Eleven in particular.

These two tractates prove anomalous for the categories I have invented, because both of them contain important components that are devoted to begin with to scriptural or theological topics. Tractate Sanhedrin Chapter Eleven, for example, lists various scriptural figures in catalogues of those who do, or do not, inherit the world to come; it further specifies certain doctrines that define the norms of the community of Israel that inherits the world to come. It will therefore prove quite natural that numerous composites will attend to scriptural or theological topics. Tractate Berakhot addresses matters of prayer and other forms of virtue, with the same consequence. In the analysis that follows, therefore, I calculate the averages of proportions of various types of composites both with and without these anomalous tractates. The upshot is that a rather inconsequential proportion of most tractates, and a small proportion of the whole, of the Bavli, is devoted to the systematic exposition of either verses of Scripture or topics of a theological or moral character. Seen in the aggregate, the proportions of the eleven tractates devoted solely to Mishnah exegesis average 83 percent. If we omit reference to the two clearly anomalous tractates, Berakhot and Sanhedrin, the proportion of Mishnah exegesis rises to 89.5 percent. If, then, we combine exegesis of the Mishnah and exegesis of the broader implications of the Mishnah's law – and in the process of classification, it was not always easy to keep these items apart in a consistent way – we see a still more striking result. More than 86 percent of the whole of our tractates is devoted to the exegesis of the Mishnah and the amplification of the implications of its law; without the anomalous tractates, the proportion is close to 94-95 percent.

So the Talmud speaks through one voice, that voice of logic that with vast assurance reaches into our own minds and by asking the logical and urgent next question tells us what we should be thinking. Fixing our attention upon the Mishnah, the Talmud's rhetoric seduces us into joining its analytical inquiry, always raising precisely the question that should trouble us (and that would trouble us if we knew all of the pertinent details as well as the Talmud does). In this final monograph I have now demonstrated beyond a shadow of a doubt that the Bavli speaks about the Mishnah in essentially a single voice, about fundamentally few things. Its mode of speech as much as of thought is uniform throughout. Diverse topics produce slight differentiation in modes of analysis. The same sorts of questions phrased in the same rhetoric – a moving, or dialectical, argument, composed of questions and answers – turn out to pertain equally well to every subject and problem. The Talmud's discourse forms a closed system, in which people say the same thing about everything. The fact that the Talmud speaks in a single voice supplies striking evidence (1) that the Talmud does speak in particular for the age in which its units of discourse took shape, and (2) that that work was done toward the end of that long period of Mishnah reception that began at the end of the second century and came to an end at the conclusion of the sixth century.

It follows that the whole – the composites of discourse as we know them, the sequence of composites as we have them – was put together at the end. At that point everything was in hand, so available for arrangement in accordance with a principle other than chronology, and in a rhetoric common to all sayings. That other principle will then have determined the arrangement, drawing in its wake resort to a single monotonous voice: "the Talmud." The principle is logical exposition, that is to say, the analysis and dissection of a problem into its conceptual components. The dialectic of argument is framed not by considerations of the chronological sequence in which sayings were said but by attention to the requirements of reasonable exposition of the problem. That is what governs. If there is a single governing method, then what can we expect to learn about the single, repeated message? The evidence before us indicates that the purpose of the Talmud is to clarify and amplify selected passages of the Mishnah. We may say very simply that the Mishnah is about life, and the Talmud is about the Mishnah. That is to say, while the Mishnah records rules governing the conduct of the holy life of Israel, the holy people, the Talmud concerns itself with the details of the Mishnah. The one is descriptive and free-standing, the other analytical and contingent. Where there no Mishnah, there would be no Talmud. But what is the message of the method, which is to insist upon the Mishnah's near monopoly over serious discourse? To begin with, the very character of the Talmud tells us the sages' view of the Mishnah. The Mishnah presented itself to them as constitutive, the text of ultimate concern. So, in our instance, the Mishnah speaks of a quarrel over a coat, the Talmud, of the Mishnah's provision of an oath as a means of settling the quarrel in a fair way: substance transformed into process. What the framers of the Bavli wished to say about the Mishnah will guide us toward the definition of the message of their method, but it will not tell us what that message was, or why it was important. A long process of close study of texts is required to guide us toward the center of matters.

The upshot of the long series of studies that conclude here is simple. We may speak about "the Talmud," its voice, its purposes, its mode of constructing a view of the Israelite world. The reason is that, when we claim "the Talmud" speaks, we replicate both the main lines of chronology and the literary character of the document. These point toward the formation of the bulk of materials – its units of discourse – in a process lasting (to take a guess) about half a century, prior to the ultimate arrangement of these units of discourse around passages of the Mishnah and the closure and redaction of the whole into the document we now know. What comes next? Well, now that we know that the Bavli is a document of remarkable integrity, repeatedly insisting upon the harmony of the parts within a whole and unitary structure of belief and behavior, we want to know what the Bavli says: the one thing that is repeated in regard to many things. Dismantling ("deconstructing") its components and identifying them, perhaps even describing the kinds of compilations that the authors of those components could have had in mind in writing their compositions – these activities of literary criticism yield no insight into the religious system that guided the document's framers. But the Talmud of Babylonia recapitulates, in grand and acute detail, a religious system, and the generative problematic of that writing directs our attention not to the aesthetics of writing as literature, but to the religion of writing as a document of faith in the formation of the social order. So we have now to turn to the message of the method of the Bavli: what the Bavli's one voice always wishes to convey.[12]

---

[12]The following works relate to the preceding section of this appendix:

Boyarin, Daniel. *Intertextuality and the Reading of Midrash.* Indiana Studies in Biblical Literature (Bloomington & Indianapolis, 1990: Indiana University Press) xiii + 161.

Kalmin, Richard. *The Redaction of the Babylonian Talmud: Amoraic or Saboraic?* Monographs of Hebrew Union College 12 (Cincinnati, 1989: Hebrew Union College), xviii + 215.

Kraemer, David. *The Mind of the Talmud: An Intellectual History of the Bavli* (New York,1990: Oxford University Press), xv + 217.

Neusner, J. *A History of the Mishnaic Law of Purities* (Leiden, 1977: E.J. Brill) XXI. *The Redaction and Formulation of the Order of Purities in the Mishnah and Tosefta.*

Neusner, J. *Canon and Connection: Intertextuality in Judaism.* Studies in Judaism Series (Lanham, 1986: University Press of America).

Neusner, J. *Comparative Midrash: The Plan and Program of Genesis Rabbah and Leviticus Rabbah* (Atlanta, 1986: Scholars Press for Brown Judaic Studies).

Neusner, J. *From Tradition to Imitation. The Plan and Program of Pesiqta deRab Kahana and Pesiqta Rabbati* (Atlanta, 1987: Scholars Press for Brown Judaic Studies).

Neusner, J. *Judaism in Society: The Evidence of the Yerushalmi. Toward the Natural History of a Religion* (Chicago, 1983: University of Chicago Press). Second printing, with a new preface (Atlanta, 1991: Scholars Press for South Florida Studies in the History of Judaism).

Neusner, J. *Judaism. The Evidence of the Mishnah* (Chicago, 1981: University of Chicago Press). Paperback edition: 1984. Second printing, 1985. Third printing, 1986. Second edition, augmented (Atlanta, 1987: Scholars Press for Brown Judaic Studies).

Neusner, J. *Judaism: The Classical Statement. The Evidence of the Bavli* (Chicago, 1986: University of Chicago Press).

2. The Riddle of the Bavli: A Literary-Analytical Solution
A Reprise of the Next Six Monographs

Describing the literary character of the Talmud of Babylonia requires us to answer questions not of contents but of context: how does the document relate to prior writings of the same origin, namely, writings attributed to the sages of Judaism of the first seven centuries of the Common Era. In point of fact, we may without difficulty differentiate three types of writings: [1] writing that is not shaped by documentary requirements, [2] writing that is not shaped by the documentary requirements of the compilations we now have, and also [3] writing that is entirely formed within the rules of the documents that now present that writing. The first task in describing the Bavli is to ask whether or not the document is coherent and purposive, in which case we may indeed classify it as a document of integrity and cogency, one that makes a statement, or whether it is simply a conglomerate of free-standing

Neusner, J. *Language as Taxonomy. The Rules for Using Hebrew and Aramaic in the Babylonian Talmud* (Atlanta, 1990: Scholars Press for South Florida Studies in the History of Judaism).

Neusner, J. *Making the Classics in Judaism: The Three Stages of Literary Formation* (Atlanta, 1990: Scholars Press for Brown Judaic Studies).

Neusner, J. *Midrash as Literature: The Primacy of Documentary Discourse.* Studies in Judaism Series (Lanham, 1987: University Press of America).

Neusner, J. *The Bavli and Its Sources: The Question of Tradition in the Case of Tractate Sukkah* (Atlanta, 1987: Scholars Press for Brown Judaic Studies).

Neusner, J. *The Bavli That Might Have Been: The Tosefta's Theory of Mishnah Commentary Compared with That of the Babylonian Talmud* (Atlanta, 1990: Scholars Press for South Florida Studies in the History of Judaism).

Neusner, J. *The Bavli's One Voice: Types and Forms of Analytical Discourse and Their Fixed Order of Appearance* (Atlanta, 1991: Scholars Press for South Florida Studies in the History of Judaism).

Neusner, J. *The Formation of the Babylonian Talmud. Studies in the Achievements of Late Nineteenth- and Twentieth-Century Historical and Literary-Critical Research* (Leiden, 1970: E. J. Brill).

Neusner, J. *The Integrity of Leviticus Rabbah. The Problem of the Autonomy of a Rabbinic Document* (Chico, 1985: Scholars Press for Brown Judaic Studies).

Neusner, J. *The Rules of Composition of the Talmud of Babylonia. The Cogency of the Bavli's Composite* (Atlanta, 1991: Scholars Press for South Florida Studies in the History of Judaism).

Neusner, J. *The Talmud of Babylonia. An American Translation* (Chico, then Atlanta: 1984-1993: Scholars Press for Brown Judaic Studies).

Neusner, J. *The Talmud of the Land of Israel. A Preliminary Translation and Explanation* (Chicago, 1983: University of Chicago Press), XXXV. *Introduction. Taxonomy.*

Neusner, J. *Tradition as Selectivity: Scripture, Mishnah, Tosefta,* and Neusner, J. *Midrash in the Talmud of Babylonia. The Case of Tractate Arakhin* (Atlanta, 1990: Scholars Press for South Florida Studies in the History of Judaism).

traditions, with no program or viewpoint of its own. In the monographs surveyed in a prior article, *The Talmud of Babylonia: System or Tradition? A Reprise of Seven Monographs,* I summarized the research that led me to conclude the Bavli indeed forms a coherent statement of its own.[13] Moving beyond those results, in the six monographs summarized here I address two distinct problems. The first concerns the definition of what I conceive to form the Bavli's cogent statement. If the Bavli really constitutes a document of formal integrity, as I have already shown, then can I point to traits of substantive coherence as well? I conducted monographic experiments to yield data in response to that question in [1] *The Bavli's One Statement,* [2] *The Law behind the Laws. The Bavli's Essential Discourse,* and [3] *The Bavli's Primary Discourse. Mishnah Commentary, Its Rhetorical Paradigms and Their Theological Implications in the Talmud of Babylonia Tractate Moed Qatan.* The second question has concerned the Bavli's relationship to prior writings, both redacted in something like the form in which we know them, and also not redacted in any document we now have, but nonetheless available to us in clearly differentiated form. I want to know how the framers of the Bavli have utilized received writings. These monographs are [4] *How the Bavli Shaped Rabbinic Discourse,* [5] *The Bavli's Massive Miscellanies. The Problem of Agglutinative Discourse in the Talmud of Babylonia,* and [6] *Sources and Traditions. Types of Composition in the Talmud of Babylonia.* For the convenience of colleagues interested in the problem I address but unlikely to work through the detailed monographs I have completed, I summarize the results I have reached on these two important questions.

---

[13]These monographs are as follows:

The Bavli and Its Sources: The Question of Tradition in the Case of Tractate Sukkah (Atlanta, 1987: Scholars Press for Brown Judaic Studies).

Making the Classics in Judaism: The Three Stages of Literary Formation (Atlanta, 1990: Scholars Press for Brown Judaic Studies).

Tradition as Selectivity: Scripture, Mishnah, Tosefta, and Midrash in the Talmud of Babylonia. The Case of Tractate Arakhin (Atlanta, 1990: Scholars Press for South Florida Studies in the History of Judaism).

Language as Taxonomy. The Rules for Using Hebrew and Aramaic in the Babylonian Talmud (Atlanta, 1990: Scholars Press for South Florida Studies in the History of Judaism).

The Bavli That Might Have Been: The Tosefta's Theory of Mishnah Commentary Compared with That of the Babylonian Talmud (Atlanta, 1990: Scholars Press for South Florida Studies in the History of Judaism).

The Rules of Composition of the Talmud of Babylonia. The Cogency of the Bavli's Composite (Atlanta, 1991: Scholars Press for South Florida Studies in the History of Judaism).

The Bavli's One Voice: Types and Forms of Analytical Discourse and Their Fixed Order of Appearance (Atlanta, 1991: Scholars Press for South Florida Studies in the History of Judaism).

I. Toward the Definition of the Bavli's One Statement. From Formal Coherence to Substantive Cogency

The Bavli's One Statement. The Metapropositional Program of Babylonian Talmud Tractate Zebahim Chapters One and Five (Atlanta, 1991: Scholars Press for South Florida Studies in the History of Judaism)

When a document says the same thing about many things, it presents not only propositions but a metaproposition, a substrate that frames the teleology of its recurrent propositions. Since in the prior set of seven monographs I proved that the Talmud of Babylonia, a.k.a. the Bavli, says a great many things in only a single manner, everywhere appealing to a severely restricted rhetorical repertoire that serves throughout, I here ask the question, how are we to know whether, in saying in one way a great many things, the document's authors propose also to say one thing about a great many things? At stake in the answer to that methodological question is the identification of the metapropositional statement implicit in an exceptionally diverse and intellectually prolix piece of writing. Once I have demonstrated how to identify the metapropositional program to which propositional inquiries repeatedly point and even suggested one of the main points of that program, I shall know how systematically to identify the Bavli's metapropositional program in a large sample of the whole. I dealt in this monograph with Bavli Zebahim Chapter Five. My results proved somewhat complicated, so I begin with an explanation of the context in which I read this chapter. For at issue here is, when does a list become a series, or, in broader terms, how does static thought become dialectical?

Static thought is represented by the taxonomic method of the Mishnah. The Mishnah portrays all things at rest, a beautifully composed set in stasis, a stage on which nothing happens. The Bavli portrays all things in motion, a world of action, in which one thing leads to some other, and nothing stands still. All of this is accomplished in a shift in the received mode of thought, and the shift is set forth in the metaproposition, fully exposed, in the reading of two paragraphs of the Mishnah. We now consider what I conceive to be the counterpart program to the one that, in my view, the Bavli's sages inherited from the Mishnah and spelled out in tedious and unending particulars. To understand what is fresh and important in the Bavli's metapropositional program concerning the nature of thought, we have to call to mind what they inherited, for what they did was to impose the stamp of their own intellect upon the intellectual heritage that the Mishnah had provided for them. The Mishnah teaches the age-old method of scientific thought through comparison and contrast. Like things follow like rules, unlike things, the opposite rules, and the task of thought is to show what is like something else and therefore follows the rule that governs that something else, or what is unlike something else and therefore follows the opposite of the rule that governs that something else. So the Mishnah's mode of thought establishes connections between and among things and does so, as is clear, through the method of taxonomy, comparison and contrast, list making of like things, yielding the rule that governs all items on the list. This monograph is reviewed in Chapter Two above.

The Law behind the Laws. The Bavli's Essential Discourse (Atlanta, 1992: Scholars Press for South Florida Studies in the History of Judaism)

The logically consequent question is whether, underneath the detailed discussions is a subtext: a set of laws that yields principles, holding together a great many more laws. The Talmud transcends its origins when it speaks beyond the limits of cases and rules and frames discrete rules, pertinent to particular examples, in broad and universal laws. Where, in the Bavli, we occasionally find a sequence of unrelated cases or examples, with a single rule deemed to be pertinent to them all, or with all of them held to demonstrate one fact that transcends the details of any one, then we confront an exercise in discovering the law beyond the laws. Even though, in the Bavli, these exercises – as we shall see – are not numerous and form no preponderant part of any tractate, not even making an appearance in some tractates, they constitute, nonetheless, a distinct and important component of the intellectual repertoire and structure of the document. This monograph presents the passages in the Bavli that ask questions of generalization and conclusion, making the effort to form the detailed and the arcane into propositions of general intelligibility and universal relevance. These passages attract attention because they both contribute to the exposition of the Mishnah and also transform Mishnah exegesis from a text-bound and limited exposition into an intellectually engaging inquiry that stands on its own and forms of passages of the Mishnah a composite of a transcendent order.

My inquiry is not complicated; I want only to show that in its quest for the law behind the laws, the Bavli accomplishes what I claim in its behalf: a discourse essential to itself, different from that of the framers of the Mishnah and from that of exegetes of the Mishnah. I want to know what these discourses look like, and quite honestly I want to place on display as many of them as I can, to show in detail what I conceive to be a critical and definitive trait of the document as a whole. So I surveyed, for nineteen tractates, essays in the presentation of the law behind the law. These composites, ordinarily crafted with skill and wit, rarely leave any doubt as to their character and purpose. I call them the essential discourse of the Bavli for a very simple reason. If we want to know how the Bavli speaks in its own name, and not merely in the name of the authors out of the past whose writings it proposes to clarify or, even, merely preserve intact, it is in these composites that they will deliver their message.

II. The Law behind the Laws: Is It Permitted to Take the Law into One's Own Hands?

To exemplify the character of discourse that strikes me as not exegetical, but rather abstract, theoretical, and propositional in a sustained way – that is, the discourse I deem essential to the Bavli and indicative of its intellectual might – I present the case that drew my attention to the need to learn more about the kind of writing under discussion here. This is the item that concluded *Sources and Traditions*. The passage directly continues the one just now cited and serves the next clause of the same Mishnah paragraph. The issue comes up somewhat abruptly, in the context of the detailed exposition of the rule at hand. But once the issue is framed, it takes over, and from there to the end, it remains the same. It is to be framed as a debate:

> [1] a man has not got the right to take the law into his own hands

> versus

> [2] a man has got the right to take the law into his own hands where there will be an irreparable loss.

At that point, a set of cases will be examined, to uncover what law is implicit in the laws at hand. I should claim that, while the Mishnah commentary is helpful, the sustained debate before us is interesting, and, without what follows, the Bavli would be merely a collection of lessons, rather than a composite of important conclusions, capable of governing in situations to which the laws of the Mishnah would prove monumentally irrelevant.

F. *R. Judah said, "A man has not got the right to take the law into his own hands."*

G. *R. Nahman said, "A man has got the right to take the law into his own hands where there will be a loss."*

H. *Now all parties concur that where there will be a loss, someone may take the law into his own hands. Where there is an argument, it concerns a case in which there will be no loss. R. Judah said, "A man has not got the right to take the law into his own hands." Since there will be no loss, he can go to court. But R. Nahman said, "A man has got the right to take the law into his own hands where there will be a loss." Since he is acting in accord with the law anyhow, why take the trouble to go to court?*

I.   *Objected R. Kahana [to R. Judah's view],* "Ben Bag Bag says, 'A person should not go and retrieve his own property from the household of someone else, lest he appear to be a thief. But he should be ready in public to break his teeth and you may say to him, "I am seizing what is my own from the thief's possession"' [T. B.Q. 10:38]." [This then would contradict Judah's position.]

J.   *[Judah] said to him,* [28A] *"True enough, Ben Bag Bag is on your side. But he is a dissenting view, differing from rabbis."*

K.   *R. Yannai said, "What is the meaning, anyhow, of* break his teeth? It is, in court."

L.   *If so, the language,* you may say to him, *is inappropriate. Rather it should be,* they [the court] may say to him! *So, too, the language,* I am seizing what is my own, *is inappropriate. Rather, it should be,* he is seizing what is his own!

M.   *So that's a problem.*

N.   *Come and take note:* In the case of an ox that climbed up on another one to kill it, and the owner of the one on the bottom came along and pulled out his ox, so that the one on the top fell and was killed – the owner of the bottom ox is exempt from having to pay compensation. *Does this ruling not pertain to an ox that was an attested danger, in which case there is no loss to be expected?*

O.   *No, it speaks of an ox that was deemed innocent, and there is a considerable loss to be expected.*

P.   *If so, then look what's coming:* If he pulled off the ox on top and it died, he is liable to pay compensation. *But if the ox was deemed innocent, why should he have to pay compensation?*

Q.   Because he should have pulled his ox out from underneath, and he did not do that. [Kirzner: He had no right to push the ox on top.]

R.   *Come and take note:* He who filled the courtyard of his fellow with jugs of wine and jugs of oil – the owner of the courtyard has every right to break the jugs in order to get out or break the jugs in order to get in.

S.   Said R. Nahman bar Isaac, "He breaks the jugs to get out only if a court says he may do so; he may break the jugs to get in only to get whatever documents he needs to prove his case in court."

T.   *Come and take note:* How on the basis of Scripture do we know that in the case of a slave whose ear had been bored [as an indication that he was in perpetual service, to the Jubilee year], the term of service of which has come to an end [with the Jubilee], the owner of which has been urging him to leave, and, in the process, injured him and done him damage, the owner is exempt from having to pay compensation? Scripture states, "You shall not take satisfaction for him who is...come again..." (Num. 35:12), meaning, for one who is determined to come again [as a slave, continuing his service], you will not take a ransom.

U.   *Here with what sort of a case do we deal? It is a slave who was a thief* [Kirzner: so the owner is protecting himself from a genuine loss].

V.   *Well, up to now he hasn't stolen anything, but now he's expected to go and steal?*

W.   *Yes, that's quite plausible, since up to now he was afraid of his master, but now that he is about to go free, he isn't afraid of his master anymore.*

X.   R. Nahman bar Isaac said, "At issue is a slave to whom his master gave a Canaanite serving girl as a wife. *Up to this time it was a legitimate relationship, but once he is freed, it is not legitimate"* [Kirzner: so the master may use force to eject him].

Y.   *Come and take note:* He who leaves a jug in the public domain, and someone else came along and stumbled on it and broke it – [the one who broke it] is exempt. *So the operative consideration is that he stumbled on it. Lo, if he had deliberately broken it, he would have been liable.* [This is contrary to Nahman's view.]

Z.   *Said R. Zebid in the name of Raba, "In point of fact, the same rule really does apply even if the defendant deliberately broke the jug. And the reason that the language,* and stumbled on it, *is used, is that the later clause goes on to say,* And if [the one who broke it] was injured by it, the owner of the barrel is liable [to pay damages for] his injury. *But that would be the case only if he stumbled on it, but not if he deliberately broke the jug. How come? The man has deliberately injured himself. So that is why, to begin with, the word choice was* and stumbled on it.

AA. *Come and take note:* "Then you shall cut off her hand" (Deut. 25:12) – that refers to a monetary fine equivalent in value to the hand. *Does this not speak of a case in which* the woman has no other way of saving her husband but doing what she did [proving one may not take the law into one's own hands]?

BB. No, it involves a case in which she can save her husband in some other way.

CC. Well, if she cannot save her husband in some other way, would she be free of all liability? *Then why go on to say,* "And puts forth her hand" (Deut. 25:11) – excluding an officer of the court [from liability for humiliation that he may cause when acting in behalf of the court]? *Rather, why not recast matters by dealing with the case at hand, thus:* Under what circumstances? When she can save her husband by some other means. But if she cannot save him by some other means, then she is exempt.

DD. *This is the sense of the passage:* Under what circumstances? When she can save her husband by some other means. But if she cannot save him by some other means, then her hand serves as the agency of the court and she is indeed exempt.

EE. *Come and take note:* He who had a public way passing through his field, and who took it away and gave [the public another path] along the side, what he has given he has given. But what is his does not pass to him [M. B.B. 6:7A-D]. *Now if you maintain that someone may take the law into his own hands, then let the man just take a whip and sit there [and keep people out of his property]!*

FF. Said R. Zebid in the name of Raba, "It is a precautionary decree, lest he assign to the public a crooked path."

GG. R. Mesharshayya said, "It is a case in which he gives them a crooked path."

HH. R. Ashi said, "Any path that is over off to the side is classified as a crooked path to begin with, since what is nearer for one party will be farther for another."

II. *If that's so, then why specify,* But what is his does not pass to him? *Why can't he just say to the public, "Take what is yours and give me what is mine?"*

JJ. *That is because of what R. Judah said, for* said R. Judah, "A path that the public has taken over is not to be disrupted."

KK. *Come and take note:* A householder who designated peah at one corner of the field, and the poor come along and take the peah from another side of the field – both this and that are classified as peah. *Now if you maintain that a person may take the law into his own hands, why should it be the fact that both this and that are so classified? Just let the man take a whip and sit there [and keep people out of his property]!*

LL. *Said Raba, "What is the meaning of the phrase, both this and that are so classified? It is for the purpose of exempting the designated produce from the requirement of separating tithes. For so it has been taught on Tannaite authority:* He who declares his vineyard to be ownerless and then gets up early in the morning and harvests the grapes is liable to leave for the poor the grapes that fall to the ground, the puny bunches, the forgotten ones, and the corner of the field, but is exempt from having to designate tithes."

The rather ambitious, free-standing composition is inserted only because the framer has drawn upon our Mishnah's rule as part of his repertoire of cases and evidence. It could have appeared more or less anywhere without any alteration of its character, since what we have is a propositional essay on a problem of broad intelligibility and more than narrowly episodic interest. It is at 4.D that the real point of debate takes over. We see that the issue is tangential to the exegetical problem, but critical in its own terms. It is further noteworthy that the issue is specified in a free-standing debate, set forth at 4.E-G. The sequence of cases moves toward the illustration of arguments one might propose, but, the Bavli being what it is, we shall work through cases that illustrate arguments, precedents that constitute facts to be addressed and held together in equilibrium, not arguments framed in a philosophical manner. Our cases emerge at 4.I, N, R, T, Y, AA, EE, KK. The Mishnah paragraph before us is cited in the context of the debate, at Z. It is not distinguished in this context, and the formation of the whole goes forward entirely within the terms of the broadest nature; we never lose sight of what is at issue. Our eight cases, spread across the face of the laws of the Mishnah, are shown to address a single problem, and any other eight cases, far beyond the details of the Mishnah's law, could have served with equal effect. Now to answer specific questions:

IS THE BAVLI MUCH MORE THAN A MISHNAH COMMENTARY? No, the Bavli is not much more than a Mishnah commentary. The paramount purpose of Mishnah exegesis was realized in these inquiries into the law behind the laws. What is other than Mishnah exegesis, rhetorically and topically, forms only a portion of the whole. What is other than Mishnah exegesis, if not topically (for that is, by definition, excluded from this type of writing, which is not topical at all), is balanced, even in analytical proposition, by what merely carries forward an inquiry begun in the Mishnah itself.

IS THE BAVLI A WRITING THAT IS SYSTEMATIC OR (MERELY) AGGLUTINATIVE? The Bavli is a systematic writing, occasionally using composites drawn together by principles of agglutination that do not in general govern in the Bavli, but then ordering these agglutinative composites entirely in accord with the Bavli's own program of Mishnah commentary.

HOW RICH A CORPUS OF SOURCES IS IN THE BAVLI'S TRADITIONS? The Bavli utilizes available sources, but among them was not a set of inquiries, worked out on their own terms and within their own framework, into the law behind the law. There is no question that, here and there, work on that interesting question was undertaken; but this was mainly, though not exclusively, in the framework of Mishnah commentary, and nearly always expressed within the rhetorical framework established by a prior program of Mishnah commentary. My initial expectation was that, through routine procedures of literary analysis, I could show that there was a "layer" of the Bavli, however thin, made up of a distinctive and essential discourse of an other than exegetical kind: writing that served an entirely distinct purpose from that that defined the structure and system of the Bavli overall. But the opposite result is now before us. The essential discourse comprising an inquiry into the law behind the laws is not a distinct source, whether early, whether late, upon which the framers of the Bavli drew; it is a discourse that is essential in a different, unanticipated sense altogether. It is essential to the exegetical purpose of the framers of the Bavli, in some few contexts, to move quite beyond their exegetical frame of reference. But when they chose to do so, they in no way differentiated in the signs of rhetoric that writing from any other. All proves uniform; all is set forth as essential in its context.

The Bavli's Primary Discourse. Mishnah Commentary, Its Rhetorical Paradigms, and Their Theological Implications in the Talmud of Babylonia Tractate Moed Qatan (Atlanta, 1992: Scholars Press for South Florida Studies in the History of Judaism)

The result of the foregoing monograph is simple, repeating results attained on different bases altogether: The Bavli in form and substance presents a commentary to the Mishnah, and, to markedly lesser degree, Scripture as well. From 80 percent to 99 percent of the composites of the tractates of the Bavli – depending on the tractate – focus upon the work of Mishnah exegesis. So the next task is to catalogue the types of exegetical compositions and composites that accomplish the paramount goal of explaining the sense and meaning of the Mishnah. In this monograph I treat in particular the manner in which the Talmud of Babylonia proposes, in Bavli-tractate Moed Qatan, to read Mishnah-tractate Moed Qatan. Defining in detail what the sages of the Bavli did, and how they did it, imparts immediacy and concreteness to the general description of their writing as "a commentary to the Mishnah." Not only so, but by showing how most of the Bavli's composites, as well as the larger part of the composites formed into those composites, form a commentary to the Mishnah or a secondary expansion of commentary to the Mishnah, I provide in highly graphic form a clear picture of the structure of the document as a commentary, covering also secondary elaboration of its own commentaries.

For the most part, the Talmud of Babylonia is a commentary to the Mishnah. Let me start by giving a simple example of what characterizes the initial phase of nearly every sustained composite of the Bavli: a commentary to the Mishnah. This is what I mean by Mishnah commentary:

Mishnah-Tractate Baba Qamma 3:1
- A. He who leaves a jug in the public domain,
- B. and someone else came along and stumbled on it and broke it –
- C. [the one who broke it] is exempt.
- D. And if [the one who broke it] was injured by it, the owner of the barrel is liable [to pay damages for] his injury.

I.1   A.   *How come the framer of the passage refers to begin with to a jug but then concludes with reference to a* barrel? *And so, too, we have learned in another passage in the Mishnah:* This one comes along with his barrel, and that one comes along with his beam – [if] the jar of this one was broken by the beam of that one, [the owner of the beam] is exempt. *How come the framer of the passage refers to begin with to a* barrel *but then concludes with reference to a* jar? *And so, too, we have learned in the Mishnah:* This one is coming along with his barrel of wine, and that one is coming along with his jug of honey – the jug of honey cracked, and this one poured out his wine and saved the honey in his jar – he has a claim only for his wages [M. B.Q. 10:4A-E]. *How come the framer of the passage refers to begin with to a* barrel *but then concludes with reference to a* jar?

       B.   Said R. Hisda, "Well, as a matter of fact, there really is no difference between a jar and a barrel.'

       C.   *So what is the practical difference between the usages?*

       D.   It has to do with buying and selling.

E.   *How can we imagine such a case? If it is in a place in which a jug is not called a barrel, nor a barrel a jug, for in such a case, the two terms are kept distinct!*

F.   *The distinction is required for a place in which most of the people call a jug a jug and a barrel a barrel, but some call a barrel a jug and some call a jug a barrel. What might you then have supposed? That we follow the majority usage?* [27B] *So we are informed that that is not the case, for in disputes over monetary transactions, we do not follow the majority usage.*

All that we have here is an investigation of the linguistic properties of the Mishnah paragraph that is cited. The framer of the anonymous writing notes that a variety of other passages seem to vary word choices in a somewhat odd way. The point of insistence – the document is carefully drafted, the writers do not forget what they were talking about, so when they change words in the middle of a stream of thought, it is purposeful – constitutes a exegetical point, pure and simple.

To understand precisely what the Bavli means by a commentary to the Mishnah, we have therefore to begin with the clear picture that the Bavli asks the questions of not only the teacher, standing inside of the document and looking outward, but also of the reader, located outside of the document and looking inward. In what follows, then, the stance of the commentator now is external to the text, and the commentator wants to know why the Mishnah finds self-evident what is not necessarily obvious to all parties:

1:7-8

I.1   A.   *So if it's* **an occasion of rejoicing for the groom,** *what's so bad about that?*

B.   Said R. Judah said Samuel, and so said R. Eleazar said R. Oshaia, and some say, said R. Eleazar said R. Hanina, "The consideration is that one occasion of rejoicing should not be joined with another such occasion."

C.   Rabbah bar R. Huna said, "It is because he neglects the rejoicing of the festival to engage in rejoicing over his wife."

D.   Said Abbayye to R. Joseph, "This statement that has been said by Rabbah bar R. Huna belongs to Rab, for said R. Daniel bar Qattina said Rab, 'How on the basis of Scripture do we know that people may not take wives on the intermediate days of the festival? As it is said, "You shall rejoice in your feast" (Deut. 16:14), meaning, in your feast – not in your new wife.'"

E.   Ulla said, "It is because it is excess trouble."

F.   R. Isaac Nappaha said, "It is because one will neglect the requirement of being fruitful and multiplying" [if people postponed weddings until festivals, they might somehow diminish the occasion for procreation, which is the first obligation].

G.   *An objection was raised:* All those of whom they have said that they are forbidden to wed on the festival **[9A]** are permitted to wed on the eve of the festival. *Now this poses a problem to the explanations of all the cited authorities!*

    H.   *There is no problem from the perspective of him who has said,* "The consideration is that one occasion of rejoicing should not be joined with another such occasion," *for the main rejoicing of the wedding is only a single day.*

    I.   *And from the perspective of him who has said,* "It is because it is excess trouble," *the principal bother lasts only one day.*

    J.   *And from the perspective of him who has said,* "It is because one will neglect the requirement of being fruitful and multiplying," *for merely one day someone will not postpone the obligation for any considerable length of time.*

What is important in understanding the nature of commentary in the Bavli is the dual stance of the commentator: inside and outside.

Now to generalize on the basis of the cases before us: What I mean by a commentary is a piece of writing that depends for its program – topics to be treated, coherence and cogency, alike – upon some other writing. We know the difference between a base text and a commentary because the base text will be cogent in its own terms, and the commentary will make sense only in relationship to the base text. And we know the difference between the one and the other because a commentary's author will always signal the text, for example, by citing a phrase or by a clear allusion, and will further identify what he then proposes to contribute. Commentaries may take a variety of forms, but the mark of them all will be the same: they make sense only by appeal to, in the context of, some piece of writing outside of themselves. But that common trait among them all scarcely exhausts the program that a commentary will undertake – or even define it. One type of commentary will follow a quite well-defined program of questions, another will promiscuously comment on this, that, and the other thing, without ever suggesting that the commentator has a systematic inquiry in mind. And, it goes without saying, the range of issues subject to comment – philological, historical, aesthetic, not to mention theological – can be limited only by the number of texts deemed by an author or compiler to deserve a commentary.

"Primary discourse," it is now clear, refers to the main lines of expression of a coherent document. When the Bavli's authorship, having cited a passage of the Mishnah, begins its statement, it always begins with attention to the cited passage. When further materials, not those of Mishnah commentary, follow, these relate to the initial discussion. So while many compositions, and even some very large composites, take shape in their own terms and stand independent of the Mishnah, when they find a place in the Bavli, it is ordinarily in the framework of Mishnah commentary, very often as a secondary expansion of what is set forth to begin with for the exegesis of what is in the Mishnah. The tractate that we have examined leaves no doubt about the coherence, with a cited passage of the Mishnah, of nearly everything in the Bavli. Materials that do not cohere either with Mishnah exegesis, or with secondary amplification of that exegesis, prove sparse indeed. When we recall that sizable components of the Bavli – numerous compositions – stand on their own and not as Mishnah commentary, we realize how much the authorship of the Bavli has done in reframing matters to serve its distinctive purpose: nearly everything that they utilized, they presented in the framework of Mishnah commentary and amplification.

Briefly to summarize my results: Here are the types of Mishnah commentary that, over all, forms the Bavli's primary discourse.

1. Scriptural Foundations of the Laws of the Mishnah

The single most commonplace and characteristic inquiry of the Bavli is framed in the question: What is the source of the rule of the Mishnah? Conventionally, this inquiry occurs in simple language, for example, "What is the source of this rule?" always with the implication, "in Scripture."

2. Authorities behind the Laws of the Mishnah

A primary exegetical question concerns whether or not a law stands for an individual's opinion or a consensus of sages. The inquiry takes a variety of forms. The simplest is, "Who is the authority behind the Mishnah's [anonymous] rule?" This allows us to find out whether we have a schismatic (individual) or normative (consensual) opinion; we may further ask whether the cited authority is consistent, testing the principle behind the rule at hand against the evidence of his rulings in other cases in which the same principle determines matters.

3. Meanings of Words and Phrases

We come to Mishnah commentary of the most conventional kind: explanation of the meanings of words and phrases of the Mishnah, appealing for scriptural parallels to set forth lexical evidence, on the one side, inquiry into the sense and meaning of sentences of the Mishnah, on the other.

4. Text Criticism. The Issue of Repetition

The matter of text criticism covers a variety of distinct inquiries. In the first sort, we want to know why the Mishnah frames matters as it does, with the generative issue being whether or not the document repeats itself. This type of Mishnah commentary is signaled by a single word, "it is necessary," and what will follow is an implicit justification of presenting more than a single rule or case. This form is not limited to Mishnah criticism; on the contrary, it is commonly used for any formulation – Tannaite or other – of a variety of cases that illustrate the same principle, and the form, brief though it is, suitably sets forth the exegetical problem to be solved. Another kind of text criticism involves the explanation of how a variety of examples hold together; the Mishnah may present three or more examples, and what we want to know is whether a stringency or leniency is conveyed by setting forth examples that do not really cohere.

5. Conflict of Principles Implicit in the Mishnah's Rules

One important issue in the Bavli's Mishnah commentary is whether or not two rules, intersecting in detail or in fundamental principle, cohere. A sustained effort characterizes the Bavli's inquiry into the harmony of the law of the Mishnah, the object of which invariably is to demonstrate that the Mishnah's law form a single, wholly cogent law, perfect in their harmony.

6. Execution of the Law of the Mishnah

At stake is where and how the simple rule of the Mishnah pertains; a Tannaite formulation of the same conclusion then reenforces the proposed reading of the Mishnah's rule.

7. The Operative Consideration behind the Law of the Mishnah

One of the exegetically productive initiatives of the Bavli will raise the question of the operative consideration that has led to a given rule in the Mishnah. That inquiry will lead us deep into the principles that are given expression in concrete rules, and we often see how entirely abstract conceptions are conceived to stand behind rather commonplace laws.

8. The Implications, for the Law in General, of the Mishnah's Particular Formulation

Here what generates the sustained discussion of the Talmud is a close reading of the Mishnah's language. This careful analysis produces an inference that has to be investigated in its own terms. Since there is no understanding the sustained discussion apart from the Mishnah's own statement, the entire composition falls into the classification of Mishnah commentary. Another mode of commentary, in the inquiry into the implications of the Mishnah's rule for law in general, involves presenting a theoretical possibility that is subject to confirmation, or refutation, by a statement of a Mishnah paragraph. That theorizing in response to a rule of the Mishnah then explores the implications of a rule of the Mishnah.

9. Settling the Point Subject to Dispute in the Mishnah

While not a principal focus of exegetical interest, some attention is given to settling the dispute presented in the Mishnah by a statement of the decided law.

If, therefore, we had to state in a single sentence the exegetical proposition, indeed the hermeneutical principle, that animates the Bavli's reading of the Mishnah – another way of expressing what I earlier called its metapropositional program – it may be stated very simply: The Mishnah is a supernatural writing, because it can be shown to be flawless in its language and formulation, never repetitious, never slovenly in any detail, always and everywhere the model of perfection in word and thought; the Mishnah is moreover utterly rational in its principles; and of course, the Mishnah is wholly formed upon the solid foundations of the Written Torah of Sinai. No merely human being could have achieved such perfection of language and of thought in conformity with the Torah. That is the point made, over and over again, in the Bavli's primary discourse.

III. The Bavli in Context: The Contextual Uniqueness of the Talmud in Relationship to Other Writings in Its Canon?

The second of the two sets of monographs turns to the question of context. What I learned here is that the Bavli really did impose its own judgment upon the entire antecedent canon, which its authorship(s) knew and utilized for their own purposes. Specifically, the Bavli is only one talmud – a sustained analytical criticism, through applied logic and practical reason, of a received document; it is a talmud to the Mishnah. But, as a matter of demonstrable fact, other documents, reaching closure prior to the Bavli, were subjected to talmud analysis along precisely the same lines characteristic of the Bavli's talmud to the Mishnah. But what the Bavli did was unique, in that only the Mishnah was subjected to a sustained, systematic, and comprehensive talmud: the Bavli's (and Yerushalmi's) polemic argued for the priority, indeed the privileging, of the Mishnah. Here I show there could have been other talmuds, serving Sifra for one instance (the one I summarize here), among various other composites of Tannaite statements, and that shows how the Bavli (and the Yerushalmi) imposed their judgment upon judgments made by others on the centrality of the Mishnah, its uniqueness.[14]

---

[14]That opens the question of how the Bavli relates to the Yerushalmi, which I plan to investigate when my Bavli translation is complete; the projected program is in these works: *The Torah in the Talmud. A Taxonomy of the Uses of Scripture in the Talmud of Babylonia*; and in the four volumes of *The Bavli and the Yerushalmi. A Systematic Comparison.*

How the Bavli Shaped Rabbinic Discourse (Atlanta, 1991: Scholars Press for South Florida Studies in the History of Judaism)

Sometime between the closure of the Talmud of the Land of Israel, ca. 400, and the conclusion of the Talmud of Babylonia, ca. 600, *talmud*, a common noun that can connote the rigorous and systematic critical analysis of a received document of Tannaite standing in the canon of the Judaism of the Dual Torah, became a proper noun, The Talmud. The Talmud was a composite of critical analysis organized around, and focused solely upon, the Mishnah. There would be two Talmuds, the Talmud of the Land of Israel and the Talmud of Babylonia, both of them limited, for purposes of structure and organization, in focus to the Mishnah. Other writings accorded Tannaite standing could have had talmuds and did enjoy that critical dialectical reading that the Mishnah did. But only the Mishnah was privileged to receive the Talmud, and all other Tannaite writings were denied the talmuds that had accumulated around them during the centuries from ca. 200 through ca. 600. Viewed from the perspective of the redactional program of the Bavli, these other analytical critical readings of documents other than the Mishnah served no purpose that the Bavli's ultimate redactors defined for themselves in their sustained reading of the Bavli and their episodic and rather sparse reading of all other writings. But those readings did serve those other documents, and in the sherds and remnants in our hands, we can see how a rigorous and systematic reading of those other writings was being written even while the Bavli's materials came forth. On redactional grounds, then, I maintain that the Bavli contains compositions and even composites that reached closure under auspices separate from the Bavli's. I further insist that it was the framers of the Bavli that dictated the shape of rabbinic discourse – not only for the future, but, more to the point, retrospectively as well: this but not that.

When the reading of the Mishnah that yielded our Talmud was under way, other documents or materials of the same status – Tannaite – as the Mishnah also were being read along the same lines. But those other *talmuds* never reached us, and although the Bavli contains ample indication that such *talmuds* could have come into being, it also contains no evidence that, in any sustained way, they did. Once we realize, in Chapters Two, Three, and Four, that ours is not the only Talmud that was under way from the closure of the Mishnah to the conclusion of the Bavli, 200-600, we then grasp how profoundly the framers of the Talmud of Babylonia reshaped all prior discourse, since they made certain that there would be only one *talmud*, the Talmud, and only one privileged document entitled to such a *talmud*, namely, the Mishnah. In Chapter Five I spell out the consequences of that realization, my claim, based on the character of the Bavli itself, that it was the policy and the decision of the framers of the Bavli to the Mishnah that no other *talmud* come to full articulation. Accordingly, the compositors of the Bavli, or the Talmud of Babylonia, preserve evidence that, just as the Talmud of Babylonia was worked out as an analysis and critique of the Mishnah, so other documents were subjected to the same kind of critical analysis. These compositors provide us with important samples of the written result of that analysis.

What we now shall see is a single example of how the analysis, in the Bavli, of a passage in the Sifra follows precisely the same rhetorical and logical rules that govern the analysis in the Bavli of a passage of the Mishnah. That fact by itself shows that the way framers of a passage of analysis and criticism of the Mishnah that found its way into the Bavli's commentary to the Mishnah is how framers of a passage of the Sifra that the Bavli has preserved for us did their work, too. It would seem to me that the prevalence of the same literary conventions in the reading of two distinct documents, each with its own indicative traits, strongly suggests the work was done more or less within the same period of literary formulation and among people responsive to the same conventions of analysis. Then a further fact will prove exceedingly suggestive. It is that the analysis of the Sifra's passage proceeds wholly in terms required by that passage and ignores the setting, within the composite of the Bavli, in which the Sifra's passage has been preserved. That seems to me to mean that the framers of the commentary on the Sifra's passage had in mind a document that would be devoted to not the Mishnah but Sifra. Then the framers of the critical analysis of the Sifra's materials proposed to produce a commentary to the Sifra, parallel to what was being accomplished for the Mishnah. But that commentary to the Sifra, that is, that *talmud to Sifra*, did not survive, except in bits and pieces in the Bavli itself. Here we see how the Sifra's materials are articulated in relationship to the Mishnah, namely, in a first-class example of how the treatment of the Sifra's passage will highlight what the Sifra wishes to show, not what the Bavli's frame of a Mishnah commentary cites the Sifra's passage to prove; the two propositions are complementary, but they are distinct. Then the further discussion of the passage at hand concerns not what is proved by the Sifra that is relevant to the Mishnah, but what is proved by the Sifra in terms important to its own framers. The distinction here is critical. The one passage wants to know how come "[from] the meal-offering of a priest who was a sinner [Lev. 7:16], the handful is taken [even though the whole of it in any case is offered on the altar], and the handful is offered by itself, and the residue [thereof] is offered by itself." The Sifra's author is going to prove that "the performance of the meal-offering rite of a priest [who has inadvertently sinned] is assigned to that priest [so that he may perform his own rite and retain possession of the residue of the meal-offering that he himself has presented]." That is, then, a talmud to the Sifra, not to the Mishnah. That proves my point, that the Sifra, as much as the Mishnah, not only could have had, but in fact did have, a talmud of its own:

IV.1 A. R. Simeon says, "[From] the meal-offering of a priest who was a sinner [Lev. 7:16], the handful is taken [even though the whole of it in any case is offered on the altar], and the handful is offered by itself, and the residue [thereof] is offered by itself":

B. *What is the scriptural basis for this position?*

C. *It is in line with that which our rabbis have taught on Tannaite authority:*

D. "It shall belong to the priest, like the meal-offering" (Lev. 5:13) –

E. the meaning is that the performance of the meal-offering rite of a priest [who has inadvertently sinned] is assigned to that priest [so that he may perform his own rite and retain possession of the residue of the meal-offering that he himself has presented].

F. Or might the intent not be to declare permitted [to the priesthood the residue] of the tenth ephah of fine flour that has been brought by a priest? [Cashdan: The verse then tells us that a priest's obligatory meal-offering is like the meal-offering of an Israelite that is eaten by the priests after the handful has been taken out.]

G. How then shall I interpret the statement, "Every meal-offering of a priest shall be wholly burned, it shall not be eaten" (Lev. 6:23/Heb.: 6:16)?

H. This then would refer to a meal-offering that the priest has brought as a freewill-offering, and as to the tenth ephah that he has presented, that may be eaten.

I. But [contrary to that line of argument] Scripture states, "It shall belong to the priest, like the meal-offering":

J. Lo, it is in the status of the meal-offering that he presents as a freewill-offering, with the result that just as the freewill-offering of meal that he presents does not yield a residue that may be eaten, so the tenth ephah of fine flour that he presents may not be eaten.

K. Said R. Simeon, "And is it written, 'And it shall be the priest's as his meal-offering'? What it says is, 'It shall belong to the priest, like the meal-offering':

L. [73B] "Lo, the tenth ephah of fine flour that a priest has brought is in the classification of the tenth ephah of fine flour that an Israelite presents.

M. "Just as the tenth ephah of fine flour that an Israelite presents yields a handful, so a handful is taken up from this offering as well.

N. "But might one then say, just as the handful is taken from the meal-offering presented by the poor sinner who is an Israelite, and the remainder may be eaten, so when the handful is taken from the poor sinner's meal-offering presented by a priest, the residue may be eaten?

O.   "Scripture states, 'The priest's as the meal-offering': In what regards the priest, it is like the meal-offering of a sinner who is of the Israelite caste, but in respect to what concerns the fire on the altar, it is not like that meal-offering.

P.   **"The handful that is taken up is presented by itself, and the residue is presented by itself"** [Sifra LXII.I.16].

IV.2   A.   *But is the rule that the rites of the priest's meal-offering may be carried out by the priest drawn from that exposition? Surely it derives from the following:*

B.   How on the basis of Scripture do we know that a priest may come to present his offerings at any occasion and at any time that he wants?

C.   Scripture states, "And come with all the desire of his soul...and minister" (Deut. 18:6).

D.   *Had I derived the ruling from that verse, I might have supposed that reference is made to something that is not presented by reason of sin, but as to something that is presented by reason of sin, I might have said that that is not the case.*

IV.3   A.   *But is the rule that the rites of the priest's meal-offering may be carried out by the priest drawn from that exposition? Surely it derives from the following:*

B.   "And the priest shall make atonement for the soul that errs, when he sins through error" (Num. 15:28) – this teaches that a priest may make atonement for himself through his own act of service.

C.   *Had I derived the ruling from that verse, I might have supposed that that rule pertains only to offerings that are presented for a sin committed in error, but not for offerings presented for a sin committed deliberately; so we are informed that that is the case as well.*

D.   *So are there really offerings that are presented for sins committed deliberately?*

E.   *Yup: deliberately taking a false oath [Lev. 5:1].*

As we proceed to IV.1, we find ourselves on familiar ground. A passage of the Sifra is introduced to prove a rule set forth in the Mishnah rests on scriptural foundations. But what that passage proves is distinct, though related: not that the handful of the meal-offering of a priest who has sinned is burned on the altar, along with the residue, but that the priest may present his own meal-offering under the specific circumstances. Then No. 2 raises a question pertinent not to the issue that has required the framer of No. 1 to introduce the abstract of the Sifra, but to the passage of the Sifra itself. And No. 3 goes forward along the same lines. That is important, because the now run-on quality of the composite is entirely routine in the Bavli; here we see that precisely the principles of agglutination that govern in the Bavli's exposition of the Mishnah are in place in the exposition of the Sifra's claims. Two simple facts follow:

[1]   The way in which the framers of the Bavli read the Mishnah is the way in which the framers of passages, in the Bavli, on

the Sifra read the Sifra. In the sample examined here, the following show that that is the fact: B. to Men. 6:3, No. 9; and the items listed below follow suit and exemplify the same fact.

[2] Passages in the Sifra that are subjected to exegesis may be read not for purposes of Mishnah exegesis but for purposes of Sifra exegesis.

The upshot is simple: whether the classification of writing be given a temporal or merely taxonomic valence, the issue is the same: Have these writers of talmuds done their work with documentary considerations in mind? I believe I have shown that they have not. Three conclusions follow:

[1] Because the modes of thought and analysis concerning the Sifra, the Tosefta, and the baraita corpus in no way diverged from those that guided inquiry into the Mishnah, I claim that the work that was done falls into the category of *talmud*, as defined earlier.

[2] And because some of these passages are sustained, I allege that, in addition to The Talmud, the one that imposes meaning upon the Mishnah, there not only could have been, but almost certainly were, other talmuds, in progress for the Sifra, the Tosefta, and components of the baraita compositions and even compilations.

[3] Where a *talmud* was taking shape around the Tosefta, the Talmud to the Mishnah would consist of the Tosefta's talmud, itself amplified and revised in relationship to the Mishnah's statements, thus, Mishnah paragraph, Tosefta amplification through restatement, in the Mishnah's language, of what the Mishnah was supposed to mean, and, third, further analysis of the Tosefta's judgment of the Mishnah's meaning and the Mishnah's unresolved issues.

The framers of the Bavli took control of, and closed off, prior discourse. They not only chose what would form the systemic statement that defined what we should call "Judaism" and what their apologists would call "the one whole Torah of Moses, our rabbi." They also privileged one document of choice, making its exegesis critical, and set in the background other documents that, in earlier times, were subjected to exactly the same engaged exegesis as the Mishnah had long enjoyed. Alongside the Talmuds to the Mishnah (the Yerushalmi and the Bavli as we know them), there might have been a variety of *talmuds* – the *talmud* to Sifra, the *talmud* to Tosefta; the Talmud that we do have, had it emerged only as a secondary development of the talmud to Tosefta, might have been a very different document from what it is. But that is not what we have.

The Bavli's Massive Miscellanies. The Problem of Agglutinative Discourse in the Talmud of Babylonia (Atlanta, 1992: Scholars Press for South Florida Studies in the History of Judaism)

Two conflicting characteristics mark the Bavli, or Talmud of Babylonia. It is, first, a disciplined and well-organized, carefully crafted piece of writing. Most of the document is formulated in accord with a few simple rules, so that it is well-organized and easily followed. The Bavli, viewed whole, is carefully set forth as a commentary to the Mishnah, and the vast majority of its composites are put together so as to elucidate the statements of the Mishnah. But in the pages of the Bavli we observe, second, very large composites, not formed into Mishnah commentaries at all. These composites do not follow the rules that govern the formation of the composites that serve as commentaries to the Mishnah. Whoever put the miscellanies together had a different program in mind. And if the framers of the miscellanies had in mind that they ultimately would be collected in a piece of writing of some dimensions, then that writing that the framers imagined bears no resemblance to the writing in which their miscellanies did end up, that is, the Bavli.

The Talmud of Babylonia therefore makes use of two distinct principles for the formation of large-scale composites of distinct compositions. Ordinarily, they brought together distinct and free-standing compositions in the service of Mishnah exegesis and amplification of law originating in a Mishnah paragraph under analysis. For that purpose they would then draw upon already written compositions, which would be adduced as cases, statements of principles, fully exposed analyses, inclusive of debate and argument, in the service of that analysis. So all of the compositions in a given composite would serve the governing analytical or propositional purpose of the framer of the composite. Where a composition appears to shade over into a direction of its own, that very quickly is seen to serve as a footnote or even an appendix to the composite at hand. Clear, governing, and entirely predictable principles allow us to explain how one composition is joined to another. Ordinarily, a sizable miscellany will tell us more about a subject that the Mishnah addresses or richly illustrate a principle that the Mishnah means to set forth through its cases and examples. In that sense, the miscellaneous kind of composite is set forth as Mishnah commentary of a particular kind. An agglutinative composite may be formed by appeal to a common theme, ordinarily stated by the Mishnah or at least suggested by its contents, and several closely related themes will then come under exposition in a massive miscellany. One common theme will be a passage of Scripture, systematically examined. A subordinate principle of agglutination will join composites attributed to the same authority or tradent, though it would be unusual for the compositions so joined to deal with entirely unrelated topics. So the principal point of differentiation between propositional composites and agglutinative ones is that the former analyze a problem, the latter illustrate a theme or even a proposition.

What then accounts for the large-scale "miscellanies"? Quite random compositions, each with its own focus, will be formed into a composite on the basis of one of three theories of linkage: [1] topic, [2] attribution, or [3] sequence of verses of a passage of Scripture. The agglutination of topically coherent compositions predominates. And this leads to a further theory on the miscellany. The conglomerates of random compositions formed into topical composites ordinarily serve as an amplification of a topic treated in the Mishnah, or are joined to a composite that serves in that way, so that, over all, the miscellanies are made to extend and amplify the statements of the Mishnah, as much as, though in a different way from, the commonplace propositional, analytical, and syllogistic composite. What appears to be a random hodgepodge of this and that and the other thing in fact forms a considered and even well-crafted composite, the agglutinative principles of which we may readily discern. In fact what we have in the miscellany is nothing more than a Mishnah commentary of a peculiar sort, itself extended and spun out, as the more conventional Mishnah commentaries of the Bavli tend to be extended and spun out. This kind of commentary collects and arranges information deemed relevant to the topic of the Mishnah paragraph under discussion, not analyzing but illustrating that topic. What appears to be odd, incoherent, pointless, rambling, to the contrary attests in its own way to the single and definitive program of the Bavli's framers. Whatever those framers wished to say on their own account they insisted on setting forth within the framework of that received document upon the structure of which they made everything depend.

Sources and Traditions. Types of Composition in the Talmud of Babylonia (Atlanta, 1992: Scholars Press for South Florida Studies in the History of Judaism)

For the title of this monograph I have taken an excellent distinction proposed by David W. Halivni in his Hebrew work of the same title, namely, *Meqorot ummessorot*, in English translated by him as *Sources and*

Traditions. This means, [1] sources as materials utilized by an authorship from what was ready-made, as against [2] materials framed by that authorship on their own account. Halivni had a very good idea for a scholarly project, but he executed it incompetently. The reason is that his entire analysis, beginning to end, rests on complete credulity: what is assigned to a given name really was said by that person, where and when he lived; there is not a trace of critical acumen in Halivni's work. For he begins his analysis of the Bavli with radically isolated bits and pieces, phrases and sentences assigned to individual names, taken out of context; I begin mine with the Bavli as a whole and I work back from the whole to the parts, stage by stage. Either his approach is right, or mine is, but both cannot be correct, and, it must follow, either his results or mine must in the end win the field. Since his approach takes for granted that what is assigned to a given authority really was said by him (or by someone in the period in which he lived who bore the same name), and since my approach is formed in response to the critical program of contemporary critical learning, which denies prima facie validity to attributions in the absence of evidence that a named authority really said what he is supposed to have said, my approach will prevail. But his distinction between traditions and sources stimulated me to some interesting inquiries.

To explain: "The sources" of the Bavli are those completed, available, and free-standing pieces of writing that the authors of the Bavli used when they wrote their book. "The traditions" of the Bavli are those composites and sustained discussions that the authors of the Bavli set forth in their writing. What I want to know is a simple matter. Upon what kinds of material did the framers of the Bavli draw when, having done their own kind of writing, which was Mishnah commentary, analysis, expansion, and amplification, they filled out their document? For as a matter of simple fact, they augmented their main writing, Mishnah commentary, with a different kind of writing altogether. That other kind of writing is so distinct from the sort that served for their principal purpose that it demands attention in its own terms. When we know what kinds of writing, other than those that formed the stuff of the document and quite different therefrom, were utilized in the framing of the Bavli, we shall know something about the sources, prepared, to be sure, under auspices we cannot identify, for purposes we do not know, and at a time we cannot determine, that ultimately flowed into the foundation document of Judaism.

It is the simple fact, shown by me in various monographs, that the authorship of the Bavli takes over a substantial heritage and reworks the whole into its own sustained and internally cogent statement – and that forms not the outcome of a process of sedimentary tradition but the opposite: systematic statement of a cogent and logical order, made up in its authorship's rhetoric, attaining comprehensibility through the syntax of its authorship's logic, reviewing a received topical program in terms of the problematic and interests defined by its authorship's larger purposes and proposed message. The samples of the Bavli I have reviewed constitute either composites of sustained, essentially syllogistic discourse, in which case they form the whole and comprehensive statement of a system, or increments of exegetical accumulation, in which case they constitute restatements, with minor improvements, of a continuous tradition.

But this brings us to the matter of "sources" – available writings, utilized but not made up – upon which the authorship of the Bavli drew for its own purposes. In fact the authorship of the Bavli made use of sources, both completed documents, and also sayings and stories, ordinarily of modest proportions. We know about the latter because these received and completed compositions, sayings or sets of sayings and stories alike, were not subjected to ultimate redaction. That fact is shown by a very simple criterion: Does this composition in all its details serve the purpose of the framers who have adduced it in evidence for their purposes? The answer is invariably, rarely in many details, never in all. In fact the received sources are given pretty much in a form quite independent of the purpose for which, in the Bavli, they are adduced in evidence. True, the authorship of the Bavli did whatever it wished with these materials to carry out its own program and to make its own prevailing statement. But while where relevant to the purposes of the framers of the Bavli, these received materials were undeniably formulated and transmitted in a process of tradition, and have been so reworked and revised by the penultimate and ultimate authorship that their original character is no longer discernible, we can identify many other such writings that were not only not reformulated but indeed not reshaped in such a way as to win for themselves a clear and cogent position in the passage in which they now appear. These latter kinds of compositions in no way define for the Bavli the syntax of argument and the processes of syllogistic discourse; all they do is supply facts for someone else's case. That is why in the instances of the compositions irrelevant to the thrust and flow of the Bavli's argument, we can still discern traces of received statements or sources.

That fact has now to be set into contrast with the view of many, that the Bavli supposedly draws upon and reshapes available ideas and reworks them into a definitive statement, hence turns sources into a tradition. The kind of material I analyzed in this monograph contradicts that view, since what we see is writing that has not been reworked at all. Let me specify the kinds of factual information that will permit me to frame a reply to the question before us. If I want to know criteria for authority and sufficiency, I have to ask about the relationship between a document and prior treatments of the topic of said document. For one critical criterion of continuity – of forming a tradition out of available sources – is the capacity to take in, hold together, and rework the entirety of a prior corpus of information, writing, on a given subject. The literary test of traditionality is whether or not the canonical statement has drawn together and reworked in a cogent way whatever lay to hand in prior writings. If the test proves affirmative, then we may propose as one substantial and necessary criterion for traditionality a particular relationship to the entirety of prior writing. If it proves negative, then the entire literary dimension of the problem of traditionality turns out to weigh the wind, measure what has no weight. A different approach to the criteria by which the entirety of the literature of Judaism forms a single canonical statement will require invention and exploration.

My survey of four tractates, documented in this monograph, yielded a small number of "sources," compositions developed in response to a program of writing, and even compilation, entirely out of phase with that of the Bavli, but upon which the framers of the Bavli clearly have drawn. I find these types and no others:

1. A sustained reading of sequential verses of Scripture,
2. Stories about sages,
3. Eposidic exposition of individual verses,
4. Proof of a proposition in no way relevant to the Mishnah or Mishnah exegesis.

The authorship of the Bavli was engaged by its own concerns, ordinarily using what it received without extensively incorporating all received materials into its own literary framework at all. So I think that there really were "sources" prior to, and in clear distinction from, the tradition that the Bavli's framers set forth. That the Bavli's authorship had access to these four classes of writing indicates that other kinds of documents and types of writing were underway besides theirs. People wrote compositions that could have been collected, for example, in lives of sages, or in collections of Midrash compilations (in addition to the handful that we have in hand). Whatever the Bavli's writers picked or chose beyond their primary foci makes slight impact upon the document as a whole. So I think that the framers of the Bavli drew upon a variety of sources in the formation of their tradition. Most of these appear to have been trivial and to have played no important part in the shaping of the document. But, when, having done their own kind of writing, which was Mishnah commentary, analysis, expansion, and amplification, the framers of the Bavli filled out their document, it was with one kind of writing that vastly expanded the document, turning the exegesis of the Mishnah into something larger and more elegant than a commentary: an essay on the law behind the laws. The authorship of the Bavli augmented their main writing, Mishnah commentary, with a different kind of writing altogether. That other kind of writing is so distinct from the sort that served for their principal purpose that it demands attention in its own terms. We now know what kinds of writing, other than those that formed the stuff of the document and quite different therefrom, were utilized in the framing of the Bavli.

Index

Aaron, 17

Abba, 69, 82-83, 120-121, 151

Abba bar R. Samuel, 69

Abba Saul, 82, 149

Abba Yosé b. Dosetai, 89

Abbahu, 56, 59, 122

Abbai, 90

Abbayye, 61, 67, 73, 81-82, 94, 114, 116, 120, 132-134, 139, 141-142, 145, 147-148, 152, 162-163, 206

Abigail, 30

Abimi, 85, 92

Abimi of Sanvatah, 165

Abin, 122-125, 139, 143

Abner, 30

abomination, 140

Abot, 6-8

Abraham, 127, 133-136, 138, 146-148, 151, 156

Abtalion, 158

Ada bar Mattena, 134

Adda bar Ahbah, 63, 123, 141, 144

adultery, 20

agglutination, 137, 155, 178, 180, 189, 197, 204, 214, 216-217

Aha b. R. Iqa, 68, 126

Aha b. Raba, 118

Aha bar Jacob, 65, 68, 138

Aha of Difti, 94

Ahab, 109

Albeck, Hanokh, 179

All-Merciful, 51, 68, 81, 99-100

altar, 13, 17-18, 20, 36-37, 42, 78, 87, 212-214

American Translation, 33, 181, 195

Ammi, 81, 125-126, 140

Amora, 94, 125, 170-171, 179, 195

Amos, 139

analogical-contrastive, 25, 36, 38

analogy, 2, 20, 34-42, 50-52, 54, 59-66, 68, 126

Anan, 150

angel, 150

anoint, 19, 37

South Florida Studies in the History of Judaism